Edwin De Leon

Askaros Kassis

A Romance of Modern Egypt

Edwin De Leon

Askaros Kassis
A Romance of Modern Egypt

ISBN/EAN: 9783744679077

Printed in Europe, USA, Canada, Australia, Japan

Cover: Foto ©Thomas Meinert / pixelio.de

More available books at **www.hansebooks.com**

ASKAROS KASSIS

THE COPT.

A ROMANCE OF MODERN EGYPT.

BY

EDWIN DE LEON

LATE U. S. CONSUL-GENERAL FOR EGYPT.

PHILADELPHIA:
J. B. LIPPINCOTT & CO.,
1870.

TO

MY FRIEND

WILLIAM C. PRIME,

OF NEW YORK,

AUTHOR OF

"BOAT LIFE IN EGYPT," AND "TENT LIFE IN THE HOLY LAND,"

WHO OF ALL AMERICAN WRITERS HAS MOST THOROUGHLY

IMBUED HIMSELF WITH THE SPIRIT OF THE EAST;

IN MEMORY OF THE MANY PLEASANT HOURS

SPENT UNDER HIS TENT IN

THE HOLY LAND,

I Dedicate

This Photograph of Eastern Life and Manners.

PREFACE.

AS the East was the cradle of the human race — the
fountain whence modern civilization has drawn its
life, its literature and its religion; and as even to this
day it furnishes the fictions that delight our childhood —
so, also, is it the only spot left on the earth's surface,
where romance enters into the daily life of the people,
and the dreams of the Poet ripen into realities.

Haunted by the memories of that dreamy land, in
which I was so long a sojourner, I cannot refrain
from recording and relating some passages from an
Eastern life — the facts of which, even without the color-
ing of romance, would seem stranger than fiction — and
weaving them into the threads of the tale now offered to
the reader.

If the incidents of this tale be not altogether true of
particular persons, they yet have their foundations in
fact; and many of the most startling revelations of
Eastern life and Eastern habits are reproduced from the

memory of the writer, with the fidelity of the photograph.

For he enjoyed peculiar facilities and exceptional advantages for seeing and learning many things, which must ever be as a sealed book to the tourist, or the trader, in the East. His official position and long residence — as well as his knowledge of the language and private life of the people — gave him opportunities of observation, of which the fruits are now displayed in this book.

Although a perpetual stream of tourists pours into and through Egypt, each winter — from the savant striving to decipher hieroglyphics, to the "Inquisitive traveller," as described by Sterne; and although books without end have been, and continue to be, written on Egypt — still as little is known now of the inner life and peculiar mental characteristics of the modern Egyptian, as of his mummied progenitors. For the Oriental is a type of human being as different from the Western, as it is possible for the imagination to conceive.

Mr. Lane's book on "*The Modern Egyptians*" probably constitutes the sole exception, as to the prose: as '*Eothen*" and W. C. Prime's charming sketches do of the poetry of that Eastern life.

The Eastern man comes in contact, but never amalgamates with the Western, for whom his nature has no real affinity — but rather repulsion — skilfully as he may adopt at Stamboul, or Alexandria, the outward usages of European civilization.

He adopts these as he does its dress—wears it in public, but casts it off in private with a sigh of relief—resuming his own more easy habits, which he has simply put by, not relinquished.

The traveller and the stranger see him only in full dress. It is only long and intimate acquaintance that admits of his being seen in *dishabille*.

Two things color the whole woof and web of Eastern society—the fatalism of "Islam," which permeates and blends with every act of its daily life—and the isolation of the Hareem, which establishes the social position of woman.

The influences of both are depicted in this book. The fatalism which governs Islam, is already vaguely understood abroad; but the position of woman in the East and her actual life there, have never been comprehended; the hitherto impenetrable veil of the Hareem having shrouded its secrets.

It was reserved for the hand of the poet first to raise that veil; and in the "*Palm Leaves*," of Richard Monckton Milnes, may be found the first true pictures of the inner life of the Orient ever given in the English tongue—as Gœthe's "*West-Œstlicher Divan*" gave it in the German many years ago. Truly does the poet of the "*Palm Leaves*" sing of woman in the East; who,

like her sister in the West — though in a different shape —
wields a power over the destiny of man:

> "Thus ever in the closed Hareem,
>   As in the open Western home,
> Sheds womanhood her starry gleam,
>   Over our being's busy foam;
> Through latitudes of varying faith,
>   Thus trace we still her mission sure —
> To lighten life — to sweeten death —
>   And all for others to endure."

The realities of the East are stranger than the dreams
of the West; and yet, since the prose extravaganza of
" *Vathek*" and the poetical rhapsodies of Lord Byron —
more than a quarter of a century ago — that rich field
has been neglected by poet and novelist alike.

From that garden, then, let us cull a few flowers; and
let the reader — taking a seat upon the magical carpet of
the Persian Prince, of the " *Thousand and One Nights*"
— be transported to the world-famous city of Old Cairo,
where our story opens. — *Inshallah !*

E. DE L.

NEW YORK, *December*, 1869.

CONTENTS

ix

ASKAROS KASSIS.

CHAPTER I.

GRAND CAIRO.

IT was evening at Grand Cairo, in the month of December; such an evening as the residents in colder climes may have fancied, but never felt. Breezes as soft and bland as those of spring whispered among the feathery foliage of the palm-trees. A soft, summery haze was settling down upon the distant range of the Mokattam hills, which alone broke the monotony of the view over the surrounding Desert.

Clearly and sharply defined through the lucid air, in bold relief against the cloudless azure of the sky, rose the sharp cones of the Pyramids—pointing like giant fingers to heaven, stately and sublime in their severe simplicity—sole record left of the great Pharaohs, whose pride had constructed them as places of sepulture.

Winding like a golden thread between the city and Great Desert—fringed with its stately palms, and bordered by palaces whose latticed windows concealed many

a fairy-like form—glittered the waters of the Nile—
Father of Rivers—not only the great fertilizer of the
land of Egypt, but the object of the love and veneration
of her imaginative people, who find saving virtues for
soul and body in its yellow waters.

The Desert, like a great sea with its ever-restless waves
of shifting sand, stretched out its vast billows beyond the
Pyramids to the far-distant horizon, as though repelled
alone from whelming the city under a sand deluge by
those mighty sentinels—which, with the Sphinx, stand
keeping watch and ward over the fair "City of the
Faithful."

Within Cairo rose, shrill and frequent, on the evening
air, all those indescribable cries and sounds of man and
beast which make Eastern so different from Western
cities—which cause Eastern life to appear so vivid and
so varied, after the hushed repose of noonday, when,
in those fervid climes, both man and nature seem steeped
in profound sleep.

"When the sun goes down all Africa dances," said
an old traveller. He might have said, "All Africa
awakens;" for dancing is not considered there a masculine accomplishment, but rather regarded as an infamous
employment.

In the very heart of old Cairo stands a huge park,
several hundred acres in area, planted with acacias and
other shade trees, filled with flowering shrubs, and inter-
sected by long avenues and winding footpaths. Rustic
seats are scattered everywhere through it; and coffee-
houses proffer their refreshment of nargileh, chibouque,
coffee, sherbet, and lemonade to its many pleasure-
seekers. This is "*The Ezbekich,*" the public prome-
nade of the citizens, native and foreign—a people as

gay, after their own fashion, as the Parisians, and quite as much addicted to enjoyment in the open air.

Around " *The Ezbekieh* " are grouped the houses of the European quarter, for most of the foreigners reside in its vicinity. Here, too, are the great hotels for the accommodation of tourists from Europe, and of passengers to and from India, who pass through Egypt to the number of several thousand each month, and make it a Babel of tongues and nationalities while the transit pours through.

At one of the open windows of the " *Hotel d' Orient* " —the best and largest of these hotels—there stood on this particular evening a group of strangers, apparently watching with amused and curious interest the panoramic view of desert, sky, mountain, and pyramid in the distance, and of the varied, many-hued, and pictorial current of life in the street below.

The party consisted of a man of middle age, with portly figure and ruddy, open face, whose florid complexion, clear blue eyes, and square-built frame indicated Teutonic origin; though, in fact, he was an American citizen by birth as well as nationality.

Cornelius Van Camp was a fine specimen of that species, now almost extinct in America, a genuine Knickerbocker. His blood yet ran slowly and coolly through his veins—not at that mad gallop with which it circulates through those of Young America, who eats fast, drinks fast, lives fast, and dies very fast, indeed. To look upon him, one might see he was a solid man in all respects; in mind as in body—a trifle obstinate, perhaps, yet thoroughly reliable.

Near him stood a young man and a young girl, in both of whom could be traced a strong family likeness to their portly progenitor, though sharpened into American angularity in the first instance, and softened into rare womanly loveliness in the second. A tall man, of aristocratic face and mien, whose costume and long yellow whiskers—no less than the many straps that crossed and recrossed his chest, supporting spy-glass and all the other paraphernalia of a British tourist—spoke him unmistakably an Englishman, lounged against the window-sill, apparently more occupied in gazing on the fair face near him than on the strange sights and scenes beneath.

Another female figure completed the group; and it was one that contrasted strikingly with the fresh and youthful loveliness of the girl, whose arm was around her waist. For this lady was neither young nor lovely; and there was little freshness and roundness in her face, or person. On the contrary, she was angular and bony, with high, severe features, and a sour expression of countenance—her prominent and beady black eyes concentrating their rays to a focus through a pair of large round glasses set in steel frames. Those eyes seemed to look out scornfully and suspiciously on all external objects; while the erect rigidity of the spare form and the pursed-up expression of the pinched lips indicated a protracted spinsterhood, which man delighted not nor woman neither. She looked, as she was, the maiden aunt of the fair young girl—professor of one of the sternest creeds and possessor of one of the stiffest spines in all unbending New England. She was a strong-minded woman of the purest Boston school, which takes its metaphysics from Emerson, its morals from Theodore Parker, its manners from the Puritan Fathers; and which finally considers there can be no salvation outside of New England !

Such was Miss Priscilla Primmins, who on this bright

evening stood, an unconscious foil, by the side of her blooming young relative, looking down with grim, defiant austerity on the lively scenes below.

And yet it required a mind severely schooled, to avoid being interested and fascinated by the combination of the gorgeous and grotesque in the strange panorama defiling through the narrow streets beneath the window, and winding away among the alleys and avenues of the *Ezbekieh.* Nor were the sounds less varied than the sights; from the deep, grunting bass of the complaining camel, to the resonant bray of the donkey; the hoarse, guttural imprecations of the Arab men, and the shrill, shrieking treble of the donkey boys; with the occasional passage of a marriage or funeral procession. followed by singing or wailing women. Ever and anon the advent of some Egyptian noble would be announced by the running *saïs*, or groom, clearing the way in advance for his Arab steed, by loud cries of *" Oa yer Ragl! Oa yer Bint!"*—(Get out of the way, O man! Get out of the way, O woman!). —accompanied by sharp strokes of the stick he carried, if the warning were unheeded.

Jostling each other on the narrow streets were the most incongruous medleys of humanity — Dives and Lazarus: the haughty Egyptian Bey, or Pasha, on his fiery Arab, with housings of cloth of gold, and bridle gleaming with precious stones, side by side with the Fellah peasant, perched like a monkey on his small donkey; or the Arab woman straddling the same useful but humble animal, man-fashion, her knees almost reaching her nose, her figure wrapped like a bundle in a black silk cloak — only two glittering eyes visible through the impervious veil. Then would follow a long train of hideous, spectral-looking camels; the tail of each tied to

2 * B

the nose of his successor—their soft, shapeless splay feet resembling huge sponges, and making no sound as they filed past, with their long, crooked necks and serpent-like heads swaying from side to side.

Next in the midst of this swaying, surging tide might be seen the sturdy form of some British tourist, perched on a donkey, almost small enough to permit the rider's legs to drag on the ground, and followed by the yelling donkey-boy, clad in his scant blue shirt, and crying aloud in Arabic, to the infinite amusement of the natives: "Son of a jackass, ridden by the son of a jackass, go faster!" Meanwhile the unconscious traveller is blandly trustful, and dreams of no insult from the small offender he imagines in terrible awe of him.

The young girl turned her bright eyes, full of animated interest, upon the elder maiden, as she exclaimed:

"Oh, aunt! is not this wonderful? Does it not look to you like a page torn from the Arabian Nights? Why, these are the very people there described—the one-eyed water-carrier, the veiled woman, the old story-teller under the tree, and the wicked black man from the Hareem!"

The rigid face of Miss Priscilla Primmins grew more rigid still as the young Edith thus appealed to her, and, in a voice which corresponded with her face, she coldly answered:

"I think it a very improper spectacle to let a young lady's eyes rest upon, Edith! And I only wonder that a man of your father's good sense should permit you to witness such indecent exposures of person as these people make habitually! It may all be very picturesque, but I know in Boston we should consider it highly indecent. Improper sights and bad smells seem to me the leading characteristics of Cairo."

"But, my dear aunt!" persisted the younger woman, who was determined not to share the fate of Cleopatra's pearl, and be dissolved in the vinegar of her acid relative, "you *must* own that it is totally unlike any other place, or people, in the world : that it is a gay and glittering pageant, not entirely composed of the unpleasant things you mention. Oh! look there, for instance! See that group of Fellah men and women under the palm-tree, listening to the old story-teller. Is not that truly Oriental? And it's not the least improper!"

"Very Oriental, no doubt," grumbled the spinster. "Half-naked savages squatting in a circle, and smoking filthy pipes that poison the air! Sir Charles," addressing the Englishman, "what do *you* think of these Arabs my niece so raves about?"

"Rum lot of beggars!" growled the Englishman, languidly. Then, rousing himself by an effort, he added : "Creatures that possess all the disagreeable qualities of the monkey, without the useful addition of being able to swing from a tree by the tail. I have served in India, and know the Blackies well. All the same — everywhere."

Now Miss Priscilla — albeit a staunch republican in theory — adored a live lord with that strange inconsistency common to our countrymen and women abroad. Still, she felt it incumbent upon her to repel the Englishman's views upon the "man and brother" whom Boston delighted to honor — so she made a feeble protest :

"I fear, my lord, you are prejudiced against the African! If you will but read —"

"A thousand pardons!" hastily broke in his lordship; "I plead guilty, bow to the judgment of the court, and will admit that you have 'washed the Ethiop white!'—for really this climate is too hot for any mental effort.''

The ancient maiden smiled grimly, retired from the window, took up a volume of Orphic Sayings of Alcott, and abstracted herself from the contemplation of the improper external world. Sir Charles glided into the place she had left vacant, and, with a faint smile, said to Edith:

"I thought the enemy would retire before my assault on the strong position; but you must not imagine I am insensible to the influences of this place and hour, nor"—and his voice softened—"to that of her who lends it its greatest charm by her presence."

"Positively a compliment from Sir Charles the Cynic!" laughed Edith. "Wonder upon wonder! I shall nearly begin to believe in Egyptian magic next!"

"Say rather in American," replied her companion, adopting her own tone of banter. "But I must tear myself away, for I see your brother Harry is impatient to be off to the Bazaars. We pledged ourselves to a solemn old Arab merchant to repair at sunset to smoke pipes with him and select some trash. So, *au revoir!*"

The two young men left the room together; the elder Van Camp had thrown himself at full length on an ottoman in the corner, and was thinking—accompanied by a running bass from his nostrils. The ancient spinster was absorbed with Orphic utterances, with her back to the girl. Edith remained alone at the window, her arms resting on the cushion that covered the sill, and her eyes sometimes fixed on the scene below, sometimes wandering over the distant prospect of palm-trees, pyramids, river, and desert. There was nothing sad or troubled in the reveries into which she plunged as the sun set and the crowds on the street dwindled into an occasional passer-by; for very fresh looked she in her young loveliness, evidently "in maiden meditation, fancy-free."

The quick tramp of a horse on the street below her window, followed by the cry of a running *sais*, "*Oa!* *Oa!*" startled her from her revery. Glancing down, she saw as gallant a cavalier as ever won bright glances from the eyes or sweet words from the lips of ladye faire in the good days of chivalry; and once having looked, her gaze was attracted and riveted to its object. The cavalier was a man in the first bloom of youth, who sat his magnificent white Arab charger with an easy grace that spoke of perfect horsemanship. He was richly clad in the Eastern dress; but the unshaven head —over which, however, he wore the red Fez cap—proclaimed him to be no Mussulman. The rich housings of his Turkish saddle, and the precious stones that ornamented the bridle and headstall, proved him to be a personage of rank and wealth; a fact equally announced by the air of command stamped on his face and person.

The *sais*, a Berberi, black as night, with his bare ebony legs lithe and sinewy as those of a greyhound — clad in a white shirt, with a crimson sash tied round his waist, and a snowy turban on his head, waved in his hand a short staff, with which he struck out right and left to clear the way for his master.

As the long, swinging stride of the Arab horse bore his rider under the window of the hotel, the latter chanced to look carelessly up, and as his glance fell on the bright countenance of the American girl—so marked in such a place—he revealed his own face, which was in perfect harmony with his graceful figure and rich costume. For that face was one on which painter or sculptor would have gazed with rapture as a fitting model for the young Antinous, so perfect was the outline of the clear-cut delicate features, relieved by the resolute expression of the mouth, and the calm serenity of the eye. Though young and beardless, save a slight silken moustache, the impress of passion, tempered by thought, was already stamped on the broad brow and the lines about the corners of the mouth. His complexion was darker than that of a European—a rich, clear olive, through which the blood seemed to glow, like light through an alabaster lamp; while the lips were as delicately chiselled and of as ripe a red as those of a woman.

The gloved hand with which he restrained the fiery impatience of his steed, who chafed and fretted like a stag-hound preparing for a bound, seemed equally delicate and muscular. The proportions of his figure were concealed below the waist by the ample Turkish trowsers, falling in heavy folds even to the shovel stirrup that concealed his foot; but it was easy to see that the frame, at once slight and supple, was firmly knit and capable of great endurance.

But the character of the face was given by the eye—large, black, and lustrous, with slumbering depths of unrevealed passion lurking in it. Now liquid with tenderness, now flashing with anger or mirth, the white possessing that peculiar opaque hue, like porcelain, seen only in the eyes of Eastern men, and the iris contracting and dilating like that of the lion—there seemed a hidden fascination in the glance of this stranger that sent a sudden thrill through the fearless bosom of the young girl.

Equally strong seemed the impression produced on the Oriental by this lovely apparition, so different from his own dusky countrywomen — set, as it were, in the stone framework of the window. By an involuntary movement, his contracted arm curbed in his steed so suddenly and so sharply, that the powerful Turkish bit tore open his delicate mouth until blood flecked the foam he champed upon it as he recoiled upon his very haunches. The rider kept his seat, unmoved by the sudden and violent shock, but relaxed the rein to relieve the tortured mouth. Maddened by the pain and by the sudden check, the gallant horse, snorting with wrath till his dilated nostrils glowed to a bright red, bounded straight up into the air, and, by a succession of rapid, frantic plunges, sought to displace his rider.

The struggle was violent but brief. Vain were all the efforts of the furious steed to unseat his tormentor, who inflicted punishment on flanks and sides with the sharp shovel stirrups, and wrenched his mouth with the terrible bit, till the desert-born, panting, trembling and exhausted, abandoned the unequal contest and stood quivering in every limb, but perfectly still, his eye glaring with mingled rage and fear. Then the rider spoke a few soothing words in Arabic, and patted the arched neck of his favorite as though in reconciliation, and the noble beast seemed to recognize the friendly overture and acknowledge it. With the nearly human intelligence with which the pure-blooded Arab horse seems endowed, he turned his head toward his master in a mute response, then stood quiet and still, as if carved from stone.

With the flush of exertion and excitement hardly dying from his face, and still lingering in his eye, the rider once more glanced up at the casement, and their eyes met; his, full of admiring wonder — hers, full of an interest and sympathy that brightened the usually calm face into a glory like that of one of Correggio's saints. That electric spark of sympathy, which can sometimes flash through the eye from one soul to another in a second's space, ineffaceable, enduring, eternal — rapid and subtle as the lightning's flash, and sometimes as blasting — passed now between these two existences, but a moment before utterly unknown to each other — even now strangers. A look, a glance, a moment's vision — how one of these may alter the whole current of a life, opening fountains of bright or bitter memories all sealed before ! For in every human experience can be found the truth, that the great heart-quakes of our lives have been preceded by some such trivial incident, unregarded at the time, yet really the harbinger of the new soul-birth.

From the large luminous eyes of the Oriental there flashed upon the maiden a glance full of fire and wonder— of open, undisguised admiration, but still not disrespect-ful. Then, with one word to his steed, the impatient animal bounded forward like a deer, and both horse and rider were lost to the maiden's gaze, in the shadows of the fast-falling night.

Edith Van Camp was not at all what is called a roman-tic girl. She was not prone to indulge in foolish fancies, or idle dreams, for her organization, mental and physical, was too healthy, and her Dutch blood and American training had not been the nurses of sentimentalism. She piqued herself upon her common sense ; and had laughed off, hitherto, all attempts to awaken the poetic and dreamy element slumbering in her nature.

She therefore felt annoyed and irritated at the strange fascination she had experienced from the momentary presence and startling glance of the stranger; and still, as she strained her eyes after horse and rider under the dim shadows of the trees of the *Ezbekieh,* she murmured to herself half unconsciously:

"He *is* like my girlish dreams of Haroun al Raschid!"

Just then from the high minaret of the mosque El Aksar, near the hotel, suddenly pealed out on the stillness of the night the warning cry of the Muezzin, floating down through the quiet air like a prophetic voice from heaven: "*Allah il Allah! Mohammed resoul Allah!*"— (There is no God but God! and Mohammed is the messenger of God.)

It startled the girl from her revery. Though conscious no eye was upon her, with a bright blush she smiled faintly at her own fancies; then frowned impatiently to herself as she muttered: "I do believe there is magic in this climate!"

Passing within the chamber, she proceeded to rouse from his meditations her refreshed sire, whose nasal melodies were now on the trombone; and her respected aunt, whom Orphic sayings had reduced to a performance on a shriller but similar instrument.

3

CHAPTER II.

ON THE EZBEKIEH.

WHO that has ever passed a night in Cairo can fail to recall the memories of the *Ezbekieh*, and the glimpses into fairy-land it gave him? Who can forget that enchanted spot, so thoroughly Oriental in all its features and surroundings — so thoroughly steeped in the drowsy, sensual spirit of the East?

The streets are silent and deserted; the hum of labor has ceased; the houses are all closed, and a few twinkling lights from the lattices alone indicate that this vast hive of humanity, with its half million of inhabitants, is not a City of the Dead. For the shops are all closed, and the prowling wild dogs alone traverse the narrow, deserted streets, so thronged with eager, noisy life a few hours before. Occasionally a solitary wayfarer, bearing a paper lantern in his hand to light his way through the dark and crooked streets, may be seen hurrying home; otherwise, they are empty.

One spot alone is full of light and life, and that is the *Ezbekieh.* There all is gayety and animation. Innumerable lamps, of varied colors, hang suspended from the trees and in front of the coffee-houses, which are driving a roaring trade in coffee, sherbet, lemonade, confection-

26

ery, and pipes. Crowds of people of every nationality
are strolling up and down the leafy walks, or sitting on
the chairs and benches in front of the chief coffee-houses,
where small, round tables are placed for the refreshments
ordered. The bubbling of the water-pipes, or nargilehs,
makes a peculiar music; the amber mouth-pieces of
chibouques are pressed by bearded lips of Turk, Arab,
and Christian; while the foreign fair ones, who are out
in full force, do not disdain to smoke cigarettes in the
intervals of conversation and flirtation; for the foreign
element at Cairo — though not so large at that time as at
present — numbered then some four or five thousand
persons, chiefly Greeks and Italians, but intermixed with
every continental nationality. All of these, as old residents, had contracted many of the strange habitudes of
the country.

The Eastern man is the most tolerant of human beings,
so that every individual there could indulge his own
peculiarity of costume or manners, without remark; and
the *mélange* on the *Ezbekieh*, therefore, was something
most curious to contemplate. Independent of the European residents, and the swarm of tourists, Egypt itself
numbers no less than sixteen different races among its
native and transplanted population. Each one of these
is distinguished by some peculiarity of costume or of
manner. There you saw men of all shades of color,
different types of race and variety of costume, from the
half-naked Fellah, or peasant, the stark-naked *Santon*, or
Saint, the richly-clad Turk, and the straight-laced European, all blent, mingled, and fused together, under the
leafy canopy, sipping coffee, smoking, and swallowing
sherbets, as they lounged up and down, conversing together in a perfect Babel of blended tongues of every
known dialect of Eastern and Western language.

Here native jugglers were performing wonderful feats of sleight of hand, or strength, swallowing live snakes, and piercing themselves with sharp knives. A little farther on a blind old man was beating furiously on a drum of fish-skin, and a wild-eyed Arab girl twanged with her dusky fingers a darabuka, or rude guitar, droning a monotonous chant to the accompaniment, while a dancing-girl exhibited graceful but most lascivious postures — far outstripping the modern ballet, over which hang enraptured now the fashionables both of Europe and America.

Crouched on the ground is the old story-teller, rehearsing for the thousandth time some rude version of the Arabian Nights' Entertainments, to a circle of half-naked peasants, squatted on their hams around him — moving them alternately to laughter and to tears. Soldiers in the Egyptian uniform of tight white jacket and baggy breeches of the same color, with gaiters reaching to the knee, shuffle past; and richly dressed Arnaouts, or Albanian soldiers, in the picturesque Greek costume — gold-embroidered jacket, with white fustenelles, or plaited shirts, and sash girded round the wasp-like waist — swagger by. Ruthless ruffians these last; neither Turk nor Christian, but a compound of the worst vices of both — armed to the teeth always, with pistol-butts ostentatiously protruding from the sash on each side, and rows of brass capsules, containing cartridges, ornamenting their breasts, till they look like walking arsenals.

On that part of the *Ezbekieh* fronting the Hotel d'Orient was an open space before the chief European coffee-house. In this were ranged the seats and tables already spoken of, and a European band, composed of refugee musicians, chiefly Italians, from time to time discoursed most excellent music. Around these, as a centre, were grouped most of the European residents of Cairo, as well as the visitors; and among the latter were the party of travellers to whom the reader has already been introduced.

Miss Priscilla Primmins had preferred remaining at the hotel, through the double fear of contracting a cold in the open air, and the secret dread she entertained of every half-naked Arab, in whom she saw a fanatical ruffian, who believed paradise his reward for assassinating a Christian.

"I have never yet passed an evening on Boston Common," she replied to Mr. Van Camp's invitation; "and it is a far nicer place than this barbarous grove: so I do not see why I should disgust myself by mixing with those dirty savages over yonder. I have a sweet poem of Whittier's here, which will amuse me until your return."

So the party went without Miss Priscilla, to the great delight of the young men, who looked upon the spinster much as Coleridge's wedding-guest regarded the Ancient Mariner.

Sitting under the acacias, listening to the music and chatting pleasantly over all the strange sights and sounds around them, under the silvery brightness of a Cairene moon, which gave light enough to read by, our new friends were enjoying themselves thoroughly.

Sir Charles was talking to Edith, who rattled away in response right merrily, when suddenly she stopped in the midst of a sentence, and colored so violently, that neck, brow, and bosom grew crimson, while her eyes wandered back and forth from one particular acacia-tree. A man was leaning against it, in the full light of the lamps in front of the coffee-house.

Her blush and confusion were not noticed by the Englishman, who was not a quick or accurate observer; but

3 *

his glance, following hers, also rested on the face and
form of the lounger under the acacia.

"By Jove!" he exclaimed, "what a handsome fellow
that Turk is! He is a perfect stunner! Never saw a
finer fellow to make a beauty man in a crack corps, if he
only had an inch more, and wore uniform instead of
bags. Miss Van Camp, there is a model Oriental for
you!"

Edith only murmured something in reply. Her eye
had already caught the form and features so strangely
and so indelibly impressed upon her memory by a single
glance. But after a moment she rallied, and replied
rather indifferently:

"Oh, yes! Good-looking enough, doubtless, but very
probably like most Egyptian views — good to look at only
from a distance. The difference between the various
classes in the East, they tell me, consists chiefly in dress,
and the pipe-bearer and the pasha are equally ignorant
and brutal."

"Well, perhaps so," responded the Englishman, "but
that is really a fine animal, nevertheless. Reminds one
of a Bengal tiger; very agreeable to look at, quite beautiful and gentle in appearance, but a terribly sharp claw
concealed under the velvet paw. I know a man when I
see him, and depend upon it, that fellow yonder is one."

"Really, Sir Charles," laughed Edith, in her old
manner, "I shall begin to believe you have contracted
an unfortunate attachment for this — I cannot say 'fair'
unknown, for he is very dark. But I fear he observes he
is the subject of our remark."

As she spoke, the person whom they were discussing
prepared to move on, throwing, as he did so, a rapid
glance at the young girl, in which she thought there was

a gleam of recognition. Just at the moment, Harry Van Camp, who had been smoking a chibouque at a little distance, sauntered up to where his sister sat.

"Look at that Turk, yonder," Sir Charles said to him. "He comes up to my ideal of what an Eastern prince ought to be. Is n't he a crusher?"

But Harry did not answer, and only stared hard at the stranger with a puzzled expression of countenance.

"Surely that face is familiar to me," he muttered to himself. "Where can I have seen it often before? It is not a common one." And after a moment, a sudden recollection flashed over his face, as he cried:

"By jingo! it must be my old chum at Eton, Askaros Kassis! We used to call him the Egyptian prince over there. He and a batch of other young highnesses were sent over to be educated by old Mehemet Ali, and I always heard he was a great swell in his own country. I 'll try if it is n't he, at all events."

So, as the Egyptian sauntered slowly off, the younger Van Camp, making a detour, passed in front of him, looking full and inquiringly at him as their eyes met. Over the dark features of the Egyptian passed the same shadow of doubt and half-recognition that had flitted across the American's a moment before; but his face lit up with a sunny smile as Van Camp advanced with outstretched hand, and cried:

"Why, Askaros, is it you, old fellow? And have you forgotten your old friend, Harry Van Camp?"

"No, indeed," replied the Egyptian, in perfect English, but with a slight foreign intonation. "One does not forget old friends so readily—at least in the East," he added, laughing. "But I had not the faintest idea you had recrossed the Atlantic since we parted at Eton, you for America, I for Egypt. But as you are here now, you must let me try and do the honors of my country for you."

Then the young men plunged into a long talk about old schoolmates, interspersed with reminiscences shared together, of the past happy college days, when the younger Van Camp was finishing his education in England.

Their colloquy ended by the Egyptian's promising to call on the ensuing morning at the hotel, that he might be presented to his friend's family, and constitute himself their *cicerone* while in Cairo, for, on looking around to find his party, after his long talk, Harry found his father and sister had left the *Ezbekieh*, and as the hour was very late, had probably retired for the night.

Next morning at breakfast, while he was relating to his sister his discovery the night before, and giving a glowing panegyric on the high qualities of head and heart of the Egyptian, the latter's name was announced, and Askaros entered the room. He advanced with easy grace to greet his friend ; but a new light came into his eye and a deeper glow tinged his dark cheek, when he found that the sister was the same lady by whom he had been so impressed the evening before. She also seemed slightly confused, although — prepared by her brother's revelation, and sustained by that superior tact which seems a natural gift to women — she suffered no sign of it to appear ; greeting her brother's friend cordially, but with apparent unconsciousness of ever having seen him before.

Mr. Van Camp, senior, was very cordial in his reception of Askaros ; but Miss Primmins was so astonished at witnessing the deportment of this "native" — who, as she afterward expressed it, "actually acted and spoke like a civilized Christian ! and even understood English !"

—that her usual volubility forsook her, and she sat staring at the young man with eyes and mouth wide open, as
though he were some new and strange specimen of natural history.

After an animated colloquy, chiefly relating to the
objects of most interest in and around Cairo, the young
man rose to leave.

"From what you tell me," he said to Mr. Van Camp,
"your party have already seen the ordinary sights of
Cairo, such as dragomen usually show to strangers. You
have seen the Citadel, the Mosque of Mehemet Ali,
Joseph's Well, and the Bazaars. You have spent an
evening on the *Ezbekieh;* but there are many peculiar
things in this country not on public exhibition, and for
some of these you must permit me to be your *cicerone.*
Have you yet dined in Turkish fashion? Ah, you have
not? Then honor me by dining with me to-morrow, and
I will show you a specimen of that performance. Of
course I include the ladies; and we will only dine thus
to gratify your curiosity. As your son has doubtless told
you, I am a Copt and a Christian, and my habits, as well
as my faith, are fashioned after your models."

So saying, with the graceful salutation of the East—
touching with his right hand his brow, lips, and heart,
with a gesture full of ease and dignity—he bowed low
and left the apartment.

There was a brief pause after his departure. It was
broken by the amazed Primmins, whose spell seemed
broken as he left the room; and whose tongue seemed
suddenly loosened, like the famous frozen horn of the
Baron Munchausen.

"Well!" she said, with a gasping sigh, "if I write this
to Beacon Street, they never will believe it! I scarcely

C

can trust the evidence of my own eyes and ears. Why, this Egyptian Turk, with his baggy—what was I going to say! I mean dress—except that his face is a little yellow, acts and talks just like any one of the young men you meet on the Milldam, a fine afternoon, in sleighing-time! But I don't believe one word about his being a Christian, although he said he was. That is all nonsense, of course."

"Why, aunt, did you not hear him say he was a Copt, not a Turk or Arab?" cried Edith; "and do you not know the Copts claim to be the earliest Christians, and look down with contempt on the Greek and Latin Catholic Churches as only upstarts of yesterday?"

"Well, my child, if you only had read that blessed Theodore Parker's works, you would know that all these old forms are nothing but superstitions and priestly contrivances; and that the only pure religion on earth is to be found, not in the East, where it was born, but in our *Down-East*, where it has become national and universal. But your father gets angry when I talk philosophically, and has old-fashioned notions, so I will say no more. But I *must* believe a Turk is a Turk, though he can speak English and act like a Christian!"

As Miss Priscilla Primmins, with all her philosophy and philanthropy, got rapidly red in the face and loud of voice whenever contradicted—glaring fiercely through the glass bow-windows on her Roman nose—her niece thought it prudent to drop the subject.

But the Englishman, who had been an amused listener, here interposed.

"I am sorry to disagree with Miss Van Camp," he said gravely. "But you are right, Miss Primmins. How can men expect salvation, or claim to be Christians, who live, dress, eat, and sleep in such outlandish fashion as the Egyptians? Why, they say their prayers in the streets, five times a day, instead of going to church once a week in black dress-coats; and their religion is made up of precepts of high morality, which the silly fellows actually practise as well as preach — including universal toleration: and finally, they have never heard even of the Puritan Fathers!"

The ancient spinster bridled up with delight at such commendation from such a source.

"Do you hear that, Edith?" she cried, triumphantly.

"Oh, yes! aunt, I am listening," answered the younger woman, half amused, half provoked at the cool irony of Sir Charles. He saw it, and chose a less serious theme.

"Do you propose accepting this invitation to an Eastern dinner, Miss Primmins?" he asked.

"Oh, yes, indeed! I am really curious to see how and what the creatures eat," answered the lady addressed.

"Has it not occurred to you there may be some risk in the experiment?"

"Risk! how, or what?" A look of vague alarm gleamed through the spinster's spectacles. Sir Charles drew nearer, looked fearfully around, lowered his head, and in a deep whisper hissed the one word: "Poison!"

"Good gracious! how shocking! what put such a horrible idea into your head?" screamed Miss Priscilla, her face becoming ashy pale, while her lips quivered piteously.

"Queer beggars these — hate all Christians — fond of poisoning 'em — put it in the coffee. Have you never heard how common it is in the East? Books of travel full of it. Why, they think it a passport to paradise to poison an unbeliever — don't think women have any

souls, so less scrupulous about them even than men!
Hope I have n't alarmed you.　Thought it only right to
give you the warning.　I have an antidote myself; always
carry it in my vest-pocket.　Good day.''

"But—Sir Charles!　Stop a—moment!" gasped the
spinster, strong-minded no longer under this dreadful
idea.　"This gentleman Egyptian is a friend of Harry's.
He says he is a Christian.　*He* would do us no harm.''

"Very true.　Had n't thought of that.　But,'' he added,　mysteriously, "who can vouch for his—*cook?*　He
is no friend of ours.　*Apoplexie foudroyante* they call it
here.　Very common, I assure you.　Do not be alarmed ;
my suspicions *may* be groundless.　At least, *I hope so.*
Good day.''

And with this parting arrow, serious and solemn as
ever, the Englishman sauntered out of the room, leaving
the chaste bosom of Miss Priscilla a prey to mingled
emotions of terror and curiosity.　But the latter part of
this conversation had not been heard by Edith, for Sir
Charles never ventured to quiz her aunt so outrageously
in her presence.　The young girl had returned to the
window, and, with her head resting on her hand, seemed
to be gazing out upon the street, while she was in reality
indulging in one of those sweet day-dreams that never
survive the period of early youth.　For the cold, harsh
realities of the world soon dispel them, as the morning
mists are chased by the day-god from the mountain's
brow, never to return until the evening shadows set in
dim and gray on the threshold of coming night.

What she was meditating upon would be difficult to
tell—perhaps clearly to describe would have been impossible even to herself; for the strange and unaccustomed
images of men and scenery around her, as well as the

intoxicating influences of the climate, were developing
the latent romance of her nature, and a confused throng
of strange thoughts and new fancies were flitting through
her brain. Prominent in all these phantasmagoric visions
were the face and form of the young Egyptian. The
music of his low, sweet voice still lingered in her ear, as
she leaned from the casement, and the soft wind fanned
her cheek and stirred gently the waves of her brown
hair.

Edith's life hitherto had been without care and without much thought. She had seen little of society, having
just completed her "finishing" at a fashionable New
York boarding-school; and had merely rushed at tourist's
race through Europe. Her mind and her heart, therefore, were both as pure, and had had as few characters
impressed upon them, as a virgin page.

What hand should trace those characters, and whether
they were to be poetic or prosaic, depended much on
chance — if, in the government of this world, there be
such a thing as chance under the mysterious ordinations
of Providence: if what we blind mortals call by that
name be not a link of that unseen chain which binds
every creature to the footstool of its Creator.

The mother of Edith had died while she was yet an
infant, and the girl had never known the softening influences even of an adopted mother's kindness and care.
The rigid Priscilla Primmins had made an attempt to
take charge of her brother-in-law's household after the
death of her sister — who was unlike her in every respect — but, finding she could not live out of Boston, had
soon abandoned the effort. Edith had no other near
female relative, so all the wealth of her affectionate heart
had been lavished upon her father and brother, who re-

4

paid it with full measure. But this absence of a mother's watchful care had given the young girl an independence of thought and feeling, and a decision of character, rare for one so young. She gave rather than took advice from her placid, easy-going father and rather fast brother, who was an incarnation of young New York in its sporting and fashionable phase—tempered slightly by his early English training—and was not particularly clever nor possessed of marked ability of any kind.

Abandoning herself to that dreamy indolence of mind and body, that perfect rest which the Easterns call "*keff*," and for which we have no distinctive word, because life with us is a fret, a hurry, a race, a conflict—Edith let an hour slip by, when the clatter of horse's feet suddenly awakened her. Looking toward the sound, she again saw the young Copt, on his milk-white Arab, slowly passing the *Ezbekieh*. Askaros looked up and bowed as he passed, with a sunny smile that disclosed under his silky moustache a row of teeth glittering white. As she returned the salutation, Edith blushed, she scarce knew why, and hastily withdrew, in some confusion, from what her own heart now whispered her had been a romantic watch for the Eastern cavalier, who now began to fill a dangerous share of her maiden meditations.

"Askaros Kassis!" she murmured. "It is a strange, odd name, but surely a very pretty one."

CHAPTER III.

THE SERPENT-CHARM.

TWO hours after noon on the ensuing day the party from the Hotel d'Orient set out to visit the house of Askaros, and to partake of the Eastern dinner he had caused to be prepared for them. Their young host himself had called for them, and with thoughtful care had caused his *saïs* to bring, for the use of Edith and her aunt, two of those remarkably fine white donkeys which are more prized in Egypt than ordinary horses. These, both in size, spirit, and pace, are very different animals from the wretched little creatures which alone are seen in Europe. Standing as high as a small horse, full of life and spirit, carrying themselves with proud, erect head and arched neck — and with gait so easy you may carry a glass of water without spilling it, as they amble along — they are the best animals imaginable for ladies' use; the European side-saddle being substituted for the native one when strangers ride them.

The narrowness of the Cairene streets forbids the use of carriages, except in particular quarters of the city, and, even in these, is accompanied with inconvenience and even danger: so, as the house of Askaros was in the narrow and confined Copt quarter, it could only be reached on horseback or on foot.

It was with great difficulty that Miss Primmins could be induced to mount the odd and wicked-looking donkey which was assigned to her; and it was only on the solemn pledge of Sir Charles that he would walk beside her all the way that she finally consented. The men of the party were all on foot, for the distance was not great; and, after passing through the *Mooskie,* or street of European shops, and winding through many narrow by-ways — whose houses jutted over their heads, with each successive story protruding farther forward until only a narrow strip of sky could be seen between them at the roof — they reached a garden gate set in a high stone wall. This gate Askaros opened with a clumsy wooden key, that turned a wooden bolt within, and the party entered a cool and spacious garden, where the palm, the orange, and the citron grew amid rich exotic flowers and shrubs that filled the air with a rich, dense perfume.

The tall, slender stems of the palms — rising to the height of thirty feet without a branch — like Ionic columns, gave the place the look of a cathedral — an effect heightened by the odor, as if of incense from perfumed censers that rose on every side. The illusion, too, was aided by the solemn silence that reigned in this retreat, after passing suddenly out of the noisy streets of the city, where the clamor of man and beast is perpetual, and the harsh Arabic gutturals rise in a chorus of discordant sounds around the pedestrian.

Inspired by the resemblance just noted, and deeply impressed by the sudden silence and solemnity of the palm-grove, Edith murmured half aloud:

" 'The groves were God's first temples ! ' "

The quick ear of the Englishman caught the quotation, and he answered, " Very true, Miss Van Camp. The quotation is true as poetical ; and this grove does look deucedly like a cathedral. But the groves have been the devil's temples, too — as witness the Druids — not to mention the witch-burnings on your side of the water. I verily believe your respected aunt now believes the long-eared fiend she is riding to be Sathanas in disguise, leading her into this his domain. We only need his original snakeship here to make the impression perfect.''

As he spoke this laughingly, walking a few paces behind the young lady's donkey, Sir Charles was surprised at receiving no other response than a blow from the sudden recoil of her donkey, so sudden and violent as to throw him out of the pathway.

At the same moment a stifled shriek broke from the lips of Edith, who had been thrown to the ground, and had just risen to her feet. She stood immovable, as though from terror, trembling in every limb, her lips parted, and her blue eyes — a strange mixture of fascination and horror in their staring orbs — fixed upon a point in the shrubbery just before her.

At the sound of her shriek, Askaros, who was a few steps in advance, leading the way, turned suddenly round ; and his gaze, following hers, was instantly riveted on the same object, with somewhat the same fascination.

From the midst of a thick clump of shrubs, at the foot of a huge palm, gleamed forth what seemed two living coals ! and beneath it — coiled in a huge bulk like the cordage of some mighty ship — fold above fold, sinuous,

4 *

undulating, writhed the knotted convolutions of a slimy serpent! The eye of Askaros bent upon the burning spots, that made a gleam in the dusky shade of the shrubs, till he could distinguish the erect head of the monster — its forked tongue moving rapidly backward and forward in its poisonous jaws — while from the greenish eyes, full of evil fire, sparks seemed to scintillate.

Then, glancing from the grim terror to the maiden, the heart of the young Egyptian stood still, the hair bristled on his head, and the blood in his veins seemed to freeze; for that wondrous influence which the serpent eye exercises over man, bird, or beast — commonly known as fascination, which science may deride, but experience has confirmed by testimony of many men in many lands — had wrought its strange spell over her gentle spirit. Her first impulse of terror and flight had not only been arrested, but changed into apparently far different sentiments; and repulsion and horror had been succeeded by what seemed attraction — even pleasure!

Her sudden flight was checked, changed to an attitude of eager expectation — her body bent forward — her lips apart — her hand placed to her ear — a yearning interest manifested in each strained feature of her speaking face. Still her large blue eyes, the pupils unnaturally dilated, strained into the copse; and she stood there, under the sombre shadow of the palm, the living embodiment of that exquisite creation of the chisel that has made its sculptor's fame — the listening Nydia of Pompeii.

Her parted lips moved slightly, and her hand raised itself with a languid motion.

"Hush!" she murmured, as one speaking in a dream.

"Do not break that heavenly music. It sounds like the song of the angels!"

Then, on the second, a hoarse, hissing whisper grated through the clenched teeth of the Egyptian, who stirred not hand or foot, but with a single glance warned back the astonished group, who were about pressing forward:

"Stir not. Speak not—if you love her! *It is the cobra-di-capello!* They only strike when angered—movement will be death!"

A chill struck to the heart of his listeners as they heard that dreaded name. They shuddered and obeyed.

Motionless as the rest, but with every muscle braced as if ready to spring between the girl and the serpent—to interpose his own body as her shield, if necessary—and with his eye riveted upon the monster, the Egyptian watched its every movement, as the crest rose and fell, and the scales of the sinuous bulk writhed and twisted in its dark-brown coils. Large drops of sweat rolled from his contracted brow, his breast heaved like that of an athlete after a deadly strain, and blood dripped on his white silk vest from the lips his sharp white teeth tore in his agitation. Anxiety strained to agony was stamped on every feature, but, with marvellous self-control, he stood still as if hewn out of stone!

Moments, that seemed hours, passed. Twice the cobra raised his flattened head, projected the ominous cowl over his red eyes, braced his stiffening coils, and seemed preparing for his arrowy spring. Then twice the Copt, bracing every muscle, seemed ready to launch himself between the monster and its prey.

But twice the serpent lowered his head and relaxed his coil; and twice a deep gasp from the overburdened breast of the man proved one peril past—one strain over.

The rest of the group—stupefied by the peril, and sure that the Egyptian knew best what the fearful situation required—implicitly obeyed his warning.

Suddenly, while all remained in this horrible suspense, there sounded from the other side of the wall the low, wailing notes of the Egyptian reed-flute, followed by a peculiar call. As the Copt caught the sound, his face brightened, and he breathed the deep sigh of relief, for he recognized the call of the serpent-charmer, so well-known in the East. The cobra seemed to hear it, too. Through his vast and sinuous bulk there seemed to run a shuddering thrill. His uplifted crest sank; his huge folds sullenly and reluctantly unwound; and, turning his head in the direction of the sound, he stretched his full length over the intervening sward. A second and shriller blast of the flute, followed by a louder call, broke through the dead stillness; and then the serpent slowly twisted round its gross body, and, with a gliding motion, dragged it off in the opposite direction—its course indicated by the waving of the shrubbery as its slimy folds worked through it with a rustling sound.

When the cobra first turned his head, and released the maiden from the spell of his glittering eye, a slight shudder shook her frame, and she leaned eagerly forward, as though to follow his movements. The next moment her eyes contracted, the lids closed wearily, her trembling limbs refused to support her, and she would have fallen heavily forward, had not Askaros rushed up and sustained her fainting form on his sinewy arm.

Then the whole group advanced at once; and even the acid spinster—softened into demonstrative affection by the fearful peril past and hideous doom so late averted — took the inanimate form in her arms, and bestowed all a woman's care and tenderness upon it.

The father's heart was too full for words. Tears rose to his eyes, a red flush conquered the ashy pallor that had covered his ruddy face the moment before; he seized the hand of the young Egyptian and wrung it hard in silence. But the old man's eye spoke his thanks more eloquently than any words.

Harry Van Camp was more demonstrative. He poured out his thanks and praises on Askaros vehemently and incoherently, swearing he never could forget that to his coolness and self-command his sister owed her life.

The Englishman — to whom danger was familiar in the tented field and deadly Indian jungles, where he had the renown of a great tiger-slayer — had blenched under this new peril, in which his experience and his manhood availed nothing. Undemonstrative, like all his country-men, he neither by word nor gesture to any of the party indicated his admiration of the Copt's conduct; but he muttered to himself under his brown beard:

"By Jove! I said he was a man at first sight, and he has proved himself one. Any fool could have rushed in, as I thought of doing; but it required nerve and will to do the thing neatly as he did it! The fellow's a regular trump, by Jove!"

Slowly Edith's eyes unclosed. Languidly she raised her drooping head from the supporting arm of her aunt, and said wearily:

"Why, what has happened to me? I never fainted before. The last thing I remember was the sound of such sweet music! It seemed to come from aërial harps, touched by the fingers of angels. Oh, such beautiful sights! processions of fairies and beautiful beings, that beckoned me to come; but I seemed spell-bound, and could not move. I never felt such strange sensations before; and now I feel weak and weary, and *so* drowsy."

And the fair young head sank passively back once more, and the eyes closed in quiet slumber.

"Bear her quietly in," said the Copt, pityingly, "and let her repose an hour. Then she will be perfectly well again. We Egyptians understand this serpent-fascination, which you Western people deride as visionary and unreal; though I have heard, in America, also, it is not unknown. But wait a moment, and I will arrange this matter better."

Turning to one of the Arab *saïs*, who had charge of the donkeys, he gave some hurried orders in Arabic. Both of them started off at a round trot, and soon returned with a rude litter, on which they placed the sleeping girl, and trotted off again up a broad avenue that led to the house; Miss Priscilla resuming her donkey, and accompanying them.

The men walked slowly after; and Askaros, turning to Mr. Van Camp, said:

"I owe you, sir, an explanation and an apology — an assurance that I never dreamed of the possibility of such peril to your daughter in these gardens. They are too carefully overlooked to permit the presence of such venomous things without our knowledge. This cobra had evidently escaped from one of the snake-charmers, whose note of recall doubtless saved a sad catastrophe. The sound that attracted him, you, of course, heard, and he is by this time in safe custody again."

"Snake-charmers!" said Mr. Van Camp; "who and

what are they? And are there really men who venture
to keep terribly poisonous snakes like that as familiars?"

"Yes; we have a class who claim—and do possess—
the power of attracting these venomous reptiles," replied the Copt. "They enjoy a perfect immunity from
the poison of serpents. I have, myself, seen them on
the desert, charming a cobra from his hole, and handling
him with perfect unconcern. But what their secret,
their spell, or their antidote may be, is known only to
themselves." ·   .

"But how do they 'charm' them? In what way?"

"By music and a peculiar cry, both of which you
heard practised with success on the truant who appeared,
and really was, so menacing to us. This is a strange
land of ours, and there are many strange things in it
which we ourselves would vainly attempt to explain.
But we cannot shut our eyes to things we see around us,
although they are opposed to probability, or are in defiance to natural laws and to established principles."

"Is the cobra, then, a very venomous snake?" inquired Harry.

"Most venomous: to any than those possessing the
spell or secret of which I speak, his bite is certain and
speedy death," was the answer.

Mr. Van Camp shuddered at the idea of the peril his
darling had so narrowly escaped, and felt yet more
grateful to her preserver. For he believed, truly, that
nothing but the coolness and self-possession of the young
Egyptian had averted the danger; and he further believed that he had been prepared to risk his own life for
hers, had the cobra made his spring. Askaros divined
what was passing in the old man's mind, and changed
the topic, as well as the current of his thoughts.

"Come, let us not dwell on such a disagreeable theme," he said. "The Eastern philosophy is to live in and enjoy the present, and leave past and future in the hands of Allah, our God, as well as theirs. '*Kismet*,' or fatalism, is their buckler and sword against all the ills of life, and submission to it their religion. Let us borrow this philosophy; and you, my friends, forgetting the unwelcome and uninvited guest now disposed of, turn your thoughts to the novelties I am about to show you in the way of an Eastern house and an Eastern entertainment. For, see, here we have safely arrived at my own threshold at last. Enter, and consider the house and all it contains your own!"

CHAPTER IV.

A DINNER À LA TURQUE.

THE dwelling of the Copt, which stood in the midst of this garden, had, in fact, formerly been a favorite palace of Ibrahim Pasha, the warrior son of Mehemet Ali. This prince had swept like a conquering flame over Syria, returned to Egypt, acted as regent during the madness which darkened the last days of Mehemet Ali, and died before him—Abbas assuming the regency until the death of his grandfather. The estate of Ibrahim Pasha had been divided among his heirs, and, as usual, his palaces had been sold. This one was purchased by the father of Askaros, who, in addition to his hereditary wealth, had accumulated a large fortune by bold and successful speculations, having figured in the *rôle* of Eastern merchant and·banker on a large scale, and as one of the millionnaires of Cairo.

The external appearance of this vast pile—built of granite stripped from the larger Pyramids, as are many of the more solid buildings of Cairo—was more imposing than pleasing. It was in the old Saracenic style, with massive walls rising sheer up, with no door or windows below to relieve the frowning exterior—only broken higher up by a kind of covered balcony, with lattice-work of wood curiously carved and interlaced, admitting light and air. Standing or sitting behind these lattices, the male or female inmates could see all passers outside, and themselves remain unseen.

Nothing but this blank wall presented itself from the exterior. The dome rose into a cupola, from which stretched away long wings on either side, making the building very spacious, while very gloomy-looking. The tourists could see no door by which to enter ; but their guide and host, applying a clumsy wooden key to a small orifice in the wall, shot back a wooden bolt within, and a small wicket-door swung back. Through this they entered a large square court, with the palace built around it, the interior space being open to the top of the cupola, which let in light through small ovals of glass stained all colors.

A sort of colonnade, like the cloisters of a convent, ran around it under the projection of the second floor of the building, with benches or rude divans, which served the purpose of seats by day, and of sleeping-places by night, for the inferior servants of the household; for, while in Europe the domestics occupy the highest story of the house, in the East they occupy the ground-floor. Day and night the *Bowab*, or porter, sits or sleeps inside of the gate leading to the entrance of the house. The *Bowab* of this establishment was an ancient *Berberi*, with a white beard, and his sole duty was to guard the gate — an institution we recognize in a refined shape in the French *concierge.*

A broad flight of marble steps led up to the first floor, and, removing the heavy silk curtains, which were the substitute for a door, Askaros ushered his guests into an apartment more truly Oriental than any they had yet seen.

It was a very long room, its lofty ceilings ornamented with the most elaborate wood-work, covered with tracery of the most exquisite patterns—the beauty of the work and the minuteness of its finish being something marvellous. The walls were of a sort of mosaic of inlaid wood, as were the floors, polished until as slippery as glass, with narrow strips of the richest Persian carpet running round the room to walk upon; heavy rugs of the same Persian looms being placed before each of the low divans occupying alternate niches in the wall of the apartment.

These divans were of the most luxurious description; low—not elevated more than six inches from the floor—broad and deep, and covered with rich silk brocade. A profusion of down pillows, covered in the same way, was strewn over each of them.

In one corner of the apartment stood a shining brasier of burnished brass, resting on a low tripod. This was intended for the reception of burning charcoal, at such rare times as the coldness of winter rendered a fire necessary, and constituted the sole substitute, in any Egyptian house, for the European grate. This, with the divans, constituted the furniture of the room, save a few *koorsies*, or hexagonal stands of rich wood—about two feet in height, and inlaid with mother-of-pearl squares—intended for resting small trays of refreshments or glasses of sherbet.

In the very centre of the room was a marble fountain, with its broad basin, into which slowly trickled a stream of pure water through a graceful swan's-head carved in marble; for, as it was winter, the fountain was not in full play. In summer it threw up large jets of water, that descended into the basin in graceful spray, and cooled the atmosphere delightfully.

"This is our reception-room," said Askaros, "and here is my father, to whom I will present you. Unfortunately, he is an Egyptian of the old school, and neither speaks nor understands any of the European languages."

There were no windows of the ordinary kind in this apartment, but at a height of perhaps twenty feet were several large latticed casements without glass, to admit both light and air, with movable silk curtains, which by a cord could regulate the supply of each. Following the direction of the host's eyes through the obscurity of the darkened room, the travellers saw at the divan, at its other end, what seemed a large bundle of silk, surmounted by a snowy beard. This bundle rose and advanced toward them, displaying the figure and face of a tall and venerable old man, darker in complexion and more rugged in feature than the young Copt, yet bearing strong resemblance to him.

The old man was dressed in the ancient Copt costume — a voluminous turban of snowy muslin, a close-fitting under-vest of striped Syrian silk, over a snowy shirt, with a long, loose, sad-colored silk gown, open only to the waist, and there girded with a heavy silken sash. Red slippers, with pointed toes, completed the costume.

He advanced and greeted his son's guests with that mixture of grace and dignity so common among the Orientals, motioning them to take seats on the divans near him, and reserving the place of honor, next himself, for the eldest of the party, Mr. Van Camp. He was a venerable-looking man — apparently of great age, but neither the fire of his eye was dimmed nor much of his natural force abated. Pipes and coffee were immediately brought in by the attendants, and furnished a pleasant substitute for conversation — the son in the East considering it respectful to remain silent in the father's presence, and the father being unable to converse except through an interpreter. In this manner the old man said to Mr. Van Camp:

"My daughter is attending to yours. I have just received a message stating that she is quite restored, and that they will soon join us; for you know that we are Christians, and do not veil our women, except in public, nor prevent strangers, properly introduced, from seeing them."

Then the whole party puffed vigorously at nargileh, or chibouque, exchanging but a few words, and in low tones. Then attendants came in, bearing trays, on which were sweetmeats in a large saucer; each guest took up one of the many spoons upon the tray, dipped it in the saucer, took a mouthful of the *confiture*, then laid down the spoon. Glasses of sherbet, lemonade, and different-colored liquids were also proffered from time to time, as were *fingans*, or egg-shell cups, of delicious Mocha coffee.

In this way an hour passed; and thus we will leave them, while, making use of the spell-words that opened the cave for Ali Baba, we penetrate into the *Hareem*, or women's apartments, on the floor above, in the western wing of the palace, and see who the fair inmates are, and how employed. Passing up the stairway—which on this flight was narrower and built of stone instead of marble—and taking a few steps through an antechamber, we pass under a crimson silk curtain into a long, narrow apartment, slightly smaller than that below, but finished and furnished much in the same style. This room is one of a *suite*. Divans are scattered around it, and the marks of female occupancy are distinctly visible

5 *

in the oval mirrors, combs, and brushes scattered over the *koorsies,* or little pearl-inlaid stands already described.

On one of the divans, half reclining, half supported by the silken pillows, was stretched the graceful form of Edith. The languor of her late swoon had almost passed from the expressive face, and the blue eyes were gazing into the dark orbits of a young girl kneeling near her, with her elbows resting on the divan, and a gaze of mixed curiosity and shyness fixed upon the fair stranger. This was the young El Warda, the adopted daughter of the elder Askaros, whose face and figure, while equally lovely and attractive, contrasted singularly with those of the American girl.

She was a true Eastern beauty—a type of the women who, though "soft as the roses they twine" to all outward appearance, yet conceal under that lazy languor passions volcanic in their fierceness, when once awakened by love or jealousy. Although scarcely more than a girl in years, her face and form had the ripened maturity of perfect womanhood; for in the East all fruits ripen far earlier.than in colder climes, and women mature and fade more rapidly too. The girl who now knelt by Edith's divan was really but fourteen years of age, but she seemed six years older; for her full, lithe form was fully developed, and the neck and bust moulded in perfect symmetry. Her face was round and full, and the warm kisses of the Syrian sun had given a deep brown tint to the skin, which was yet clear and smooth, with a rich sunset glow suffusing it. Her eyes—large, almond-shaped, and lustrous, with an expression of dreamy melancholy in them—would have given an air of indecision to the countenance, but for the long firm slope of chin and lower jaw, which told of resolute will. The features were refined, small, and chiselled; the lips full, pouting, and voluptuous.

She wore a tight-fitting crimson velvet jacket, richly worked in gold, over a white satin chemisette, likewise heavily embroidered, and with a row of small gold buttons up the front, which was cut very low, and open enough to display much of the lovely neck and bosom. She also wore a *shintyais*, or pair of full Turkish trowsers, of rich silk; and falling loosely over these was a straight skirt, or petticoat, of the same material, which terminated in a train behind, and gave much the same effect as the European skirt. Round the slender waist passed a golden girdle. The perfectly shaped little feet were thrust into dainty little slippers, and on her head was set a little round cap; both cap and slippers being of crimson · velvet, embroidered in gold to match the jacket. Her lustrous black hair, soft and fine as silk, but in thick and heavy masses, was plaited and hanging down her back in two long braids, the ends being fastened with gold coins, pearls, and bright bits of ribbon.

Both in face and figure, dress and carriage, she presented a most striking contrast to the blonde Edith: and even a greater one to the spare spinster, whose angular proportions were unrelieved by crinoline, and whose bombazine dress clung to her thin figure with affectionate tenacity.

Though far from ungraceful in her movements, there was a startled shyness about the girl that made her almost seem awkward, in spite of the natural undulations of her lithe form. She resembled rather a half-tamed fawn, half sportive, half terrified, than a well-conditioned young lady.

The orphan child of a near relative, adopted by the

elder Askaros many years before, when the absence of his son in Europe made a void in his house and heart he found it necessary to fill, El Warda had gradually grown to be considered a real daughter by him, and a sister by the young man.   Whether it was a sisterly affection which brought the hot blood to her face whenever the name of the latter was mentioned or his step sounded on the stairs, she herself would have found it difficult to tell, for she was as yet too young, too happy, too inexperienced to analyze her own sentiments and emotions.   Her education had been perfected by an old Frenchwoman, long resident in the East, and she had thus obtained some information on general topics, and a sufficient mastery of French to speak it fluently, and chat away with Edith, in a shy, constrained manner at first, but finally in a more cordial and unreserved strain.

During this careless talk, in which Edith asked questions and El Warda answered them, the young American first learned, to her surprise, how utterly different and repugnant were an Eastern and a Western woman's ideas both of propriety and of pleasure.   For the native Christian of the East, though differing in faith from the Mussulman, yet carries into his life, manners, and morals many of the peculiar customs and prejudices of the Turk, especially as regards his estimate and treatment of women.

With all of them the woman occupies a subordinate position — is not regarded as an equal or a companion, so much as a plaything, to be petted in the homes of the higher — a kind of upper servant in the households of the middle classes.   The wife of the Copt, Armenian, Syrian, or Greek Christian, brings in with her own hands the tray of refreshments, and, after meekly serving guest and husband, retires or remains quietly in a corner, without expecting to be addressed or to take part in the conversation. If spoken to, she glances at her husband to respond for her; and seems so fearfully embarrassed, no stranger repeats a second time the well-meant but painful politeness.

When these women go abroad, they also veil themselves, and it is considered a high compliment for a strange man, even in the house, to be permitted a sight of the face of an unmarried woman.

El Warda had, however, obtained some information as to the habits and manners of the Western women from her old French governess, and, to Edith's surprise and amusement, plied her with questions such as an intelligent child might be supposed to ask. Miss Primmins, who understood no language but her own, and who was troubled with dire apprehensions concerning a cramp in what she termed her "limb," in consequence of the unaccustomed contraction of that member from sitting crouched so long upon the divan, sniffed audibly and defiantly as she breathed an inward vow never again to subject herself to such trials.

There were several female servants, black and coffee-colored, standing in respectful postures and absolute silence around the room, and one of these, now approaching El Warda, informed her that the dinner awaited only the coming of the ladies.

Passing down the steps, and turning into a small but lofty apartment adjoining the great saloon of reception, they found the party already awaiting them, and the ceremony of a dinner *à la Turque* commenced. But as there was no table visible, nor any preparation for dining, our travellers were greatly mystified.

In the centre of the room, however, Edith observed a large *souffra,* or stand, around which were ranged cushions to the number of their party. Upon an invitation from Askaros, she seated herself upon one of these, El Warda taking that next to her, and the rest of the party assuming their places, with the exception of Miss Priscilla. She, indeed — through the double apprehension of poison and of cramps — strenuously resisted all invitations to join the circle, alleging sudden indisposition as her excuse.

The party being seated, a slave passed noiselessly around, distributing rich damask napkins with gold borders, which each guest, following the example of his host, gravely tucked, bib-like, around his neck. Then two other slaves followed, one bearing a large silver basin with perforated bottom and a reservoir beneath, and carrying on his arm a very soft and fleecy Turkish towel ; the other holding a large silver pitcher of fresh water.

Instructed what to do, Edith first held out her hands over the basin while the slave poured water over them — the Easterns, with a refinement of cleanliness we might well imitate, always washing hands and face in running water. Then, when she had dried her hands upon the towel, the slave sprinkled a few drops of rose-water, or other delicate perfume, over them. The same ceremony was gone through by all the party ; and then and there the slave deposited a large silver tray upon the *souffra* round which the guests sat. This was the soup, which was served in little bowls, a large, round, and flat piece of bread being also placed before each guest, like a plate. The soup finished, the next dish was brought in.

"Behold your dinner !" said Askaros.

The guests looked, but their faces lengthened perceptibly, for this dish was only a young lamb, roasted whole.

Neatly turning up his right sleeve, the master of the house, with his thumb and finger, tore deftly off large flakes of the flesh, and deposited them upon the pieces of bread before each guest, that being the only plate furnished ; and for knife and fork, only those that nature had provided for the primitive man. The lamb was roasted with pistachio-nuts, and was tender and delicious in flavor. It struck the strangers with wonder to see how skilfully and how gracefully the old man managed this peculiar carving, and how daintily he selected the best tidbits for his neighbors. But what astonished them still more was the perfect cleanliness with which the Egyptians ate, while the Europeans presented greasy faces, and greasy fingers too.

Upon tearing open the lamb, by seizing his two fore-legs, the opening disclosed a roasted turkey; tearing open the turkey, behold a roasted fowl; and within the fowl a pigeon was discovered! Then the guests supposed the tale was told. But no! Within the pigeon was an egg in the shell. Surely it is over now, thought the guests. But fresh surprise awaited them, for, on breaking the egg, in the very centre was a ring, of the rich uncut ruby, more prized in Egypt than the diamond. This, with courtly grace, the venerable host proceeded to place upon the finger of Edith, despite her protestations and reluctance at accepting a gift she knew must be of such great value. But Askaros having assured her his father would feel both hurt and offended if she persisted in her refusal, she felt compelled to accept the princely offering.

A brief pause ensued, after these labors of the table, before the second course — consisting of an infinite variety of made dishes, cooked with a skill and cunning that astonished the strangers — succeeded. Then came sweets and ices.

The banquet was concluded by the appearance of the head-cook, bearing in his arms a great palace in confectionery, which as a work of art rivalled anything they had seen before — the Easterns being as perfect in their manufacture of such things as even the best French *chefs*.

At a sign from his master, a slave handed Edith a long willow wand; and at the same instant El Warda rose from the cushion next Edith, and passed to the other end of the room, where the ancient spinster sat chewing the cud of sweet and bitter fancies, and watching the proceedings with mingled sensations of suspicion, scorn, and curiosity, sharpened by hunger, which the savory fumes from the dishes had aggravated.

Edith took the wand, and, prompted by Askaros, struck smartly one of the towers of the castle of confectionery. It fell in fragments, but the girl started back in alarm, for something living struggled out from those fragments with a whirring of wings, and a snow-white bird rose into the air above their heads. Circling around the table, it hovered over them, and finally settled down on the left shoulder of Edith, pressing its soft head caressingly against her cheek. She saw it was a beautiful carrier-dove, and commenced to fondle it and smooth its ruffled plumes. But the bird seemed restless, and pecked at her gently with his beak, as though impatient, and seeking to attract her attention.

"He brings a message from the Genii," said Askaros; "or, as you would say, from the Queen of the Fairies.

If you wish to find it, detach the ribbon from his neck."

The girl obeyed, and when the ribbon was detached, she drew by it, from under the carrier's wing, a small silken bag. Opening this, she saw a scroll of white satin, with Arab characters emblazoned upon it in gilded letters.

"'Translate it for me!" she cried; and Askaros repeated:

"This house and all it contains is yours. *Salaam Aleikoum!* (Peace be with you!) Search again in the bag," he added; "there may be something more."

As she plunged her fingers into it, they encountered a hard substance, and, drawing them out, she saw what resembled two lockets of gold. On the back of each, in a circlet of precious stones, were traced Arabic letters — set in the front of each a dull yellow stone, not unlike an amethyst, but more cloudy and less brilliant.

"The Arabic letters," explained Askaros, "are your name and your aunt's. These are amulets to be worn over the heart as a protection against the Evil Eye — the stones come from Mecca. This is a Turkish superstition, and yet, I regret to say, that most of the native Christians, and even many of the foreigners who have been long here, believe in it. Will your aunt and yourself condescend to accept them, in my father's name, as souvenirs of the honor you have done him by this visit to-day?"

"Really," said the young girl, smiling, as her aunt, coming forward, accepted the gift in her own and her niece's name, and both bowed their acknowledgments to the elder Askaros, who bent low his head and laid his hand upon his heart — "Really I shall begin to believe that this is an enchanted castle, and that you are a fairy

6

prince, and your father the old Caliph Haroun in disguise. But tell me one thing : how came the bird to perch on my shoulder, in preference to another's?"

"Nothing more simple," responded the young man. "He was trained to perch on El Warda's shoulder, and a small red ribbon, which you will now see pinned on yours, was his lure where to perch. El Warda left her cushion by your side, not to confuse him."

"Very clever dodge, by Jove!" said Sir Charles. "That really did puzzle me. Perfect sell! Begun to believe myself that our charming host and his venerable father were a pair of wizards, and might fly away with the ladies through the top of the roof. But my fears are now dispelled. Pity to spoil the romance of it by an explanation, however. Curse of the age everywhere!"

The slaves now approached once more with basin and goblet, and the same ceremony of bathing in running water, which had prefaced the dinner, closed it.

Then the head of the household gravely rose, his flowing robes and long white beard giving him the dignity of a patriarch, and, extending his hands, asked a blessing in Arabic for all around the board.

Then all his guests rose also, the female portion reascending to the upper apartments, where sherbet and coffee were served; the men reclining at ease on the luxurious divans, and inhaling the fragrant latakia, or stronger tumbac of Persia, from chibouque and nargileh —the latter made of silver inlaid with gold, in rich arabesque of fruit and foliage traced upon the stands. They were four feet high, and the bowls, containing rose-water, were made in some of them of ostrich eggs set in silver, and their flexible tubes were ten feet in length.

It was near midnight when the whole party returned

to the *Hotel d' Orient,* bewildered and delighted by the strange scenes that had passed under their eyes during the last few hours. But before they left the house, the younger Copt had laughingly said :

"I have kept my promise, and given you an entertainment thoroughly *à la Turque.* Such is the way our people habitually live : such is the ordinary life of my father's family, but with one exception. Such is not *my* life ; for, as the spoiled child of the household, I am allowed the privilege of living *à la Franque,* as they term it, or like a European. The jealous temper of Abbas Pasha, our Viceroy, and his hatred of everything European, make conformity to Eastern usage in dress and mode of life essential as well as politic."

Lifting the curtain of the door, he passed out, followed by the foreigners, and led the way through many long and winding passages, that indicated the vast extent of the building. Suddenly applying a key to a small, low door, he passed another narrow passage, and, lifting a curtain, displayed a spacious suite of rooms. They consisted of parlor, library, bed and bath-rooms, and were perfect and elegant in details of appointment, being fitted up in the most luxuriant European style.

"This is my home," he said. "Here I venture to assume my English habits and tastes, with my English toilet and studies. I should otherwise have relapsed into a barbarian, as have many of my old classmates since their return from Eton. So you see, my friends, I live two lives — an outer and an inner one. To-day shall be marked in my calendar with a white stone, for to-day Europe has come to me, instead of my pretending thus to go to it."

CHAPTER V.

AN EGYPTIAN VICEROY IN PUBLIC.

ABBAS PASHA, grandson of Mehemet Ali, sat on the throne built up and cemented by the craft, cruelty, and courage of his great progenitor, so aptly termed the "Napoleon of the East."

The line thus far had been an ominous one; the race seemed destined to be as fated as was the old classic house of Pelops, in the Greek tradition, on which the gods had hailed down all and every species of woe and horror, and all those ghastly terrors which have come down to us through the tragedies of Sophocles and Euripides.

For the visitation of God had first fallen upon the great head of the house himself, in the fearful doom of madness; and the chosen instrument of that visitation was said to have been none other than his own daughter, Nezlé Khanum—an Egyptian Helen of Troy—for from her hand came the love-philter which was to renew his waning powers, which shattered his reason. The evening of the great monarch's eventful life alternated between moody melancholy and violent insanity, until he was deposed, and his son, Ibrahim Pasha, made Viceroy over the kingdom.

64

Ibrahim did not long survive his new dignity. Whether from his excesses — or from poison, as many supposed — the warrior's funeral procession followed close upon the pageant of his installation; and Abbas Pasha became Regent for a few months, till death released his grandfather, and made him Viceroy in name as well as in fact.

The father of Abbas had met even a more tragic fate than his sire. Sent to subdue the fierce Wahabees of the Soudan, he had been captured, and burned to death, over a fire of green wood, by those implacable fanatics, who boast themselves the only true followers of the prophet, and are aptly styled the "Puritans of the East." Cruelly was this savage act avenged; for Mehemet Ali sent the *Defterdar*, surnamed "The Tiger," the husband of Nezlé Khanum, to carry fire and sword through the Soudan; a commission he fulfilled with all the bloodthirst of the fierce wild beast whose name and nature he shared. He too was said to have perished from poison administered by the fair but fatal hand of his beautiful spouse — a tigress fiercer and more fell than her savage mate.

So when Abbas Pasha ascended that throne, reeking already with blood and crime, and tainted with the sickly odor of poison, well might he suspect and fear those who should have been nearest and dearest to him in blood and affection, and have watched for his deadliest foes among his own kindred. Popular superstition also had centred upon him as one possessed of the "evil eye" — considered a fatal gift in the East; and whispered predictions of the dreadful doom awaiting him were already made.

And the character and nature of Abbas were such as to allow bad seed to swiftly germinate and fructify.

6 * E

Sullen and suspicious, grasping at and hoarding wealth, solitary as some wild beast of the desert—he was known only to his people from his exactions and his cruelties; for his was truly a "Reign of Terror," in which neither the life, liberty, nor property of any subject was safe. His nominal suzerain, the Sultan, had really no control over his powerful vassal, and seldom attempted to exert any, satisfied with the yearly tribute punctually paid. So Abbas was free to work his own wicked will over the fertile land and over the people of Egypt, even as he listed. Such was the actual condition of the country, and such its sovereign, at the period of this tale.

Some days subsequent to the visit to the house of the Copt, as the tourists were sitting at breakfast at the *Hotel d' Orient*, they were visited by their late host, who bore in his hand a bouquet of rare exotics, arranged with that skill which seems the special gift of the Eastern man. After presenting these to Edith, he informed his friends that on this day the formal presentation to the Viceroy of one of the newly-arrived foreign consuls-general was to take place at the former's palace, the *Helmea*. He proposed taking them to this ceremony, which would afford an opportunity of their seeing and being entertained by the Viceroy.

"I can only invite the gentlemen," he said, with a smile, "for you know, in the East, woman has not yet emerged from the seclusion of the hareem. She cannot figure in such ceremonies, as in more civilized countries —yours for example," he added, bowing low to Miss Priscilla Primmins.

"Very true, young man," replied that ancient female, flattered by the appeal. "There never has been a governor inaugurated, nor a public meeting held at Faneuil

Hall, to which the ladies of Boston were not welcomed by the gentlemen. Some even have gone so far as to speak in public! Now, I do not quite approve of that, nor of woman's voting; but, as nobody votes here, I suppose *that* doesn't matter."

"The ladies of Boston figure, too, in the learned professions, do they not?" asked Sir Charles; "preach, and practise law and medicine? Am I right?"

"Certainly they do! And why not?" responded the spinster.

"Oh, certainly! Why not?" responded the Englishman, carelessly; "*Cela dépend du goût;* but if I were a married man, Miss Primmins, even at Boston, I should seriously object to my wife's getting up at night to go out and see another man, professionally or otherwise! I am not quite sure but our friends the Turks are quite right in putting some restraint on female liberty."

A wrathful answer rose to the lips of Miss Primmins at thus hearing woman's rights and Boston theories so summarily disposed of; but she remembered it was a lord who spoke, and her reverence subdued her wrath. She sniffed, stiffened her spine, bit her tongue, and was silent, somewhat to the detriment of that useful organ.

Turning to the Van Camps, Askaros resumed:

"You will naturally wish to know how it is in my power to give you this privilege, for such it is; and it will surprise you to learn that I am an employé of the consulate whose representative is to be received to-day. I am its official translator, not for the sake of the salary, but for the inestimable privilege of the protection it confers; for each and every employé, or official, of a foreign consulate here is, by usage, which is stronger than law, entitled to claim and exact protection for person and property, even against the Viceroy himself. My having accepted this protection has greatly incensed the Viceroy, whose government have thus far denied it. But I have strong friends in the consulate," he added, "and shall go to-day, in spite of a warning from the master of ceremonies to the contrary. My family were great favorites with Mehemet Ali, under whom my father held high office. Hence we are hated by Abbas, who fears and suspects all who loved his grandfather."

The Americans and the Englishman listened in silence and with much surprise to this strange explanation, which showed them that other serpents than the cobra might lurk among the sunny pathways and rose-covered gardens through which, to the casual observer, the feet of the young Egyptian seemed destined to tread. But no further comment was made on either side; and, requesting them to be ready after midday to accompany him to the foreign consulate, whence the procession was to move, the young man placed his hand over his heart, cast an admiring glance on Edith, and gracefully withdrew.

At midday he returned, and accompanied the party to the consular residence, a large house fronting the *Ezbekieh*, with the national arms conspicuously painted on a shield over the doorway, and the national flag floating from a flag-staff high above the dwelling. For in the East each embassy, or consulate, protects the ground it covers by the virtue of its own flag, and is an inviolate asylum, free from all intrusion by the local authorities or the Egyptian Government.

Formal notice of the new consul-general's intention of presenting his credentials had been given, and as formal an answer, in French, had been returned by

"His Highness, the Viceroy," announcing the time and place fixed for such reception. The hour after midday was the time, and the place one of the Viceroy's numerous palaces at Cairo, called the *Helmea.* An hour before the time fixed for the reception, there arrived and passed before the consulate-general a long line of carriages, escorted by some two hundred cavalry; the men and horses most gorgeously dressed and caparisoned, and the state carriages lined with crimson damask and blazing with gilt decorations. From these carriages descended the Viceroy's chamberlain and introducer - of - ambassadors, both of whom spoke French, and, on being introduced to the consul-general by his dragoman, or interpreter, they announced, with much form and ceremony, that they had been sent to accompany and usher the foreign representative into the presence of their august master. Pipes and coffee were offered these officials, who partook of both, and then, expressing their readiness to set forth, the consul-general, accompanied by his suite of consular officials, some eight in number, was heralded out by two janizaries, or guards, magnificently attired and armed in Oriental fashion.

These ranked with captains in the Egyptian service, and were responsible to no one but their chief. In addition to their crooked Turkish scimitars, with silver scabbards, they bore long white staffs, six feet long, tipped with silver, and having silver heads six inches in length; with which, preceding the consul-general, they struck at every one who impeded the way, with the most reckless impartiality. The functionaries of the Viceroy seated the suite of the consul-general, including several strangers whom he had invited, in the state carriages, according to precedence, and then the whole cavalcade, escorted by the cavalry, set out for the *Helmea.*

Slowly the *cortége* wound its way through the crooked, narrow, and crowded streets of Cairo; the people scattering right and left, as the wheels almost grazed them, and escaping from being crushed to death, or flattened into pancakes against the walls, by what seemed a miracle. *Saïs,* or couriers, armed with stout sticks, ran on before the horses' heads, and struck all who did not get quickly enough out of the way; so that they were followed by what seemed a chorus of curses, until reaching the palace gates. Here another troop of horsemen were drawn up to receive them; and, alighting in front of a most imposing structure, abounding in marble fountains and latticed windows, they ascended the broad steps, passed through long suites of spacious apartments, magnificently furnished in a *mélange* of Eastern and European splendor, and were ushered into the presence of Abbas Pasha, Viceroy of Egypt.

He was sitting on a divan, with his feet coiled up under him in true Turkish fashion, as they entered, but rose and advanced a few steps forward to meet the consul-general. As he did so, he saluted, by placing his hand upon his brow, and courteously motioned his guest to take a seat by his side. The Turkish gentleman never shakes hands like the Englishman or American, nor embraces and kisses like the Frenchman or Italian. He salutes his friend by touching his own heart, lips, and brow, with a gesture full of grace. The common Arab is more demonstrative. He seizes his friend's thumb and squeezes it; then slaps the other's open hand several times with his own. The ladies you are not expected to salute, as you are not supposed to be allowed the privilege of ever seeing them.

The consul-general took the proffered seat by the Viceroy's side, his suite being assigned places on the divans at some little distance. Then he glanced curiously at his companion, and saw a man apparently of middle age, of swarthy complexion, and with little beard, short and stout of figure, with bloated, sensual face, and dull, cruel eyes — one to inspire distrust, not admiration. He wore the Eastern dress, but without ornaments, except that the tassel of the red *fez* he wore instead of a turban, was looped up by a magnificent diamond; and on his finger sparkled a ruby of great size and value.

His manners, like those of all high-born Turks, were bland and polished; for in ease, courtesy, and all that constitutes deportment, the Eastern certainly excels the Western man. He may be unable to read or write, his conversation consists of bald commonplaces about the weather, and the most agreeable part of the visit, after taking pipes and coffee, is the moment of departure; but Lord Chesterfield himself could not improve the manners of the courteous gentleman, who, in his inmost heart, looks upon you as less than the dust beneath his feet — as "a dog of an unbeliever!"

Abbas Pasha, unlike the rest of his family, knew no European language; so the conversation — after the formal reception-speeches had been disposed of — passed through the interpreter, French being the medium of communication. This the interpreter translated into Turkish, the Court language, in preference to the Arabic. No one who has not tried it can tell how embarrassing it is to have his simple remark of its "being rather a warm day," gravely announced in French, to an obsequious gentleman covered with gold embroidery, who immediately dilutes it into Turkish for the edification of the

Viceroy, who, through the same medium, and with many changes of tongue, solemnly responds "he thinks it is."

Pipes and coffee, however, such as can never be had out of the East, agreeably fill up the intervals of conversation; for your Turk is a taciturn animal, and considers much talk undignified.

The pipes on this occasion were chibouques, with stems of jessamine, or cherry-wood, six feet in length — the mouth-pieces being amber, with circlets of precious stones. Some of the stems, also, had serpents of jewels winding round them. The *zarfs*, or coffee-cup holders, were also incrusted with diamonds and rubies; the cups themselves being egg-shells of porcelain, transparent as glass.

Having disposed of three relays of pipes and coffee — for as fast as one was finished, the silent, swift domestics replenished it — and having exchanged complimentary speeches with the Viceroy on their respective countries to mutual satisfaction, the consul-general rose to go. Then, at a sign from his master, one of the officials rushed up and threw over his head a gilt cord, to which was attached a Damascus scimitar — thus investing him with the *sabre d'honneur*, as a compliment from the Viceroy. Thus doubly armed, for he wore his own Court sword as a part of his uniform, the consul-general exchanged parting salutations with the Viceroy, and passed into the court-yard.

Here he found the carriages and escort drawn up to receive him; and he also beheld a handsome horse, gayly and richly caparisoned — another gift from his princely entertainer. He had been previously notified that such was the usage on the presentation of a representative of one of the Great Powers; of which there were, in

Egyptian reckoning, five only, England, France, Russia, Austria, and America — neither Prussia nor Italy having at that time risen to the dignity they have since obtained.

On returning to his consulate, the new functionary found he was expected to pay for these gifts — not to the Viceroy, but to the guard of honor — in the shape of customary presents to the amount of a hundred pounds sterling. This was distributed by his dragoman, according to a well-understood tariff, each officer and private receiving so much per head, and regarding it not as a favor but as a right — wrangling fiercely with the dragoman as to the amount, and paying not the slightest attention to the bleeding victim, who that day learned what Eastern presents cost.

Throughout the East this system of making presents and expecting much more valuable ones in return prevails, from the highest functionaries of the state to the lowest servants in your household. It is not improbable that the same system is sometimes adopted in the West also, but not so openly.

The demeanor of the Pasha throughout this interview was not only dignified and courteous, but most flattering to the recipient, who had every reason to suppose he had produced a most favorable impression — so smiling and almost affectionate was the Viceroy's adieu. He therefore returned to receive his colleagues — who, according to etiquette, were to pay him a formal visit in full uniform and state — well satisfied with the potentate of Egypt and with himself.

7

CHAPTER VI.

THE VICEROY IN PRIVATE.

THE heavy curtains of the doorway had scarcely fallen after the last of the consul's *cortége*, and the sound of retreating footsteps had not ceased to echo in the corridor, when a sudden and striking change came over the mien and aspect of the Viceroy, who had played the courteous host so well. He stretched himself wearily, like an actor who has finished rehearsing a tedious part; the smile faded from his face, and he scowled savagely after his departing guests. The countenance, so pleasing the moment before, darkened, and a frown contracted the heavy brows over the dull, blood-shot eyes, out of which gleamed an evil light. The ease and dignity of demeanor which had characterized him during the late interview, were replaced by irritable impatience and unrestrained ill-humor.

He hurled away from him the chibouque he had been smoking, so violently that the precious amber mouth-piece, surrounded by brilliants, was detached and rolled upon the floor; bounded from his divan like a wild beast, and poured from his lips a volley of terrible Eastern imprecations upon the bodies and souls of his terrified and cowering officials! When the first storm of his passion had subsided, he threw himself back upon his divan, and commanded his master of ceremonies to be summoned again into his presence.

The cowering official appeared, his knees trembling, his body bent almost prostrate, and his face exhibiting the extreme of abject fear, as he knelt down to kiss the hem of his master's robe.

Brutally repulsing the kneeling man, with a violent kick from his foot Abbas sent him rolling backward on the floor, while he screamed out mixed curses and orders that his sword and insignia of rank should be taken from him. These insults were received with true Oriental submission by the disgraced functionary, who again prostrated himself, and asked in humble tones:

"O *Effendina!* (great lord) may the meanest of thy slaves dare ask how he has incurred thy sovereign displeasure, that he may show his repentance, and strive to atone for his fault!"

"Son of a dog! grandson of an ass!—whose mother's grave may swine defile!—how hast thou dared to admit into our presence, under foreign protection, that dog of a Copt Christian, Askaros? He has dared to defy me, and laugh at my beard in disobeying my orders not to seek that protection! By the soul of the Prophet! *he* shall rue it. And explain why *thou* shalt not be sent to *Fazougli*, for thy share in this insult!"

"The life and fortunes of thy slave are thine, O Effendina!" was the trembling reply: "and thy wrath is just. But let it not fall on the head of the innocent. The fault was not mine; for the Copt had warning from me as to the will and pleasure of my sovereign lord, and so had the consul-general; but both disregarded my warning—and thy slave dared not, without thy special

orders, refuse admittance to any one in the company of
the consul.''

"*Peki!*" ('T is well!) answered Abbas, whose first burst
of wrath seemed passing over. "Still, thou shouldst have
shown better management, and impressed my wishes
more strongly. My sight has been offended by the presence of this dog! and his presumption must be punished.
Thou canst only regain my favor by showing me how
this may be done.''

"If his Highness will permit, his slave may be able
to do this thing. Already steps have been taken to
avenge my lord for this outrage,'' replied the still kneeling official.

"Come with me, then,'' said Abbas, suddenly re-
membering that the audience-chamber, filled with the
high dignitaries of his empire, was not the proper place
to discuss such matters. "Come with me, and I will
listen in private to thy explanations.'' And rising up,
attended on each side by an obsequious functionary who
supported his elbows, he shuffled out of the room,
followed by the master of ceremonies, whom all the
other courtiers carefully avoided in this hour of his disgrace. Abbas passed on to his own private apartment,
at the door of which was stationed a guard, commanded
by one of his most trusted officers; and, making a sign
to the rest not to enter, permitted only the master of
ceremonies to pass within. Then throwing himself on
a divan, he cried with fierce impatience:

"Explain thy meaning! What steps have been taken
to punish the Copt dog, who has strewn filth on my
father's grave!''

"Lord of my life! We have discovered his secret
foe in the person of his most trusted friend, who pos-

sesses all his secrets and those of his family, and whose hate can be made to minister to the justice of Effendina. That man now awaits the pleasure of my lord, who can himself question him, and learn all he has to tell."

"Admit him!" was the brief response. "But first tell me who and what he is, and how he can be useful in this matter."

"His name is Daoud-ben-Youssouf," answered the official. "During the absence in Europe for several years of the young Askaros, he was the confidential secretary of his father, and the inmate of his house; only resigning that position when the young man returned, eight months since. He still possesses the confidence of both father and son, and is the most intimate associate of the latter; for, though not educated in Europe, he knows much of the language and habits of the Franks."

"Has he been badly treated by father or son?" asked the Viceroy.

"On the contrary, Highness; they have overwhelmed him with favors!"

"Why, then, does he hate them, and seek to do them injury?"

"Highness, it is the same cause which ruined our great father, Adam. They say the daughter of the old Askaros is fair to look upon; and these Christian dogs permit their young men to look upon the unveiled faces of their women. So the young Daoud sought to gain her in marriage, and attributes the rejection of his suit to the young Askaros. So did I learn through a trusty spy I have had among the servants of that household for some time past. Therefore did I seek this youth, and had many conferences with him. Now we understand

7 *

each other. Did I dare to name such a worm of the dust in the same breath as your Highness, I should say his hatred of the Copt, Askaros, equals that with which your Highness has deigned to honor the unbelieving dog! But he insists upon seeing your Highness personally."

"He is over-zealous, or over-bold," answered the Pasha, frowning darkly. But the next moment a cruel smile wrinkled the corners of his mouth, as he added: "Doubtless, Mahmoud Bey, he is dissatisfied as to your power or authority fitly to reward him, and seeks the assurance from myself. By the tomb of the Prophet! he shall have it. Admit him."

The suddenly disgraced and as suddenly reinstated official retired backward from the presence of his master; but the moment after returned, accompanied by a slight, tall young man, clad in the Coptish dress. He made a profound, but not abject salutation, to the Viceroy, without prostrating himself, or kissing the hem of his robe; then folding his arms over his chest, seemed to await the latter's pleasure.

Abbas gazed upon him with surprise, so young and girlish-looking was the face, so gentle and subdued the expression of the young stranger's countenance; the oval outline, soft and beardless, save the mere pencilling of a dark mustache; and the smooth, fair skin, unfurrowed by a single strong line or wrinkle. But Abbas Pasha, like all Turks, was a skilful physiognomist, and he looked again and more closely upon the face before him. The Syrian suddenly looked up, and the Viceroy caught his eye and was satisfied the face was only a mask. For at that moment the passions which agitated the heart shone through the windows of the soul, and the real nature of the man was revealed, as though by a lightning flash, to the great adept in evil before whom he stood. The expression swiftly passed from the telltale mirror, and the next moment the eye was as calm and expressionless as the other features.

"A real young tiger-cat!" muttered the Viceroy, under his beard; and there was something in the gliding, elastic movement of the body, and in the sleepy softness of the greenish-brown eye of the young Syrian, that made the comparison an apt one. His dress was that of the ordinary Coptish accountant—a full black turban over a closely-shorn, but unshaven head; a long gown of striped Syrian silk, falling like a robe to his feet, and a white under-vest, with a row of small silken buttons, coming up high on the neck, around which he wore no covering of any sort. A Syrian sash wound around his waist; and into this was thrust a large silver inkstand, supported by its handle within the folds, and a large pen of the same material. The only ornaments he wore were the signet ring on the forefinger of his right hand, and a large diamond on the little finger of his left. After gazing on him some time in silence, the Viceroy spoke : "Mahmoud Bey tells me you know something which it befits me to hear," he said. "You are permitted to speak."

Steadily and calmly the Syrian replied :

"May the shadow of Effendina never be less! I am told by Mahmoud Bey that your Highness seeks some information as to the public administration of Askaros, the elder, whose private *Wakeel* (secretary) I was, when he was *Khasnadar*, (treasurer,) under the reign of his late Highness, Mehemet Ali. Although Askaros was my employer and my patron, yet, Highness, my first duty is to my Viceroy, and I am ready to reveal all I know. Ask, then, and it shall be answered.''

A red flush passed over the face of Abbas, partly of pleasure at securing so useful a tool ; partly of anger at the calm audacity of the beardless boy, whom he considered as less than dust beneath his feet, in thus daring to assume community of purpose between them. He did not, therefore, deign to reply to the Syrian, but, turning to Mahmoud Bey, coldly said :

'' Tell him that I approve of his zeal, and that it shall not go unrewarded. I doubt not there have been grave abuses in that administration ; and he who furnishes proofs of them merits and shall have rich compensation. I shall instruct you when and how to interrogate him on the subject. Now he may go.''

The calm face of the Syrian manifested no emotion, either of pleasure or confusion, as the Viceroy uttered these words. He allowed Mahmoud Bey to repeat them to him, as though he had not heard them ; then courteously, but firmly, responded through him.

'' Say to the Effendina, that it is to him alone that I can communicate these matters in the first instance ; and that without a witness. Otherwise my lips are sealed. My life is his, but my secret is my own ; and I have that to repeat to him, I may say to none beside himself.''

The face of Abbas underwent a sinister change as the daring youth uttered these words. His swollen features grew purple with passion, and the veins rose like cords upon his temples. He clutched at the band around his neck as though it were stifling him ; and his broad chest heaved as he panted for breath. His eyes seemed to emit a dull red flame, like that of the cobra, as he fastened it upon the rash speaker who thus braved him, and dared to propose terms, as though to an equal. But ere the torrent of invective and wrath, which these signs presaged, burst forth, the young man spoke again to avert it; and this time with far greater show of reverence in his manner than he had yet assumed.

"Let not the wrath of my lord, the Effendina," he said, "be kindled against the humblest of his slaves, who means no want of reverence, nor dares disobey his sovereign will. But there are things which it befits his private ear alone to hear; and I, therefore, humbly crave a few words alone."

So saying, the Syrian bent his knee and bowed his forehead in the dust, in Oriental reverence. The cloud passed from the brow of Abbas, though the hatred rose in his heart against this astute plotter, who dared thus, as he plainly saw, to play with him. But he thought it best to extract his secret, and use before he punished him. Therefore he spoke again to Mahmoud Bey:

"I pardon the rudeness of this youth, in consideration of his ignorance, and because his lack of discretion may be compensated by his zeal. As this concerns grave public interests, I will permit him to impart it to my private ear—but stand just outside the door, and should I clap my hands, enter immediately. Come hither first." And, bending his head, he whispered in the ear of Mahmoud, "Tell Ruschid Pasha, captain of the guard, to post himself at the secret entrance just behind me; and, at the least sign of danger, to shoot this stranger. He *may* mean misceief."

Mahmoud Bey made his reverence, and withdrew.

"Now speak," said the Viceroy. "Why did you ask to tell your tale alone?"

F

"Highness, may I speak fearlessly without giving offence?"

"It is permitted you to speak!"

"Highness, I could do a great service—I can .rid you of a dangerous enemy and give you a fair excuse to confiscate his great estates and his vast wealth. And I can, moreover, tell you where to find that wealth. But, Effendina, you must let me name my price!"

"Slave!" roared the Viceroy, "do you dare propose a bargain to me, your lord and master! Do you not know that for less insolence I might have you flayed alive!—scourged to death?—or that at a word from me the rest of your life would be passed in a dungeon? Do you not know your living tomb may be gaping for you even now?"

A shudder ran through the slight form of the Syrian, but still he answered firmly:

"All this I know, O Effendina! All this I thought of before I came; but my mind is made up, and wild horses cannot tear my secret from me, except on my own terms."

The very audacity of the reply, coming from such a source, was not without its charm for Abbas, whose complex character often puzzled those who thought they knew him best. Looking over the slight figure before him, from head to foot, he burst into a roar of laughter, as though the contrast between the speaker and his words had been too much for his gravity.

"By the beard of my father!" he cried. "Who would have thought to find the soul of the Persian Antar under the frock of a Syrian scribe!—who, with no other weapons than his pen and ink-horn, braves Abbas Pasha to his very beard!—Ho! ho! ho!"—and he laughed again, until the tears trickled down his cheeks and he

stopped from sheer exhaustion. "Name thy price, then,"
he added, on recovering his breath, as though he were
still humoring a capital joke.

"My price," answered the Syrian, boldly, for he saw
he could not long depend on the changing moods of the
capricious tyrant—"My price for my secret is—death
or banishment for father and son! and that the daughter
may be given to me as my wife, with a dower of two
hundred purses, when the work is done."

"Is she then so lovely, this maiden?" asked the
Pasha, scoffingly, fixing his small eyes—over which a
dull film seemed to pass, as over those of venomous reptiles — full upon his rash interlocutor, whose cheek paled
visibly at the question.

"Highness, *no!*" the Syrian answered quickly. "She
is *not;* nor in any way attractive! It is hate, not love,
which prompts me. I seek that the daughter of mine
enemy may serve as my handmaid!"

Abbas laughed again; but there was more mockery
than mirth in this explosion.

"Fool, as well as liar!" he cried; "why seek to
deceive me! I know now the secret of thy heart, but it
matters not to me; I covet not thy maiden. Give my
council the proofs, or put them in the way to do the
things thou hast promised, and I swear by the tomb of
the Prophet, and by my own soul, the wishes of thy heart
shall be granted. But mark me well!"—and his voice
sank into a savage snarl—"if thou deceivest me—if
thou seduce my council into commencing a prosecution
that cannot be sustained and carried out without creating
scandal, here and at Stamboul— better far for thee hadst
thou never been born! For living thou shalt taste the

pains of Eblis, and pray for death as deliverance from the doom that awaits thee !

"And now, false hound, that hath turned to bite the hand that hath fed thee, go ! Among all the Nazarene dogs that blaspheme the name of the holy Prophet, can be found none so vile as thyself; but remember! thy sleek head now is under the paw of the tiger ! Go now and do thy work; but do it not negligently, or woe unto thee !—Thou art warned !

"Pollute my sight no longer with thy presence, and thy rottenness. Strange ! that Allah should have put so smooth a mask over so black a soul !"

As he closed, he clapped his hands, and several attendants entered.

"Mahmoud Bey," the Pasha said, "take your friend away. And," he added, in a lower tone, "bid him be silent as to this interview."

His orders were obeyed.

While the Viceroy had been giving his parting benediction, the Syrian's head had been bowed down on his breast, as though in deep abasement or contrition. Not a muscle of his face changed, not a nerve of his frame quivered; but his pride, which was great, writhed within him under each stroke of scorn, like a fierce lash lacerating his soul. And all the more because he knew the tyrant's words were just, did the barb fasten the arrow in the wound, to remain there festering for ever! The Viceroy but echoed the voice of his own conscience.

But as Saul wrestled in vain with the evil spirit, so did his descendant—tempted as sorely as he; and the evil elements in his nature hardened under the fire which should have melted them.

With eyes downcast, that the lurid fires that blazed in

them might not be seen, and with hell raging in the heart that seemed scarcely to beat under his silken mantle, the Syrian stripling registered another vow of vengeance, when his first debt should have been paid—and this time it was against his accomplice and his king!

And so, after having made their evil compact, prince and subject parted with hate and scorn rankling in the souls of each; and the seeds of mutual sin sown in two souls that day, were destined to bring forth bitter fruit in the future.

8

CHAPTER VII.

HAWK AND DOVE.

O N a bright morning of the succeeding week, in one of the oldest and dingiest of the tall stone houses fronting the *Ezbekieh*, sat the young Syrian, diligently engaged in writing. He was squatted on a divan covered with torn, faded, and dirty chintz, and, crouched among the cushions, wrote upon his knee, in place of book or table. Long, narrow strips of paper were strewn round him on the floor, with Arab characters and numerals traced upon them; and everything in the small room seemed dirty and disorderly, except the occupant, who looked as sleek and spotless as was the animal to which the Viceroy had likened him.

The contrast between the appearance of the man and the poverty-stricken squalid appearance of the room, was very marked; and the noises from the street would have disturbed any less concentrated attention, not to mention the fact that contiguous to this room was the stable of his donkey, whose proximity was made evident to several senses at once.

Unmindful of these various annoyances, that use had made second nature to him, the young scribe worked on; and so absorbed was he in his labors, that he only became aware of the presence of a visitor when a clear, familiar voice sounded close to his ear, and caused him to start, till he almost upset the inkstand he had taken from his girdle and placed on the divan beside him.

"*Salaam Aleikoum!*" (Peace be with you!) said the new-comer. "The bee is busy, as usual, I see, but I much doubt if it be honey he is making."

"*Aleikoum es Salaam!*" (Peace be also with you!) was the response. "I am making bread, not honey, for my labors are anything but sweet."

"Your workshop certainly is not," said Askaros, laughing. "So, unless you prefer your donkey's society to mine, or are too busy to smoke a chibouque with me, come up stairs to your sitting-room, for it is long since I have seen you, and I have many things to say."

"Most willingly will I exchange this dull work for your pleasant society," replied the young Syrian, whose manner, though deferential, was not humble toward his more fortunate friend. "I rejoice that you have visited my poor house, for I long to talk with you. You know," he added with a bitter smile, "I might as well converse with my long-eared friend in the next room as with most of my ordinary companions, who twit me with being two-thirds a Frank—thanks to your example."

So saying, he arose, and, leaving the papers strewn over the divan, locked the door, and motioned Askaros to precede him up the steep and winding stone steps which led to the upper apartments. At the head of these steps the young men passed into a good-sized room, over-looking the *Ezbekieh,* in which was none of the dirt and squalor visible below, though it contained no other furniture than long divans covered with chintz, running round its sides. It had, however, glass windows without curtains, which gave it a more civilized air. Daoud clapped his hands, and a servant appeared, who immediately proceeded to fill pipes; and, seating themselves on the divan in front of the window, the two young men coiled up their legs, and commenced smoking vigorously. Askaros spoke first.

"You do not ask me, O Daoud," he said, "the cause of my infrequent visits to you of late. Are you not curious to know?"

"Curiosity is the quality of a woman, not of a man," the other answered. "Far less does it become a friend to pry into the secrets of one so high above him. I was satisfied your absence did not arise from any offence I could have given you; and, therefore, though I missed much your society, I was satisfied with that."

"Spoken like a sage!" cried Askaros, laughing again. "But you would like to know, nevertheless, and I want to tell you."

"Of course some fair Houri has caused your absence," replied the Syrian. "I well know the temptations to which you are exposed, and the facility with which you yield to them. But I fear to give offence, else I would ask, do you not fear to anger the *Khanum*, (great lady,) whose eyes are everywhere, and whose jealousy is as fatal as her love?"

"No fear of that! for two reasons," Askaros hastened to answer. "For, though you are right, and there is a woman at the bottom of it, yet it is not the usual thing at all; and the woman belongs to and moves in a different world from ours and the Khanum's."

"One of the genii, or a fairy princess, perhaps," said the Syrian. "But cease your transports, and tell me who, what, and where she is, that my senses also may be gladdened by glimpses of paradise and the Houris."

"I can answer all of your queries in one word," responded Askaros, pointing with his finger toward the *Ezbekieh.* "Behold!"

The Syrian's eye followed the direction of the finger, and he saw the party from the hotel slowly strolling down the broad path in front of the coffee-house.

"*Ingleeze!*" he said. "*Sitta Miriam!* (Holy Virgin!) but the young one is lovely. *Binta quiesa, quiesa kitteer!* (A beautiful maiden — very beautiful!) but more like a fairy than a woman, to my taste."

"Well, is she not sufficient apology for my absence?" laughed Askaros, gayly. "I have been actually playing dragoman to the whole party for the last two weeks! You, who know how tame and tiresome sight-seeing is to me, can guess how pleasant must have been my payment, to make me go through with it."

The Syrian did not reply, but he fixed his eyes upon the young girl with a strained intensity, as though to make a mental photograph of every line in her face and figure, for some minutes. Then again he only repeated: "*Quiesa kitteer — kitteer!*"

Briefly, but with much animation, did Askaros describe to him the incidents of their acquaintance and intercourse; to which the other listened in silence until he had finished.

"Have you seen the Khanum in the interval?" he then asked again. "I tell you, her eyes never close, and she has heard of your Frank fairy long ere this. She is not to be trifled with! Those who play with panthers, must keep the fur smooth by rubbing it the

8 *

right way. And no panther was ever more treacherous
or more deadly than she."

"I know! I know!" said Askaros, impatiently.
"Trouble not yourself about that; nor couple in the
same thought, nor name in the same breath, two creatures as widely apart as the good and evil genii! The
Khanum may be a panther, but I know a spell can tame
her."

The Syrian bowed his head, as though in apology,
and changed the subject, which he saw was not an
agreeable one.

"Why, O my friend," said Askaros, affectionately,
"will you persist in your false pride, and refuse my
father's offers of service, so earnestly and so pressingly
made? Why live this hard life in this squalid house, so
repugnant to your delicate and fastidious nature, as well
as to your training, while my father's *Wakeel*, during
the years of my absence? He again charges me to
tender to you enough of capital to establish yourself in
commerce, at which you can surely accumulate a rapid
fortune; and, to spare you any sense of obligation, he
consents to accept a share of the large profits he is sure
you will make. Come, my friend, be reasonable. Accept this offer."

Tears came into the eyes of the Syrian. His impress-
ible nature was deeply moved. He shook his head
slowly:

"I cannot!" he said. "But do not think me ungrateful, nor foolishly proud, that I do not. When I
was your father's *Wakeel*, had I accepted what was
offered me, I might have been rich to-day; but I came
poor out of his service — rich only in a good character
and in your friendship; and I believe and know I can

work my own way to fortune. Even now I am not so poor as I appear to be, and prefer working my own way still. So give my best thanks to your father, and tell him this from me."

There was a pause, before assuming a graver tone, and, with an air of great concern, he spoke again, more slowly and with hesitation.

"Askaros Effendi," he said, "both you and your father know my affection and fidelity to your house, and that affection may make me nervous when there is no need; but I think it my duty to warn you that there is danger in store for you both."

"How, and from whom?" asked Askaros, impressed by the tone and manner of the Syrian; for he knew him to be no idle babbler, nor given to foolish fancies.

"From — Abbas Pasha!" responded Daoud, in a whisper, and glancing cautiously round, to be sure he was not overheard; "and the danger takes the double shape of assaulting your father for his administration as Khasnadar, and of punishing you for daring to accept a foreign protection."

"How know you this? or what induces you to suspect it?"

"Your friend, Zoulfikar Pasha, who, although not in favor, yet keeps his position near the Viceroy, and who loves you much, sent his confidential *Hakim* (physician) here to me, that I might warn you. I know of nothing further."

"You have a clear, cool head," Askaros answered, thoughtfully. "What is your counsel? What do you advise?"

"I would advise, firstly, that your father should pray the Grand Council to open and examine his accounts —

of the vouchers for which you know I have duplicates.
In the next place, I would counsel you to resign this
place in the foreign consulate, and thus propitiate the
wounded pride of the Viceroy.   Thus may you both
escape the wrath of Abbas, and be taken into his favor ;
otherwise I fear trouble is in store for you both.''

"You astonish me!'' exclaimed Askaros, opening
wide his eyes, in amazement; ''you actually would
counsel us to put ourselves—our lives and our fortunes
—absolutely without recourse into the hands of Abbas
Pasha!   What sudden blindness has stricken you that
you cannot see the greater perils yawning under that
course? Do you believe that Abbas has suddenly become
just, generous, and humane—that to the wolf can be
safely confided the keeping of the lamb?''

"My opinion of the Viceroy has not altered, nor do
I think any better of him than when we last spoke,''
answered Daoud, without raising his eyes.   ''But I do
believe the plan I propose is the best, to disarm him.
You best know how far you can count on the protection
of your consul-general, in case of violent measures on
the part of the Viceroy.   With reference to your father's
accounts, that is a matter in which your foreign protection cannot intervene.   Think on these things seriously ;
for I believe the necessity for your action may arise
sooner than you imagine.   But count always on my aid,
and command my services at all times,'' he added,
slowly; ''for the debt I owe you and your father, I hope
I may live to pay!''

He turned his head away as he spoke, as though over-
come by emotion, and struggling to suppress the strong
manifestation of his gratitude.   But had Askaros seen
the cruel, sinister smile that writhed the thin lips, and the

evil glare in the downcast eye, veiled by its long, feminine lashes, he would better have understood the equivocal promise that had just been made him. That promise
it was Daoud-ben-Youssouf's intention to keep to the
letter, if not to the spirit, with his too confiding listener
—for in his heart at that moment he felt a foretaste of the
pains of Eblis, racked and torn as it was by the conflicting
demons of Jealousy and Shame—Hatred and Remorse!

But the brow was as smooth and the face and form as
still, as though no moral tempest were making havoc
and howling wildly through his soul. For, strong as was
his trial, his strength to master it was greater still. Though
his pulses bounded through his arteries at fever-heat;
though his brain rocked and reeled under the strife of
the conflicting emotions that rent and tore him, like the
man possessed of devils in Holy Writ—still his external
calm was not disturbed; though he listened like a man
in a dream, and without comprehending the meaning of
the words which his friend poured into his ear.

Until the day of his death, Daoud never knew what
that friend said, at the close of their interview. He
heard the sounds, but they conveyed no meaning to his
mind, as they passed to it through the ear. He answered
mechanically, and must have done so fitly, for no suspicion of his preoccupation seemed to cross the mind of
his friend; and when the conversation flagged, and
Askaros rose to take his leave—affectionately rallying
Daoud on his seriousness and anxiety—the Syrian seemed
to awaken as though from a trance.

As soon as he was alone, he sighed heavily, and
grinding his teeth, muttered:

"Is it worth the price? Is it worth the price? And
is the Book right, when it asks: 'What will it profit a

man to gain the whole world, if he lose his own soul?'
If it be so, as the priests say, then woe to me here and
hereafter! But"—and the lines of his feminine countenance suddenly hardened from softness into ferocity—
"but woe! double woe! to the fools who have driven
me to this damnable treachery to gain her, without whom
my life would be but one hopeless longing!—one waking and breathing death!"

A moment he paused, with set teeth and laboring
breath; then an expression of subtle malignity crept
over the face, and blent with the ferocity that covered it
like a veil.

"But can I trust the promises of Abbas? I have read
in the parchments that the fathers loaned me, that the
Evil One never kept faith with his servants, nor paid the
price for which they sold their souls; but by some cunning juggle exacted the service, and enforced the penalty,
without fulfilling the desire of their hearts. If ever incarnate devil was allowed to plague this earth, it is Abbas
Pasha! And neither Allah nor Eblis have any sway
over him. Can I trust him? Can I trust him? And is
it yet too late to tell Askaros the truth, and save father
and son? No! no! I cannot now, if I would. For, did
not Abbas say my head was now under the paw of the
tiger? And said he not truly?"

Again a fleeting cloud from his changing mood swept
over the face, growing ever darker and ever older in its
wrath. There was bitter mockery in his tone as he spoke
again:

"My fortunate young friend, by his riches and his
influence, can secure foreign protection; but who would
trouble himself—what Frank consul would lift a finger
—if Abbas desired to crush so mean a worm as Daoud-

ben-Youssouf? But he cannot say I did not warn him —
even more strongly than I intended; for my purpose was
only to hint, not speak out, so as to keep his confidence
after his father had been summoned to the council. Had
he taken my advice, my path would have been easier.
As he did not, it is a steep and slippery one — but I shall
climb it — I shall climb it! And then — O El Warda,
— star of my youth! inspiration of my manhood! for
whom I long more than ever did Mussulman for the
green-sleeved Houris of Mohammed's heaven! — though
by crime I may win thee — yet thou shalt be mine! Yes,
in spite of earth, and heaven, and hell! Even though I
sell my own soul to clasp thee!''

As he spoke thus his face kindled into a glow of passion, and he turned his face again toward the window.
But this time his vision was attracted, not by the sights in
the *Ezbekieh* below, but fixed on some moving object
high up in air, and sharply defined against the background of the clear blue sky.

Far up in the cloudless atmosphere — reduced to a
mere speck — one of those wide-winged Egyptian hawks,
half bird of prey, half vulture, was balancing itself motionless in the air, preparatory to its descent upon a terrified
Barbary dove, which — with the rare instinct of self-
preservation — instead of flying away in a straight line,
was circling round and round, to confuse the vision and
aim of its deadly enemy.

The Syrian, though a skeptic in religion, yet, like all
Easterns, was a slave to superstition, and a great believer
in signs and omens. Fixing his unwinking eyes full on
the two birds in the broad glare of the midday, he held
his breath, and hoarsely muttered, in his eager anxiety:

"Yes! I will accept it as an omen; I am the hawk,

El Warda the dove! Whichever wins will show me my
chance of success; and I feel in my spirit that my good
star will prevail."

As though in answer to his cry, he could see, high in
air, a gleam on the feathers of the hawk's wide wings,
as he slanted them close to his sides, and with an arrowy
rush, dropped sheer down, like a plummet, through the
yielding air, his outstretched neck and contracted talons
ready for the blow. Swift as was the plunge, it was met
by a counter movement on the part of the destined victim;
for, as the hawk flashed down toward it, the dove ceased
its circling movement, and darted off in a straight line —
just in time! for the strained eye of the gazer could
scarce mark the space which intervened between the
dusky bird and his snowy quarry, as he shot down far
below, almost grazing it in his swift descent.

But, though baffled, the bird of prey was not beaten;
and Daoud smiled grimly to see how savagely and how
swiftly he checked his downward rush, opened his fan-
like wings, and soared upward again in chase of his
victim. Then ensued a trial of skill and of stratagem
between the two birds, each circling round and striving
— the one to rise, the other to keep above its enemy —
for in so doing was the sole hope of the smaller bird.

" Courage and force must win!" muttered the Syrian,
as he saw the hawk, with each sweep of its strong wings,
rise higher and nearer — narrowing the distance — while
symptoms of distress and weariness were beginning to
show themselves in the smaller bird. At length, by one
final and powerful sweep, the hawk shot up into the air,
hovered a second over his struggling quarry, and poised
for the final swoop. The dove's terror seemed to have
mastered its strength. Paralyzed by its failing hope and

coming doom, its wings almost closed, and, with a piteous piping cry, it flew straight downward, seeking shelter among the trees of the *Ezbekieh.*

With a shrill shriek, again the hawk launched himself down upon his prey, which, forgetting its fear of man in its greater terror of its foe, dashed blindly down into the bosom of Edith, where it clung convulsively; the fiercer bird swooping so close as almost to brush the face and shoulder of Edith with his wings, in the ardor of pursuit; then, baffled and disappointed, suddenly sailing away, with a clanging scream, toward the barren range of the Mokattam hills.

"Poor bird!" said Edith; "how glad I am he sought my protection, and that I was able to save him."

"You are his guardian angel," answered Askaros, who had joined her; "and many would run as great a risk for the privilege of your sympathy. But he seems very tame for a wild dove."

"He differs from men," answered Edith, laughing. "He knows his friends, and he trusts them at sight."

"Pardon me!" answered the Copt, looking more closely at the bird; "but he is not a new acquaintance: he was introduced to you two weeks since at my house. It is one of my carrier-doves, that has come wellnigh paying dear for its truant propensities. His grave was almost ready in that hawk's maw."

While this gay badinage was passing on the *Ezbekieh,* and frivolous words were exchanged between light and innocent hearts, the solitary Syrian, on his unseen watch, was moved by far other sentiments. To him the omen he had invoked was a serious thing; and the superstitious element in his nature was strongly worked upon by the issue of the trial he had set up as the symbol of his suc-

9 G

cess or failure.   He knit his brow savagely, and, gnawing his nether lip with his sharp white teeth, flung out
his clenched hand in a gesture of menace to the unconscious pair beneath, whom he identified with that failure.

"An idle story!   An old woman's tale!" he growled
scornfully and impatiently to himself.   "Why am I fool
enough to feed such fancies, or to dream such dreams?
What have the birds of the air to do with the thoughts of
man's brain, the wishes of his heart, or the works of his
hand?   Why should I, who laugh at the mummeries of
Mussulman imaum and of Christian priests alike, believe,
even for a moment, in the divinations and the omens of
the old pagan time, that I read of in Roman books?
Folly!   Folly!   So once more to hard work, to forget
such fancies; but not to forget both the love and the hate
I bear the house of Askaros."

And descending below, the once more remorseless
plotter plunged into his interrupted labors, weaving those
webs, fine as spider's threads, yet perhaps as strong to
bind his enemies as links of steel.

And so, as often happens in life — more often, perhaps,
than even in fiction — within a few short steps of each
other, three beings were busy weaving the threads of
their destinies — threads to be intertwined inextricably
one with the other.   While, all unconscious of her secret
influence over the most dangerous of these busy workers,
in the hareem-chambers of the old palace in the Turkish
quarter, sat the gentle girl, El Warda — thinking, not of
him who thought of her, but of that other, who had forgotten for the moment her very existence, in the thrill of
a newly-awakened passion.

CHAPTER VIII.

THE HAREEM OF THE PRINCESS NEZLÉ.

"GO with her to visit a — hairrum!" cried Miss Priscilla to her niece. "Trust ourselves, without the gentlemen, to be shut up among those nasty black men and those wicked women! who spend their lives in eating sweetmeats, and ogling the men from the lattices; and whose poor husbands have to lock them up at home, and send guards to watch them when they go out! I really do not believe, Edith, it is either safe or proper for us to go to such places to visit such people, whatever your father may think or say!"

"But, aunt, El Warda sends me word we are to go to the hareem of a princess — a lady of the royal blood. It will be a kind of reception, like Queen Victoria's, or the Empress Eugenie's — not like visiting a common person's hareem, by any means."

The cunning little puss, with true feminine tact, had pierced the weak point in the spinster's armor. She could not refuse to visit a princess: so, with many internal qualms, and with a miserable retrospect of what she endured in the first essay to enjoy the hospitality of Askaros, she reluctantly made up her mind for the martyrdom.

99

The permission to visit the hareem of the Princess
Nezlé Khanum, whose name has already been mentioned, was obtained for El Warda by the old French
governess, who was intimate with that high lady.   The
astute Frenchwoman had remarked, with some surprise,
the eager interest manifested by the princess at the mention of El Warda's name, and that of the young American ; and the questions with which she plied her as to
the age, appearance, figure, and features of the latter.
For Nezlé — the *Sitta Khanum*, (great lady,) as she was
generally termed — did not usually display much interest
in her own sex.   Her time and attention — unless the
gossips of the hareem and of the coffee-house belied
her — was principally devoted to the male population.
Even among that evil family she bore a name exception-
ably evil ; but such was her craft and talent, so great
was her energy and her influence, even over Abbas, that
she wielded a power and inspired a dread in Egypt,
second only to that entertained for him.

The old Frenchwoman, who, if rumor lied not, knew
more of the private life and thoughts of the great lady
than most people, left the hareem.   Hardened and
unscrupulous as she had grown during a long life as an
adventuress in the East, she yet retained some germs of
the better feelings of her youth, before becoming a social
outlaw who had fled from her country.   She felt a true
affection for her former pupil, "Warda," and feared
that the anxiety of the princess to see her and her Frank
friend meant mischief of some sort.   For she knew that
the feminine vice of curiosity found small place in the
plotting brain and masculine will of Nezlé Khanum.

But this she dared not tell even her former pupil, or
hint to the self-willed princess.   She only made an

inward vow to keep watch, and fathom the mystery if she might; and therefore she solicited permission to accompany the party on their visit, which was cheerfully accorded her.

The next day was fixed for the reception, and, at an early hour in the morning — for early rising is a common habit in the East, the noonday being devoted to the siesta — the ladies of the party, escorted as far as the gates of the princess's hareem by the gentlemen, proceeded in carriages to the rendezvous. The road was a fine, broad carriage-way, shaded by palm-trees and acacias, leading to Boulak, the port of Cairo on the Nile ; which at that time — before the completion of the railways — was a place of some importance as the port of embarkation by steamer to Alexandria, and the dépôt of goods transported thence by the river, then the only means of transit. About half a mile below Boulak was situated the palace of the princess, overlooking the Nile, and with large gardens, surrounded by a high stone wall, stretching back from it. Through this garden entrance, guarded by a file of soldiers outwardly, and by a number of eunuchs and female slaves within, the ladies of the party were now conducted, bidding adieu to their cavaliers, who were to return for them in the afternoon.

Ushered through these extensive and lovely gardens by the obsequious slaves, who glided on before them, uttering no word, the imagination of Edith was powerfully affected ; and all the strange stories of the strange woman she was about to visit — that she had heard vaguely whispered — rose to her memory.

She expected to behold a witch-like, withered woman, with a harsh voice, forbidding face, and a wicked eye, in the person of the princess. What, then, was her sur-

9 *

prise on being presented to a lady of most prepossessing face and figure, apparently not past the middle age; whose voluptuous form the Eastern costume enhanced, whose soft voice was most musical and winning, and who seemed the incarnation of gentleness and womanly grace.

Nezlé Khanum was not tall; but her figure was perfectly rounded, and her hands and feet small and symmetrical as those of a child. Her arms, bare to the shoulder under her wide sleeves, were perfectly moulded; and her every gesture and movement full of grace. The face was round and full, with small, delicate features, perfectly chiselled — the lips, perhaps, a trifle too full and sensual, as was the chin and lower part of the face.

The eyes, smaller than usual in Eastern women, were jet-black, penetrating, and very bright, with none of that lazy languor in them common to her countrywomen. Her arched eyebrows were united in a straight line by kohl, and the same pigment, traced under her eyelids, gave additional lustre to those shining orbs. Her fingertips and nails were tinged by henna to a rosy hue; and her small, plump fingers were covered with rings of great price. The manner of the princess was as bright and sparkling as her eyes. She spoke no European language, so the old Frenchwoman and El Warda acted as her interpreters with the strangers.

As the party entered, the Khanum rose from her divan, and came forward to meet them with mingled grace, dignity, and cordiality. The old Frenchwoman watched her closely, and saw that while her eye ran rapidly and carelessly over the persons of the others, it fixed itself with a penetrating and exhaustive regard on the young American. Face and figure, even to the slightest details of both,

that eagle eye fastened upon, as though to make a mental
inventory of all; yet not rudely, so that the fair object of
her scrutiny was herself unconscious of its minuteness.
Then the princess, motioning her guests to be seated,
made the usual compliments of welcome; and, slaves
entering with refreshments, she pressed all the dainties in
sweetmeats, confectionery, and fruits upon them, together
with sirups of various kinds, pink, rose-colored, and
green.

To these succeeded dainty-looking chibouques with
velvety amber mouth-pieces and slender jasmine stems,
inlaid with precious stones; a delicate, fragrant perfume,
wonderfully unlike the strong odors of tobacco, rising
like incense from their graceful bowls, that rested on
silver salvers. Seduced and tempted by the shape in
which the invitation came, even Miss Primmins forgot
her usual caution, and partook freely of the refreshments.
She even essayed for the first time to smoke a chibouque,
which feat she performed with a seriousness and severity
of aspect at variance with the employment and the occasion; but not without a certain serene contentment,
nevertheless.

Leaning forward toward El Warda, the princess, in her
soft tone, said:

"Thou art the daughter of Askaros Kassis, the ancient
Khasnadar of my father, Mehemet Ali — to whom may
Allah grant peace! Thy father and mine were friends.
So let it be between their children. Thy face and thy
presence in my hareem will ever be pleasant to me. I
hope to see them often here, now that thou hast found
the way."

To this graceful speech the young girl made fitting reply; but the brow of the old Frenchwoman grew still

darker at the unusual courtesy.   Then, turning toward
Edith, the princess said :

"Thou hast visited hareems before?   No !   Then must
I show thee something of our way of passing time?"

She clapped her hands thrice sharply together, when a
curtain was suddenly pushed aside at one corner of the
apartment, and three *Ghawazee,* or dancing-girls, bounded into the room, and commenced the wildest dancing ;
unseen musicians, behind the curtain, accompanying their
movements with the wailing music of the fife, and of the
darabouka drum.   To describe their dance would be next
to impossible, for it had in it more of St. Vitus or of
St. Anthony than of Terpsichore.

The movement was at first slow and measured, like the
opening of the Tarantula; but soon the music grew faster
and more furious, and, with the rising din, faster and
more furious grew the posturings and contortions of the
Ghawazee.   They writhed and twisted their lithe bodies
and sinuous limbs in strange muscular contortions — into
almost impossible positions — keeping time to the music
with every motion.   They advanced and retreated ; one
personating a man, another a woman, in every attitude
of timid supplication — audacious wooing, rejection, despair, angry violence, consent, successful love, rapture,
agony ! and closed the strange performance with gross-
ness too revolting for description,

The visitors, fascinated at first by the wild novelty of
the performance, were soon disgusted by its coarseness ;
especially in the great feat which was the crowning performance, the " *Naklé a ho,*" or " bee-dance ;" for
the conception and execution of this dance surpassed any
indecency of the French or American ballet corps —
very far exceeding the bounds of the most lax propriety.

The young girls and the ancient maiden averted their eyes, and fixed them upon their pipe-bowls, while this more than Bacchanal frenzy was gone through with, to the infinite amusement as well as the unutterable scorn of the princess, who regarded their behavior as hypocritical prudery. She herself applauded warmly the strongest and most indelicate parts of the performance, stimulating the dancers to yet more frantic indecencies; and when, panting, exhausted, and in sheer breathlessness, they ceased — divested almost entirely of the voluminous wrappings with which they had begun the dance — dusky models of the Eastern Venus, whose priestesses they were! — Nezlé flung to each of them a purse of gold, as her parting benison. Prostrating themselves with lowly reverence, the *Ghawazee* collected the garments they had flung off while searching for the bee, and retired backward behind the curtain.

The wrath of Miss Priscilla was too great for words; else — and had she spoken any language the princess could understand — she undoubtedly, then and there, would have given her what she termed "a piece of her mind." Outraged womanhood asserted itself in that withered bosom, at witnessing such sights herself, and permitting her niece to see them. She almost choked with indignation, and twice or thrice attempted to rise, with the intention of taking the latter from the room. But the strong hand of the vigilant old Frenchwoman, who sat next her, grasped her as in an iron vice. She could not free herself from it, struggle as she might; and a moment's reflection convinced her that she must not insult the hostess.

So, chafing and fuming inwardly, she sat still, and, to pacify her mind and tranquillize her nerves, puffed vigor-

ously at the chibouque, which an attentive slave replenished from time to time, without the spinster's knowledge.   Gradually she felt creep over her a serene indolence, followed by a slight drowsy sensation ; then, just
as the dancers retired, horror of horrors ! she experienced
a slight nausea, quickly succeeded by a deadly sickness !

Cold perspiration broke out upon her brow ; her body
felt clammy as that of a corpse ; and her brain reeled so
that she could scarcely sit upright.   With a convulsive
clutch she seized the arm of Edith, who sat next to her,
and in a sepulchral tone gasped: "Oh, Edith! I am
poisoned !   Get me away, or I shall die !"

The girl looked round in alarm, and the livid face that
stared into hers terrified her.

"Great heavens!" she cried to the Frenchwoman.
"What can be the matter?   Look at my aunt!   What
can have happened to her?"

"*Pas extraordinaire !*" replied the person addressed,
with a true French shrug, that almost concealed her head
between her shoulders.   "Madame has eaten much confectionery, and smoked many pipes ; and many persons
suffer from Eastern hospitality the first time, before they
are used to it.   She will not die this time ; *soyez tran-
quille.*"

When the illness of Miss Priscilla was imparted to the
Khanum, she was graciously pleased to insist on the victim's being removed to an inner apartment, to repose.
So the spinster was led off, passive and unresisting from
nausea, but firmly convinced in her own mind that she
never more would behold her friends.   More confirmed
was she in that impression, when she not only was laid
out on a divan in a secluded apartment, but beheld,
every time she opened her swimming eyes, two Nubian

female slaves — black as night, and with great, glaring, rolling white eyes — sitting immovable as two sphinxes on each side of her couch, and gazing with stony stare full upon her. Shuddering, she closed her eyes, and, murmuring a short prayer, resigned herself to her fate.

In the mean time the princess continued to do the honors to her remaining guests. After the dancing succeeded the singing-girls, who droned out a melancholy and monotonous chant, to the accompaniment of a kind of rude guitar, called the "*rahab.*" There was little melody and less music in the sounds to foreign ears; but they seemed to please the native listeners.

Then, rising from her seat, the princess proposed to show the house to her guests, and took them through the bath-rooms, with marble floors and fountains of marble, walls inlaid with red Egyptian alabaster, and a dome of stained glass, that threw a blood-red light into the apartments, which were heated to a temperature almost insupportable to the Europeans. Then she carried them through the various rooms dedicated to her own use, and that of her numerous domestics and slaves. Her own apartments were sumptuously decorated and fitted up with every costly luxury; those of the others, with a bare simplicity, divested even of the common comforts of the toilet or dressing-room.

The whole palace presented a strange *mélange* of lavish extravagance, costly trifles, and squalid discomfort. Though in the chief apartments French mirrors of the largest size were fitted into niches in the walls, magnificent chandeliers hung from the ceilings, and the coverings of the cushions, the tapestries, and the curtains over the doorways were of the richest materials; yet in the smaller chambers the coverings were of coarse chintz, and the frames of the divans of common wood; while large glass lanterns, containing tallow candles, gave light to the ladies of the Court.

The dress of the princess herself was of the richest description, and her hair, bust, arms, and fingers glittered with precious gems; while her attendants wore materials of the commonest and coarsest kind, in many instances torn, and not overclean.

The impression produced on the mind of the visitor was that splendor and luxury were compatible with hareem life, but that comfort was not. The princess and her attendants examined without scruple, and with the utmost minuteness, the details of Edith's costume; asking her a thousand questions about the smaller articles of feminine attire, and carrying their researches as to names and uses so far, that the fair girl was apprehensive of being reduced to the disrobed condition of the dancing-girls. Seeing that she was becoming flushed and annoyed by their investigations, the princess checked the curiosity of her attendants, and dismissed them all, that she might converse alone with her guests.

"You will pardon the curiosity of my people," she said; "but Franks are very rarely admitted into my hareem, and the Frank costume is a novelty to them; and our manners are so different from yours, that I fear they may have annoyed you."

Edith made a courteous disclaimer of such feeling, and expressed her thanks for the honor accorded her. The princess then asked her a great variety of questions as to the customs and habits of foreign women; from which, and from her comments upon the answers, Edith was surprised to observe that she rather compassionated them for the liberty allowed them, which she seemed to

construe into indifference of the men toward them.
The immodesty of the unveiled face in public also
seemed to strike her much ; and she declared the animated pictures Edith drew of the life of American
women only confirmed her idea of the superior advantages and pleasures of the Eastern, who substituted the
bath on Friday for reception; had their shopping
brought to them, and enjoyed their gossip at home; and
had abundant leisure to eat, drink, dress, sleep, and
make love, which she seemed to regard as the whole
duty of woman.

El Warda took but little part in the conversation,
though the Khanum treated her with marked courtesy.
Refreshments, such as sweetmeats and sherbets, were
brought in at intervals ; and at parting a bouquet of rare
flowers was given to each lady.   Before they took their
farewell, Miss Priscilla — rescued from her sable watchers, but still looking very pale, haggard, and wretched —
rejoined them.

The princess, turning to the old woman, said in
Turkish, in a low voice:

"Why did you tell me the Ingleeze was beautiful?
She is as colorless as a scentless white flower beside a
damask rose, when compared with the sister of Askaros !
She is as thin as a starved camel, and has no figure" —
and she glanced complacently at her own plump proportions, as though to point a contrast.   "He never can
fancy a stick like that !   I am well content to have seen
her.   As to the old bean-pole" — nodding toward the
chaste Priscilla — "she should be set up as a scarecrow !   Now relieve me of the presence of these Giaours,
for I am weary of them.   Say something flattering to
them in translation of what I have just said to you ; and

10

then take them away, in the name of Allah! or I shall
get as sick at the stomach, soon, as that old scarecrow
who swallowed so much of my smoke."

In compliance with this mandate, the old Frenchwoman made a complimentary speech of the most
flowery kind to the unsuspecting guests, winding up with
an intimation that they might now take *congé;* and the
princess, with many smiles, dismissed them.

CHAPTER IX.

UP THE NILE IN A DAHABIEH.

W ILL you do me the honor of taking a sail up the Nile in my *dahabieh?*" asked Askaros, dropping in on the hotel party a few mornings after the harem visit. "We can take donkeys down to Boulak, where the boat lies, and do old Father Nilus in fine style—a short distance up, at least."

The proposal was at once seconded by the young men, and received a smiling assent from Edith. Mr. Van Camp pleaded business with his consul, having had a difficulty with his dragoman : but Miss Priscilla alone interposed an objection.

"I am told the Nile swarms with those horrible creatures, the crocodiles," she said ; "and the wife of one of our missionaries was yesterday entertaining us with some horrible cases of young infidel converts having been devoured by them when going in to bathe. At least, to that she attributed their sudden disappearance ; for three of them went off to bathe in the Nile, after having been well clothed and fed out of our fund for several weeks, and showing a most, hopeful and edifying spirit, and they have never been heard of since. The mothers came howling and wailing to tell the sad story ;

but they likewise offered three of their younger children, very ragged and dirty, to instruct in their stead; and they were taken of course.''

A peculiar expression, surely not of sympathy, flitted over the face of Askaros. Strange as it may seem, it more resembled amusement: though he said nothing in direct reply. But Sir Charles did.

"Very affecting tale, indeed, Miss Primmins. Remarkably well told, too; only I do not see the crocodile in it, or under it. More like a fish-story. These Arab beggars remind one wonderfully of the Indians, in the way they impose on the missionaries! I have not the shadow of doubt, the same crocodile will devour the three other children, just so soon as they are sufficiently clothed and fattened to make it an object."

"Shocking, Sir Charles! How can you talk with such levity on such serious subjects! What do you think, Mr. Askaros? Are there not crocodiles in the river near here?"

"As to your first question, madam," answered the young man, gravely, "I would prefer not to answer it; for I really know nothing of the matter. But I can assure you, on my honor, you will see no crocodiles where I propose taking you to-day. And when you see my dahabieh, you will be satisfied that on board of her you will be as safe as on one of your fine American steamers. She is more like an English yacht than a row-boat."

"But is there no danger of — of sea-sickness?" persisted Miss Priscilla. "My poor head cannot stand much rocking, especially since my visit to that horrid hareem."

"None whatever," was the comforting reply. "The

river will be as smooth as glass, and you will glide over it with almost imperceptible motion. So I hope you will discard your fears, now that your doubts are dispelled, and give me the pleasure of your own and your niece's company.''

A pleading look from Edith settled the question with the spinster, who was very good-hearted at bottom, and really very fond of her niece ; so she promised, with a sigh, to matronize the excursion, and followed the young lady up stairs to make preparations for it.

''Why did n't you answer my aunt's question about the crocodile story?'' young Van Camp asked Askaros. '' It was a heavy sell on the missionaries, of course ; but why did n't you say so?''

'' It is a delicate subject to speak of, for us especially,'' answered the Copt. '' We native Christians — of whom the Copts claim to be the oldest branch, the original Church — are not on good terms with the missionaries. They regard us as little better than the heathen ; while we dispute their right to come to Christ's own birthplace—the cradle of His Church—to teach us points of doctrine or discipline, and give us lessons in faith. Hence we rarely meddle in any way, either for good or bad, with the well-meaning people who come out as missionaries. Their efforts to 'convert' us we look upon as very curious. Yet they try it.

'' The Arabs practise all kinds of impositions upon these poor missionaries. Of this you have had a specimen to-day ; and really they are so plausible that any new-comer, or person unfamiliar with their ways, would be deceived by them. The Fellah women, especially, are the best natural actors I ever saw. What wonder, then, that they deceive these foreigners?''

10 *   H

"You had better not say all this to my aunt," answered Harry, smiling. "The old lady believes in these missionaries, even though they do not bring out rum with the Bibles, as was the universal custom of our New England Puritans, in their conversion of the heathen."

"No, I shall not," answered Askaros; "for these poor people would have a hard time to live, were they not supported by the contributions of their countrymen, since they all have many children and large families, which is a scandal also to the Latin Christians."

Here the conversation was interrupted by the appearance of the ladies, equipped for the expedition; and, sallying out of the hotel, the party soon found themselves the centre of an animated, struggling mass of donkey-boys and donkeys, the former noisily and vehemently competing for their custom.

"Berry fine donkey, mum! him John Bull!"— "Mine Yankee Doodle, miss! nebber fall down!"— "Dis one Slow-Coach!—lady name him so yesserday!"

Such were the cries and invitations which rose from the ragged rout of dirty boys, whose knowledge of scraps of all spoken languages is one of the most remarkable things in Cairo. And this knowledge is coupled with immediate detection of the nationality of the stranger, which they flatter by addressing him in his proper tongue.

Selecting some of the most desirable specimens of these sagacious brutes—resembling exaggerated rabbits— the party galloped off toward Boulak; each animal followed by its owner, who persuaded it along with a sharp-pointed stick in the flanks when it relaxed its speed.

The dahabieh lying at Boulak was a very pretty specimen of these Nile craft, having been freshly refitted and
painted, with its large sails white and spotless as snow.
She carried a crew of ten men, to row or push her along,
when the wind was not sufficient to fill the sails. She
had an upper cabin, running half the length, fitted with
divans; and an upper deck, with cushions strewn over it
for seats, and an awning to keep off the sun. Askaros
welcomed them on board, gave his orders, and they were
soon running rapidly up the placid stream of the Nile,
propelled with arrowy rapidity by the large sail.

The shores, fringed with date-palms, seemed to glide
away from their view through the soft haze which over-
hung earth and sky: the long lines of camels, plodding
along the banks, and the awkward water-oxen—their
bodies hidden under the water, and only their hideous
heads protruding from it—seemed sliding off from them,
as in a panoramic picture. Earth, air, and sky were all
so hushed and still, that the only sound breaking the
breathless calm was the melancholy, creaking sound of
the sakkia, or rude water-wheels, turned by oxen, on the
shore, or the ripple of the water, as the swift dahabieh
cleaved its way through, against the strong current.

These soporific influences of the scene and hour, assisted by the fatigue of the long donkey-ride, and aggravated by the lunch with pale ale proffered by Askaros
after first coming on board—proved too much for Mr.
Van Camp and his sister, the elders of the party. Both
gently closed their eyes, to shut out the glare, and both
were soon steeped in oblivious slumber. Harry and Sir
Charles went to the upper deck to enjoy the scenery, a
long pull at their nargilehs, and an occasional shot at the
wild ducks, which—roused from the shady nooks in

which they were disporting—constantly flew over the passing boat.

The young Copt and the American girl were left alone. They were just passing one of those Arab villages that look so picturesque at a distance, so squalid and filthy on near approach; and, passing out of the cabin-door, they stood together near it and gazed upon the picture. The dome and minarets of the mosque crowned the centre of the village; around it grouped the mud huts, shaded by the drooping boughs of clustering palm-trees; while the bright blue dresses of the women, and the even gayer costumes of the men, with the shapeless forms of the sleepy camels, constituted a scene never presented but in the Orient.

But though the maiden's gaze was riveted on the picture, so novel and so striking to her, the eye of Askaros rested—not on earth, or sky, but on the face and form beside him, with an intensity that caused her to blush and turn uneasily toward the door, as soon as she observed it. But the young man arrested the movement by a pleading look; and said, in a low tone:

"Stay one moment, I implore you! For I must tell you that I no longer have power to conceal within my breast. Scorn me! crush me, if you will, with your contempt! that one so far beneath you in all things, yet has dared to lift up his eyes to one so far above him. But I must tell you—that I love you! Not with the calm, tame love of your cold West; but with the fiery, burning heat of my own East, where the blood rushes from eye to heart like the swift current of the Nile!

"Pardon my presumption and pity my folly! but, oh! lady, fairer far than the wildest dreams of our romancers have pictured—give me one ray of hope, or—I shall die!''

Had a lightning-flash broken suddenly from the serene blue vault above them, it could not more have astonished the maiden than this sudden and unexpected avowal. A red flush crimsoned brow, neck, and bosom, then left her deadly pale: her lips moved, but no sound came from them; and she cast a look, half bewildered, half beseeching, on the young Egyptian. Gathering hope from her silence and agitation, and mistaking their meaning, he again burst forth into an incoherent rhapsody of mingled adoration and entreaty, as though beseeching some being from a higher sphere.

''I know how different are your usages from ours!'' he cried. ''I know how far inferior in all things am I —untrained, half-educated barbarian—to you! perfect flower and rich fruit of the highest civilization! I know how your maidenly modesty must be shocked by such words, from the lips of one but yesterday a stranger— unworthy to unloose even the latchet of your shoe! But as yonder glorious sun deigns to send down his rays, giving light and life to the meanest of created things— so, from your height far above me, give but one little ray of hope to this heart, that now and for ever must beat for you alone! God has given me some gifts with which he has endowed your more favored race. I will devote all my energies, all my powers, to make myself what will be pleasing in your sight! I will abandon home, country, friends—everything! and adopt that home and that career which pleases you. All that I have—all that I am—body—soul—brain—heart!— all I offer to you absolutely, to control and dispose of—

more than repaid, if one approving look, one smile from you will recompense me for it!''

He ceased from sheer exhaustion of overwrought heart and brain; his eye — full of unspeakable devotion — strained with the intensity of passion upon her own.

In reply came the soft, low tones from her lips, in accents faltering and tremulous with mingled sorrow and shame:

"God forgive me!'' she said, ''if any word, or look, or act of mine has raised false hopes in a heart so noble, and so fresh as yours. For I never dreamed that such wild visions had entered your brain, else I should have dissipated them at once and forever. What you have said is madness. Our lives — our thoughts — our destinies — have, and can ever have, no link to bind them together! In race and character, habits and ideas, we are and must ever be as utterly dissimilar, as though we inhabited different worlds!

"I can pardon and forget the insult you have offered one you scarcely know, by speaking thus, only on condition of its never being offered again; for it *is* an insult to speak such words to a young girl, who three weeks since had never seen your face, or known of your existence, and who even now knows almost as little of you. These may be the customs of the East, where women are but servile playthings — mere toys for men! They are not of the West!''

Recovering her self-possession as she spoke these words, and almost warming into indignation as she proceeded, she once more moved toward the cabin-door. But the Egyptian gently, though firmly, detained her; laying his hand upon her arm with a gesture of entreaty, and with despair stamped upon his speaking features.

"Lady, you do me wrong!" he said. "Sooner than utter one word that could give you pain, or one syllable that savored of disrespect, I would pluck out my tongue from its roots. If I sinned against your maiden modesty, by aught that I have said or done, punish me by banishment from your presence — no crueler torture could be inflicted on me. But the tongue of Askaros has never lied; and I swear to you by my mother's grave! that in this thing I have sinned through ignorance of the ways and usages of your people, which I thought allowed free utterance between man and woman of the thoughts of their hearts, when they were pure — and deemed it no shame.

"In sorrow and contrition now do I see how great was my folly, to dream that you had ever for a moment viewed me other than as a creature of another race, and of another nature than your own. In that knowledge lies my heaviest punishment — the atonement of my wild frenzy! Pardon and forget it; and never again by word, or look, shall any repetition of it offend you! But banish me not, I pray you! from your presence hereafter. That is all the boon I ask!"

As he uttered these words in proud humility, the young Egyptian knelt down with a movement full of grace and gentleness; and taking Edith's passive hand, pressed his lips lightly upon it. Then laying his own right hand upon his heart, he bent his head in lowly reverence, as though to an empress, and glided swiftly to the other end of the boat, leaving the young girl too rapidly to permit a reply.

Slowly, and moving like one in a dream, the young girl — whose virgin heart had been, for the first time, so suddenly and so painfully stirred from its repose into womanly consciousness and introspection — moved back

into the cabin, and sank upon a divan with her face buried
in her hands, vainly striving to collect her scattered
thoughts.

Had she spoken truly to Askaros? And did she really
feel the indignation she had expressed at his avowal?
No! she felt within her inmost soul the confession he
had made her was not without a subtle and secret charm;
and that the recollection of it had sent a pleasing thrill
through her heart, that still fluttered as wildly as an untamed bird, first clutched by the hand of its captor.

Did she return his passion? No! she felt that she did
not; and she was terrified by the vehemence of his
language and the violence of his feelings, which his
Oriental fervor had exaggerated. But she also acknowledged to herself that she was not fancy free; though, as
yet, she had nourished only romantic dreams and shadowy
visions, into which no thought of reality had entered, no
plans for the future, with her as yet a blank.

Was what he proposed possible? Could the time ever
come, when this young Eastern Antinous could be more
to her than one of those bright memories of her brief
Egyptian experience, blending in the picture of mosque
and. minaret, palm-trees and camels, veiled women and
turbaned men; like the figures in the foreground of some
painted landscape, which the eye loves to rest upon — a
thing of beauty and a joy forever! No, a thousand times
no! He was, and must be ever to her, what she had
named him at first sight — Haroun el Reschid; a revival
of the enchanted tales which had bewitched her childhood, but, like them, never entering the domain of actual
life.

Had she encouraged his hopeless passion? She acquitted herself on that score; for she had carefully

suppressed any indication even of the romantic interest she felt in him. She was still weaving the threads of her fancies and thoughts in her newly awakened consciousness, when the two other young men came tramping noisily into the room, talking and laughing loudly enough to awaken the elders from their profound slumbers ; and created a diversion in her thoughts, bringing her back from her dreamland into that of reality.

"Great sport!" cried Sir Charles. "Lots of wild fowl! Supplied our larder for a month with ducks, not to mention a pelican Harry shot, 'which hath an ancient and a fishlike smell,' as the divine William expresses it."

"Were you only shooting at ducks?" inquired Mr. Van Camp, stretching himself. "I fancied I heard a volley followed by a scream, just as I was losing myself in a doze. I thought you had killed some larger game than wild fowl."

"Harry shot at a buffalo, mistaking him for a crocodile," answered the Englishman. "Beast was in the water, with his head hidden in the rushes. Harry took his back for the god of the ancient Egyptians, peppered him badly with small shot, and made him scamper up the bank in double quick. I'm not quite sure he did'nt bag an Arab woman too, she screeched so. Suppose, however, it was only sympathy for the beast, though, whose hide much resembled hers in color and toughness, as she stood knee-deep in the rushes where the fellow broke cover, wringing linen and her hands!"

"You fired at the buffalo, too!" cried Harry, rather sulkily, nettled as well at the imputation on his sportsmanship as at the laughter that greeted Sir Charles's recital. "Why, you shot first! Why do you put it all on me? and you missed the thing, besides."

11

"Very true, my dear boy," was the serene response. "So I did; but I shot at him on the same principle as your American novice did at the calf he mistook for a deer — to miss it if it was a calf, and hit it if it was a deer. On the same principle I proceeded to miss the buffalo that was not a crocodile, and now make game of you for not doing likewise. But where is our host, and where is dinner? for smoke and coffee sit lightly on the stomach!"

Sir Charles's spirits seemed to carry him away as if he had been a schoolboy rather than a six-foot soldier; for, with a deep salaam, he turned to Edith before any one could answer.

"Ah! fair lady, hast thou sent away the Egyptian prince on some impossible errand to remote Bagdad!" he said; "and wilt thou not summon him back, that the humblest of thy slaves may partake of the dinner of expectancy on the cushions of contentment; and subsequently smoke the chibouque of digestion on the divan of postprandial repose?"

As though in response to this invocation, and before Edith had made up her mind what badinage to reply, Askaros glided into the room, with that noiseless step characteristic of Orientals. Short as had been the time since Edith had seen that countenance convulsed with strong emotion, it was now as serene and as placid as ever, although she thought she could detect a shade of deeper gravity than ordinary lurking under its repose. He studiously avoided her eye, and did not approach her, but answered Sir Charles in his own vein, announcing that dinner, *à l'Arabe*, would soon be served, as he had received an intimation to that effect from his favorite Nubian attendant, Ferraj.

Almost immediately the Nubian entered, bearing the tray, and the guests did full justice to the viands of Hajji Mohammed, the Arab cook, who had exerted all his skill to subdue the palates his dainty viands and peculiar *plats* excited. For in the concoction of sauces —the secret spell of all cookery—the Arab cook equals, if he does not excel, the French, whose artists have stolen from the East many of their secrets in this science, as well as others, without acknowledgment. The people to whom Europe and America owe their numerals, their algebra, and their metaphysics, have bequeathed many culinary discoveries, whose first professors have slept the sleep of the embalmed many thousand years, beside the mummies of Pharaoh and Rameses.

The Nubian, Ferraj, who served the repast, was the favorite slave of Askaros, to whom he was devoted with a spaniel-like affection and fidelity. As he moved about the cabin he attracted the special attention of Sir Charles, who, turning to Askaros, said :

" Fine creature, that of yours ; splendid specimen of ebony carving ! He's the best I ever saw, with none of the peculiarities of the Simian species about him. No more like the 'man and brother' Boston and Exeter Hall howl over, than Harry's crocodile was like the genuine article. Must have been painted black; he could n't have taken it the natural way. Our niggers in India are better than the ' Eboskins,' but don't come up to this standard. Where and how did you pick him up? Would like his duplicate amazingly ! "

" He is my friend as well as my favorite slave ; one of nature's own noblemen," replied the Copt. " I bought him, when a boy, from one of the *Jellabs*, (slave-dealers,) for a hundred piastres. He is a Nubian, not what you term negro; and, in his own way, has the pride of a prince, and much better principles than many who own that title. Truthfulness, courage, and fidelity, are his great characteristics. His value to me is above rubies, for I could safely trust my life in his hands. As you see, his slavery does not sit heavily upon him, nor his chains gall him much."

"I can understand," broke in Miss Priscilla, severely, "how the heathen and benighted Turks, who worship cats and crocodiles, can hold their brother men in bondage; but how you, who profess to be Christians, can reconcile yourselves to practise or to countenance such a sin, is beyond my comprehension! Why do you not liberate this unfortunate young man? who is your brother, though his face is black!"

"Can't see the family likeness; can't, 'pon my soul!" muttered Sir Charles to Harry. "But must have been by another mother. Miss Primmins knows no scandal, I hope, about the respected father of our respected host, whose family affairs we should not pry into."

"Sir Charles, you must certainly have drunk too much of that arrackee!" cried the spinster, whose sharp ears had caught the remark; "and I shall retire if you continue this vein of conversation."

"My dear lady," replied the Englishman, courteously, "I beg a thousand pardons; but I really did not intend my remark to reach your ear, as you seem to suppose. '*Honi soit qui mal y pense*,' you know; but let us change the subject."

CHAPTER X.

PERIL AND RESCUE.

WHILE they were dining, the dahabieh had turned, and was rapidly descending the stream on her return. The sail was lowered, and they dropped down with the current, which, as it was the season of high Nile, ran at the rate of some five miles per hour. The crew put in their oars and pulled lustily, keeping time in a sort of rude chant, its words improvised by one of their number, while the others joined in the burden of the song in a sort of chorus. This scarce awakened an echo from the flat banks of the river, but sounded musically over the water. The boatmen wore only the coarse blue shirt and fez cap of the country, their brawny arms, chests, and legs bare, and resembling bronze statues more than men — moving backward and forward all together, with the regularity of machinery, at the dip and stroke of their oars.

And so the dahabieh glided down the current with her freight, until, near Boulak, the whole party came out upon the upper deck to enjoy the fresh evening air; for the sun was rapidly declining, and the fiery splendor of noonday was succeeded by the softened shadows of coming night.   Suddenly Edith uttered an exclamation of surprise and pleasure.

"Oh, how lovely!" she exclaimed, pointing to Rhoda Island, just then coming into view.   "Is that the mirage we have heard of, or is it a real island?   It more resembles a glimpse of fairy-land.   '*Uno pezzo di cielo caduto in terra,*' as the Italian poet says.   What is that lovely spot, and how is it named?"

"That is Rhoda Island," Askaros responded; "and very lovely indeed it is, for both nature and art have rivalled to make it a little paradise.   The marble palace you see gleaming yonder, with its steps sloping down to the water, and its terraced gardens of rare exotics in front and rear, is the favorite retreat of Ismail Pasha now, as it was of his father, Ibrahim, formerly.   Every inch of this little island of the Nile has been beautified, and all the resources of our Eastern gardeners exhausted. Look at the tasteful little kiosks and pleasure-houses scattered at intervals, and gleaming white through the vistas of trees!   Is it not really, as you have said, a fairy-looking spot?"

"It is indeed," answered Edith.   Then clasping her hands impulsively together, she said, as if to herself, and unconscious of a listener: "Oh! how I should love to visit it."

"Nothing can be easier," returned Askaros, as though in reply to a remark made to himself.   "My dahabieh draws too much water to approach the steps, and the ordinary gate of entrance is closed; but I have attached to this boat a light *caïque,* made on the model of those at Stamboul, in which I can easily take you to Rhoda, if your aunt will accompany you.   It will only accommodate four persons, so one of the gentlemen and myself can row you."

A look of sweet entreaty from Edith to the spinster extracted from her a grim assent to the proposal; and Sir Charles insisted on being second oar, having been famous in former days as the crack "stroke" of the "Oxford U. B. C."

This being settled, the dahabieh was soon run into the farther shore and made fast, while the graceful *caïque* — looking like an Indian bark canoe, only sharper, shallower, and slighter — was soon floating like a cork upon the water.

Shutting her eyes, and resigning herself to the inevitable drowning she saw awaited her, Miss Primmins heroically stepped into the frail skiff, which rocked fearfully as she did so, and crouched with Edith on the cushions in the stern. Askaros and the Englishman took the light oars, turned their backs to the ladies, and, with a warning from the Egyptian that neither of them was on any pretence to move from her position, as the *caïque* was very easily upset, they shot out into the stream, struggled a moment against the current, then darted, with bird-like movement, over the rippling waters.

"Very nice, indeed!" said Miss Primmins, leaning forward as she spoke, but suddenly recalled to herself by a dip of the frail bark that almost emptied her into the river. "Good gracious, what a cranky little thing!"

"Be careful!" cried Askaros; "you came near oversetting us that time, Miss Primmins. Sit still, if you wish to cross safely; for a dip in the Nile at high water is no joke, I assure you."

Thus admonished, the spinster sat pale and trembling, and her apprehensions were aggravated by the next remark of Sir Charles, who sought to play upon them.

"You asked about crocodiles this morning, Miss

Primmins," he said, "but you forget a far more dangerous creature the Nile often conceals.   I mean the hippopotamus!   Have seen him in menageries; would be a mighty ugly customer to meet in such an egg-shell as this."

"Good heavens!" almost screamed the terrified woman.   "You don't mean to tell me that hideous and terrible creature lives in this river?   Turn back, oh, good young men, turn back!   Put me on shore anywhere!" and she wrung her hands in hysterical terror, not daring otherwise to move.

Askaros was about to reassure the trembling victim, whom the strangeness of her situation, and superadded nervous excitement, deprived of her usual common sense, hard, shrewd, and not to be imposed on.   But before he could speak, shrill, high, and keen rang a shriek from Miss Priscilla; and, turning their heads simultaneously, both men beheld her staring fixedly on a monstrous head, with broad flat nostrils, and wild, rolling eyes, that rose slowly above the surface of the stream close to the elbow of the terrified spinster.   Then, ere Askaros could shout, "A water-ox! sit still!" he saw the gaunt form of Miss Priscilla precipitate itself forward frantically, felt the frail *caïque* tremble from stem to stern, and the next instant all four were plunged into the swollen and turbid waters of the Nile.

Sir Charles, too, saw the peril at a glance, and turned to clutch at Edith, to save whom, at that moment, was his sole thought, utterly regardless of the peril to his own life.

As though by a lightning-flash, at this instant of supreme peril, his own love for her stood revealed for the first time to himself.   He would save her or perish with her.

But his heroism was frustrated; for, as he turned, he suddenly felt the bony arms of Miss Priscilla tightened

around his neck to the verge of suffocation, while the spare
form clung to him with the desperate tenacity of a drowning woman, as they went down together under the turbid
waters of the rushing river. Wrenching himself free
from her desperate death-grip, as the fainting fingers relaxed, but retaining his hold of her hair, the practised
swimmer rose again to the surface, supporting the head
of his burden above the water. His eye, thrown despair-
ingly around, could see no other struggling forms upon
the surface of the stream ; but the next instant his dreadful
suspense was relieved. The surface bubbled, broke, and
the form of Askaros rose from the depths, bearing on his
arm the sunny, but dripping head of Edith, its wealth of
dishevelled curls floating over the breast of her rescuer
from the slimy mud of the Nile bed.

The fair girl was insensible, hanging like a dead weight
on the supporting arm of the Egyptian, who floated himself and his precious burden as easily as though in his
native element; and, with a deep sigh of thankfulness,
the Englishman saw that she was safe from immediate
peril, under that protection.

"Beware of the under-tow!" shouted Askaros, perceiving him. "Do not try to swim ashore, or turn back.
The deep mud is as treacherous one way as the strong
current the other. Keep afloat only, and rescue will soon
reach us from the dahabieh. They must have seen our
accident."

He was obeyed and his prediction verified before even
he expected ; for no sooner had the *caïque* overturned
than half a dozen dusky forms plunged from the side of
the dahabieh into the water. Seizing on a small boat
attached to her stern, they manned it, grasped their oars,
and pulled lustily to the rescue ; Ferraj, the Nubian, acting

I

as steersman, and exhorting the rowers to renewed effort with such vigor that his black face glistened with the moisture that gathered over it.

Only a few seconds — which seemed hours to the anxious but intrepid men supporting their frail and fainting charges in the water — and they were dragged on board the boat; the women wrapped in shawls, brought by the thoughtful care of the Nubian, and restored to consciousness.

The languid eyes of Edith rested, as they opened, first upon the anxious faces of father and brother; and she smiled a wan smile to reassure them.   Then turning her glance to the other side of the boat, where stood the dripping figure of Askaros — his face still pallid from emotion, and his form still trembling from the violent exertions he had made so lately — she stretched out her hands in mute gesture of supplication and gratitude toward him, and murmured:

"Twice saved from a dreadful death!   How can I ever be grateful enough?"

The quick ear of Sir Charles caught the low tones, and partly their meaning, and a fierce pang of jealousy thrilled through his awakened heart; but his native generosity of soul conquered.   He turned to Mr. Van Camp with more dignity and gravity of manner than he habitually assumed, and said, pointing to Askaros:

"Sir, your thanks are due to that gallant gentleman, for having saved the life of your daughter, imperilled through my thoughtless folly and ill-timed jesting.   For it I ask pardon of both the ladies, but more especially of Miss Primmins, to whom I owe a double apology; though I never dreamed my silly speech could lead to serious consequences, till that hideous water-ox rose, and the mischief was done.''

Miss Priscilla, from her mummy-like swathing of shawls, feebly twittered a pardon to the frank Englishman, mingled with protestations that he had been ''her saviour,'' etc., while Edith flashed upon him a bright glance of approval, that sent sunshine to his soul. Mr. Van Camp and his son wrung the hand of Askaros in true American fashion, even to the infliction of physical pain. Edith only looked her gratitude; but it cannot be doubted he preferred that mute recognition to the more violent demonstrations of father and son; or even to the flattering testimony of the Englishman, whom, with the quick eye of love, he recognized as his rival.

Sobered and rendered serious by the almost tragical termination of their day's pleasure-excursion, there was little said by any of the party on their ride back to the hotel. On reaching it, the ladies retired to their rooms, and Askaros to his home, to change their still wet clothing, and adopt the necessary precautions after their unexpected cold bath in the waters of the Nile.

But that day was the turning-point of three lives; and the after destiny of each and all the three was first shadowed and commenced with that sail on the dahabieh. Each of the three had learned many new things, and awakened to new self-consciousness within a few hours; but none of them could conjecture, even dimly, the future of the others, nor their relative relations one to the other in the coming years. Time alone — a greater reader of riddles than the Sphinx — could solve the problem of what those future destinies might be.

As Askaros stood on the threshold of his home, he paused, turned his eyes upon the spot where the serpent-charm had manifested itself upon the young girl — then a stranger to him, but now the very light of his life — and muttered :

"Were I a Mussulman, I would say it was *kismet* (destiny) ! Twice have I been made to save her life at the risk of my own ; yet my passion only excited her scorn to-day ! But the look she gave me this evening almost repaid me for the morning — for all ! "

So, with the blind fatuity of all real lovers — pressing deeper into his heart the barb that rankled there — clutching at the shadow of a hope where there seemed really none, and confounding gratitude with affection — the young Egyptian, with a lighter heart, entered the house and passed into his father's presence.

CHAPTER XI.

THE BULBUL AND THE ROSE.

NIGHT had fallen upon the city of Cairo, and the shadows projected from the tall houses into the narrow streets looked like solid masses of black stone, so clear and brilliant was the moonlight. The stars, large and lustrous, like great lamps suspended from an azure dome, shone with that clear, white light peculiar to their lustre in Eastern heavens — unknown to the watchers of the cloudy skies of Europe or America.

It was on such nights, and through similar streets and scenes, that the good Haroun el Reschid was wont to take his rambles with his vizier Giaffir, in search of strange adventure. So let us now follow the footsteps of one of his innumerable imitators in nocturnal rambles under Eastern skies, whose mission was very dissimilar to that of the famous caliph, though not without its romance and its danger, too.

About midnight might have been seen a man, apparently young and vigorous, wending his way through the outskirts of Boulak, choosing the most obscure streets, as though to avoid observation, until he reached the high stone wall of the palace of the Princess Nezlé

Khanum, which, as before described, faced on the Nile. There was nothing in this man's appearance and dress to distinguish him from one of the ordinary occupants of the quarter, except that, on his left hand, when he raised it, there sparkled a precious stone, and that the hand itself did not resemble that of the common laborer. What was unusual was that he bore no lantern to light his way; which both law and custom, as well as safety, required.

Concealed under the shadow of the wall, he carefully groped along in the obscurity, occasionally disturbing some prowling or slumbering wild dog, which, snarling fiercely, and menacing the intruder with its sharp white teeth, sullenly and reluctantly retreated before his steps. But as the Egyptian wild dog never barks — partaking of the savage nature of his ancestor, the wolf, in that respect — no warning of the visitor's stealthy approach was given to the guardians of the hareem, if, indeed, any person in its vicinity was awake at that late hour; the Orientals all retiring early to rest.

At length the man stopped, and tapped three times at a particular spot on the wall. Immediately a small gate, invisible before, swung within noiselessly, opened by an unseen hand; and, as he stepped into the garden, the door closed as swiftly and noiselessly as it had opened — indistinguishable as before from the wall. The man softly clapped his hands three times, and suddenly appeared before him a veiled female figure, shrouded from head to foot in the *abba*, a voluminous black silk cloak, worn by the Cairene women in the streets.

"*Salaam Aleikoum !* You are waited for," she said, in Arabic. "The Sitta has long been expecting your arrival. Come quickly, for you know she likes not to be kept waiting, and, if her impatience rises to wrath, it is a consuming fire!"

The untimely visitor returned her salutation, but followed her footsteps in silence through the solitude of the garden, to which the black shadows of the trees gave a gloomy and sinister aspect that reflected the shadows in his own soul. For his was not the mien, the bearing, or the step of an impatient lover hastening to his mistress; but rather that of one who reluctantly performs a duty not to be avoided, or who responds to an invitation he may not refuse. They passed through the shrubberies into the palace by a small door, which his conductor opened with a wooden key, followed many winding passages, and ascended a narrow stairway, when the visitor found himself alone in a lofty chamber, furnished with all the luxury of the East — a chamber which he, unfortunately, knew only too well.

It was the private boudoir of the mistress of the hareem; and the latticed window, overlooking the rushing torrent of the Nile, was open, giving glimpses of the waters which boiled and bubbled below, as they raced hoarsely past, glittering like gems in the bright moonlight. The man cautiously approached the open lattice, and peered curiously for an instant on the rushing river below, whose waters, as it was high Nile, rose to within twenty feet of the window.

He turned away after a moment, however; and, seating himself on one of the silken divans, was soon sunk in so deep a revery, that he did not hear the rustling sound that announced a woman's presence, and started when a soft hand was laid caressingly on his brow, and a soft voice inquired:

"Is my young Antar dreaming, or asleep, that he needs waking?"

The young man, starting up, made a profound and respectful salutation, as he answered:

"The night is always dark for me, until the evening star comes to light it with her presence. But one thought can fill the soul of any mortal happy enough to be admitted here; and that is of her I now see before me."

"Well sung, my bulbul!" said the lady, unveiling as she spoke, and disclosing the imperious beauty and bold bright eyes of Nezlé Khanum herself. "But thou shouldst not compare me to aught so cold and distant as a star! The bulbul ever chants his love-song to the rose. And am I not worthy to be deemed a rose?" she added softly, glancing down over her own voluptuous form, and fastening upon him the unholy light of eyes full of sensual fire.

"A rose thou art, indeed!" cried the youth, with genuine passion in his voice. "A rose, indeed! a full-blown rose, whose perfume and whose loveliness intoxicate the senses and the soul! The song of the bulbul must ever be addressed to thee, O light of mine eyes and blood of my heart!"

The face of the princess glowed with gratified vanity at these impassioned words, poured out with burning ardor—either felt or feigned—by the lips she loved best. With all the *abandon* and recklessness of an Eastern woman—who flings all modesty and all reserve to the winds, and whose sense of shame seems utterly to disappear with the veil that has concealed her face—she threw herself on the divan beside her lover, and lavished upon him all those terms of endearment of which the Eastern tongue is so profuse. She removed the fez cap that he wore, and toyed with the short, clustering curls of his hair; and, reposing her head upon his breast, looked up into his face with a soft glow on her features, and a tenderness in her eye, that transformed her into another woman from the eagle-eyed and imperious Nezlé Khanum of every day. She seemed to renew her own youth with proximity to this young lover, the beauty of whose face and form were well calculated to inspire admiration in the heart of woman.

The hours glided away, and the interview had been prolonged until the first faint streaks in the Eastern sky heralded the approach of dawn. The young man glanced up through the open lattice, and said:

"The morning hour approaches, and I must tear myself away from paradise before the dawn: and the bulbul has not yet been told, why the rose summoned him to her bower so urgently on this most favored of all the days of his life."

As he spoke, the face of the princess, so radiant and so loving until now, suddenly changed its expression. The smile faded away from her lips, the light of love from her eye, and the soft glow of gratified passion was succeeded by the red flush of anger. She half withdrew her form from the encircling arm of her lover, and removed her hand from his brow, where it had rested caressingly. Then a cold, cruel expression crept over her countenance, and gleamed out of her glittering eyes. She seemed suddenly to have recalled some painful and irritating memory, which the presence of her lover had caused her to forget, but which his words recalled. Her tone grew measured and hard as she replied:

"There was a time when the bulbul needed no messenger to summon him to the bower of the rose! when

12*

the garden where she dispensed her perfume was haunted by his presence; and when his wings could not bear him swiftly enough back to her, from other wanderings. But now it is different. The bulbul must be lured back; and no sooner has he been snared, than his wings flutter impatiently to fly again. But the pretty bird should know" —and she cast upon him a look full of menace and of mockery—"that this cage is strong, and he may be made to sing in captivity, as other birds have before him. For the rose has thorns as well as sweetness ever; and those who have tasted the one, may feel the other too!"

There was no love now in the face or in the eyes that looked upon him, and the man felt his peril—saw, too late, the trap into which he had walked blindfold. But he summoned all his courage and his craft to meet the emergency and baffle the danger.

"Why is the star of my night so suddenly overclouded?" he asked, with real or feigned anxiety. "Why is her light withdrawn from her worshipper? What sin has her servant committed, that the ire of the great lady should visit him? He is innocent of intending offence—ignorant of having given any—and why should the Khanum speak as though to one who had provoked her displeasure? If his visits have not of late been frequent, it was because he feared to intrude without invitation; for it needed but the intimation that he would be welcome, and behold him at the feet of her who has honored him with her favor!'

"Thou hast the tongue as well as the sleek skin of the serpent," answered the princess, half relenting, half offended. "But thou knowest I possess the serpent-charm, and can handle thee with impunity. Thou hast not spoken truly to me; thou hast acted falsely and treacherously, too. And to the pale, scentless Ingleeze lily thou hast chanted thy love-lays, in place of the full-blown rose! Lie not to me, for I well know how the shameless face of that unveiled woman hath been seen with thine on the *Ezbekieh*, day after day! To the scorn and shame of womanhood, she hath cast love-looks on thy dainty face in the sight of all men; even to the mockery of the donkey-boys of the streets. Further do I know, how the shameless Infidel, in defiance of all modesty and decency, hath passed a whole day in thy house!'' — and the princess spat upon the ground in token of loathing. "I know, too, the story of the tame serpent, with which thou didst deceive the poor silly Ingleeze, and that other trick of upsetting the shameless thing in the Nile mud, to parade thy bravery again before her! Yet, with her kisses warm upon thy false lips, thou darest come and talk of love to *me*, while I am weak fool enough to listen, forgetting all these things, and all my just resentment, like a silly girl! Have I not spoken truly? Answer, O man of double face and forked tongue!''

Over the face of Askaros — for it was he to whom the princess spoke — there had, in spite of his self-control, passed many changes, as the furious woman went on. Apprehension, indignation, rage, shame, and disgust rapidly chased each other over his expressive features; and when the princess ceased, from sheer exhaustion, overpowered by the passions that raged within and tore her like so many devils, he raised his crest haughtily.

No trace of humility or of reverence in his face or voice now, but, with a steadfast light in his eye, and resolve written on his dilating nostril, he stood like some wounded lion brought to bay, and confronted the proud princess with a pride equal to her own.

"Lady," he said, "for the first time since we have known each other, you have spoken words of scorn and insult to me, which no man might utter and live. Those words I might forget and forgive, possibly pardon, for I know they spring from a jealousy fierce as it is unfounded. But you have coupled with my name that of another, which has no connection with either of us — the name of one, the purity of whose life and thoughts neither of us can imitate, scarcely comprehend — one as widely apart from us and ours, as though she were one of the Houris of whom your imaums speak! I swear to you, by my life and soul, that your suspicions are unfounded; for I am nothing to this Ingleeze woman, nor she to me. And furthermore, if that will not content you, let me tell you, that when I, in my mad folly, dared to speak of my admiration, she repulsed it, as you would that of the meanest of your slaves! If, then, I have had a short madness, and been unfaithful to you for a few brief moments, the folly is past and gone. Now I resume my allegiance, and ask forgiveness from the most enchanting of her sex. Well do you know, fear never could move me, or I never had entered here; or, having once entered and escaped, would never have returned."

Neither by word nor gesture did the princess interrupt him while he spoke, but she drew a deep, long breath when he had finished, as though her patience had been sorely tried, and again burst forth in stormy wrath.

"Dog of a Giaour! and son of a line of dogs!" she screamed. "Rightly have I been punished for stooping to defile myself with the society and presence of a wretched Copt, lowest, meanest, and basest of the mongrel spawn of Nile, which my great father trampled under his victorious foot, and used as men use other rubbish, to aid in building the empire which his line rule to-day. Was it not enough, that my condescension should be abused and my kindness betrayed, but that thou shouldst dare compare to my disparagement, thy Infidel paramour from the barbarous lands of the West, here to my very face, and in my own palace? Dearly shall that insult cost thee! I am a woman, it is true, but a woman of the blood of Mehemet Ali; and never did man or woman do him wrong, and live to boast it! Never again will thy pale-faced mistress, with her hair of withered straw, look on that girlish face of thine, or kiss those dainty lips. The Nile, from which thou rescued her but yesterday, shall sport with thy graceful form, and be thy bed to-night! An Infidel like thee, whose doom must be the fall from the Narrow Bridge of Al Sirat into perpetual fire, needs no time for prayers, as a Mussulman might."

She paused again, exultant malice and fiendish hate stamped upon every feature of the face which seemed suddenly to have sharpened and grown old, under the fiery heat of the simoom blast of passion sweeping over her soul.

Her destined victim did not quail. He felt his peril, but, like a brave man, braced himself to meet it worthily, if he could not avert it. Yet he did not seem utterly desperate, and as his eye glanced warily round the room, it rested for an instant on the open casement, and he drew nearer the princess, who, pacing rapidly up and down the room like an enraged tigress, had now paused near the window; and through it now softly came the first fresh breath of the awakening morn.

"Khanum," said Askaros, "are you very sure your

spies have not deceived you? that the things they have
told you are not lies, coined out of their own false hearts,
to win gold and favor from you, and to destroy me,
whom they hate for many reasons known to you?''

A cruel smile convulsed the lips of Nezlé.

"There spoke the craft of the Copt!" she snarled;
"ever more resembling woman than man, and striving
to escape by artifice dangers he has not the courage to
avert! Know then, O wise youth! that my informants
were not my spies, but of thine own household — ay,
even supposed to be of thine own base blood! The girl
El Warda, whom the world deems thy sister, was my
informant! She came to me" — and a derisive smile
again curled the cruel lips — "to pray me for a love-
philter to win back thy most precious affections, stolen
away by this Ingleeze, as the silly child believed. I gave
the philter to the fool; but I repaid myself by obtaining
all her secrets, and thine!''

This revelation fell on the young man with a stunning
shock. For the first time, as by a lightning-flash, he
saw the real state of the heart of his reputed sister. Of
this he had never dreamed.

But at the same time he saw how the danger of his
position was aggravated; and how useless, after all she
had heard and knew, would be any attempt to conciliate
or mystify the princess. Rapidly he made his resolve,
and prepared to act.

"Princess," he said, drawing still nearer, until he
stood close beside her, "these recriminations and explanations are useless, and can only tend to make us
both say words we shall regret hereafter. I have made
confession of my fault, and implored thy forgiveness.
Give it to me, by the memory of our past love, which

will renew itself, warmer and fresher after this short storm, and then let me go, for the day already begins to dawn in the East.''

"That day thou shalt never behold!" fiercely answered the princess. "Slave! dog! Giaour! thy blood be on thine own head! An hour hence, and thou shalt feed the fishes of the Nile, and thy vile name and viler treachery be washed away from my memory, even as thy carcass shall be washed from my palace-door by those rapid waters!''

And she pointed to the window, where the rushing tide, swollen and turbid, raced past in its sullen flow.

Swiftly she turned away from the window, confronted the Copt, and raised her two hands, as if to clap them together to summon her slaves. But rapid as was her movement, the young man's was more rapid still. Ere she could bring the hands together, he had seized her left wrist and held it, as in an iron vice, close down to her side, preventing the meditated summons. Her next movement was as sudden as his had been. Her right hand flew to her bosom, and a small, keen poniard flashed over his head, aimed full at his heart, ere he had time to suspect or avert the act. Instinctively he threw up his left arm to protect his heart. Down upon that guard the sharp steel descended, driven with the whole strength of maniac fury — rent its way through outer jacket of thick cloth, and through the folds of shirt and undershirt; then, grazing, tore open the fleshy part of the muscular forearm, round and white as that of a woman.

The blood spouted from the wound, as hand and dagger dropped to the side of the baffled murderess. Her face changed from rage to fear, as she cowered before the roused wrath of her destined victim — the feverish, fitful rage of woman yielding to the more concentrated wrath of man. For the face of Askaros had undergone an alteration as startling as that in her own. The devil that slumbers in the depth of every human heart had been unchained ; and the magnetic contagion of evil had been communicated from her leprous soul to the hitherto generous heart of the young man, stained already by her with sin, and now on the verge of being blackened by irremediable crime !

From the predestined victim, he suddenly rose over her as the doomsman — the avenger. And, with the lightning-like rapidity with which thought can travel in moments of immediate peril and impending death, the long catalogue of her crimes rose like accusing angels before the mental vision of the wicked woman, whose life had been a long defiance to the laws of God and man — a warfare against humanity.

For in the set and rigid face, with contracted brow and pitiless eyes, that bent above her, she saw no mercy — no hope ; and in his right hand was raised the dagger wrested from her, ready to strike the moment he apprehended treachery in any call, or gesture, or effort to summon aid.

So stood these two beings, whose criminal tie had been so suddenly and so violently severed — lovers, lisping endearment to each other in softest whispers but a moment since — now foes, whom the death of one, or both, could only separate to all human seeming ; one a baffled homicide in act, the other a predestined murderer in intention, with the shadow of their mutual crime hanging like a pall over both.

Askaros spoke first, though the silence, seemingly so long to both, had been of scarce a minute's duration.

"Is the dagger poisoned?" he hissed into her ear. "Is this wound of mine mortal? I must know, for two lives depend upon the truth."

"It is *not!*" she sullenly responded; "though I wish it were. I had meant my stroke to be too sure to need poison, else had I supplied it, to make my vengeance certain!"

"Will you swear it? Will you — but, folly! What oaths are not worthless to you? What in earth, or heaven, do you hold sacred? Will you hold out your arm and let me scratch it, to prove the truth of what you say?"

With a return of her former haughty and defiant bearing, the princess silently stretched out her right arm for the test; a slight, scornful contraction of her mouth indicating her contempt for what she considered the Copt's cowardice. But the movement seemed to satisfy him without further proof.

"I will not shed one drop of your blood," he said. "I am satisfied there is now no other poison running riot in my veins, save what my unholy love for you has left there. No; the dagger was not prepared with your usual forethought. Had it been otherwise, two corpses instead of one would have been found in this chamber; which has doubtless heard the death-groan of many men better and braver than I! For now I know that Cairene gossip lied not, when it told those tales of Nezlé Khanum, that I disbelieved until now. Princess, farewell! for never will we look upon each others' faces in this world again."

"You speak confidently," replied the Khanum, whose

13   K

audacity rose as the immediate danger receded; "you seem to forget that egress from this palace is not so easy without my permission. As well might a lost soul cross the bridge of Al Sirat over the fiery gulf, as any strange step pass in safety through this palace, or those gardens, to the outer world. You may slay its mistress — a daring act for a brave man, opposed by an unarmed woman! — but hence you cannot and you shall not pass, by my free will, or orders!"

"Trouble not yourself for my safety, O charming hostess!" answered the young man, calmly — cutting a strip of linen from his sleeve, and binding his bleeding arm as he spoke: "I know my path, and need no password from you. Nor fear I any peril from your armed mercenaries, to travel it — if not in safety, at least unmolested by you, or yours. Repent your past life, and strive to amend it, that the rude lesson I had to give you may not be lost. Neither in love, nor in hate, shall you look upon the face of Askaros again — who now shakes from his feet the dust of this palace of abominations, and bids it and you farewell forever!"

As he ceased, and the astonished woman stood spellbound and bewildered by his words and meaning, he vaulted lightly on the framework of the open lattice, stood for a second, and then plunged headlong into the raging and rushing flood that howled beneath!

Recovering from her stupor of astonishment at the suddenness of his disappearance, the princess rushed to the window, and by the uncertain light of the early dawn, peered with mingled curiosity and anxiety on the flood, into which the daring youth had so rashly precipitated himself. She strained her vision to discover aught beside the turbid surface of the stream, whose current swept

down rapidly, with a hoarse murmur, some few floating
pieces of drift-wood; but she did not see anything resembling a human head or a human form, within the
range of her vision.

Wearied by the useless search, and chilled by the raw
morning air, with a shudder she turned from the window
and closed the lattice, as though to shut out the memory
as well as the sight of what was passing below. A softened sentiment, almost of pity, blended with her exultation at her own escape from peril, and the destruction of
her old lover and new foe, who had thus executed her
vengeance on himself, and spared her a new crime.

"Poor boy!" she muttered, "he was very young to
end so soon; and so handsome, too," she added, regret-
fully, "while the men seem to me to grow uglier and
more stupid every day. Was he mad, to take that leap?
No living lover of mine took it before — though many
have passed through it without their knowledge or consent!"

She yawned wearily; then, after a moment, added:

"But he will keep my secret now, that is a consolation;
though I do feel a foolish softness about his fate, I never
felt for another's. But Allah made this world for the
living, not for the dead: so 't is useless to think; and,
doubtless, it was his kismet to die. Ingleeze can never
steal him from me now! But I shall look like a witch
from want of sleep; so now for a pipe of hashish, a
good sleep, and to commence a new experience and look
for a new lover to-morrow!"

Then yawning again, and wearily stretching her graceful limbs, the Egyptian princess glided to her own private
chamber, to forget in the fumes of hashish — and the
death-like slumber it would summon — the agitations of

the last few hours; to forget the tragic fate of the youth she had first tempted and seduced, made a plaything of, and finally hunted to his doom.

Let us drop a veil over the waking and sleeping thoughts of that incarnate evil in woman's form, to whom sin was a solace, and crime a pastime—a Circe, who brutalized the souls as well as the bodies of men, yet who died peacefully in her bed at last.

CHAPTER XII.

NEW LOVE AT OLD LUXOR.

EVENING at Luxor, on the Upper Nile : the rays
of the setting sun gilding and softening her majestic
ruins with a glory that seemed a reflection of the past,
when the City of the Hundred Gates was without peer or
rival in the ancient world — when, through those long
avenues, guarded by their grim stone sphinxes, poured the
subjects of the Great Rameses, many of whom the traveller sees as mummies to-day.

For, amid the ruins of the city we call Thebes, still
enough remains to excite the wonder of the modern
world ; so gigantic is the scale on which her structures
were erected — so colossal the fragments which even the
ruthless hand of Time has failed utterly to destroy.

Standing on the threshold of that vast temple, which
still overlooks the eternal Nile, and looking across the
yellow waters of the Great Father of Rivers — far away
we see towering the mighty statues of Memnon and his
mate, like twin giants keeping watch and ward over what
is left of Luxor on the one shore, and the Memnonium
on the other.

Over earth, air, and sky — over the half-buried relics
of the ancient city, and the mud-huts crouching under

the columns of its colossal ruins — even as the Egyptian of to-day is dwarfed by comparison with his predecessor, though not his progenitor, in that land — over all these brooded a solemn silence.

The influence of the scene and of the hour was strongly felt by a party of tourists, who had spent the day rambling among the ruins of those mighty structures; and who were now grouped together in the great hall of the temple, sitting on fragments of fallen columns and the shattered statues of colossal kings — fallen from their high estate in their temple, as in history.

In the party we recognize the familiar faces of our friends of the *Hotel d' Orient*, who for several weeks have been making the usual Nile trip, and are now about to retrace their steps. They have almost determined to ascend the river no farther, in consequence of the receipt of letters from Europe which compel the speedy return of at least one of their party. A passing steamer, bound for the First Cataract, had that morning brought these letters, forwarded from their Cairene banker; and to Sir Charles especially their tidings were most important. They gave him news of the sudden death of his elder brother, who had been killed by a fall from his horse while hunting, making him the presumptive heir to the family title and estates.

Miss Primmins had been profuse of expressions of sympathy and tearful condolence when the news was imparted to her; but Sir Charles, with characteristic frankness, had declined to wreathe his brow with weeping-willow. He had explained the matter to his American friends with his usual candor.

"It may, perhaps, seem unfeeling to you," he said, "but really I cannot affect any great grief at my brother's death; for I scarcely knew him. A poor devil of a younger son, I was sent out to India as a cadet when quite a boy, and have never set eyes on him since — our lines in life and all our associations being widely apart. And I do not believe, from all that I have heard of him, that he was a very lovable person — never married; and, as my father is very old and infirm, I may expect soon to come in for the family title and estates. The latter are very large indeed; and, though I am more of a Bedouin than of a country gentleman, still my birth and descent make me feel I am fit for something better than nigger-killing and tiger-hunting. So, under the circumstances, you must not think me a brute, if I am not overwhelmed with grief."

"Brute!" screamed the spinster in shrill denial. "The heir to a coronet and twenty thousand a year — a brute! Noble young man! I honor your fortitude in bearing this blow with such composure!"

A singular smile passed over the Englishman's face as he answered, with a half-shrug:

"I must hurry back to England therefore, for my presence will be essential there now. But," he added more seriously, and with a slight hesitation in his usually blunt manner, "but I can sincerely say I *do* grieve at leaving, unfinished, this delightful excursion, and at losing the society of friends for whom I entertain so warm — a regard!"

So it was settled Sir Charles was to leave them next day — taking passage for Alexandria on the steamer that brought the letters — while the Americans continued their upward voyage in their dahabieh as far as Assouan and Philæ — perhaps as the Second Cataract and Nubia.

SITTING together on the fallen granite statue of some great Egyptian king, who had lived and loved two thousand years before, on this sunny evening, were the Englishman and the American woman—so oddly thrown together in this remote corner of the earth, from homes so widely separated.

Sir Charles was unusually subdued and silent—even absent; his usual gay *insouciance* was gone, and an unwonted seriousness, amounting even to sadness, showed in his face and manner—and even in the inflections of his voice, when at rare intervals he made brief and irrelevant remarks.   At length, after a long pause, which seemed equally embarrassing to both, and which both seemed equally desirous and powerless to interrupt, he broke the awkward silence.

"Miss Van Camp," he said, gravely, "you know I leave you to-morrow, and the chances and changes of this world are such that God only knows when we shall meet again."

"Yes," answered Edith, softly; "but I hope we may meet again, and before very long."

"It may be a matter of indifference to you—it doubtless is so!" the Englishman went on, warming as he spoke.   "But before I go I *must* tell you it is far from being such to me.   It is true you have known me but a little while, and I am not vain enough to believe you care much about me; but it will be a source of more than pleasure—of infinite joy—to me, to hear from your own lips that I am more than a mere stranger!"

He refused to notice, if he even saw, the sharp, quick start she gave, and sudden gesture of her hand, raised as if in warning, and continued: "Tell me I am more than a passing acquaintance, and that I may be allowed to return and perfect a friendship which, to me at least, has been so delicious a privilege!''

A glowing blush overspread the fair face of the girl, more at the tone in which this speech was made than at the simple words themselves. She fixed her eyes steadily upon the ground, and, after an apparent struggle with her voice, spoke with much hesitation:

"I assure you, Sir Charles, that I — that *we* all shall miss you very much. I do not look upon you as a casual acquaintance at all, and nothing would give us greater pleasure than to continue the intimacy I — we formed in our wanderings together.''

He made no immediate answer, and another pause, longer than the first, ensued. Edith seemed to be examining with great minuteness the rubbish strewn around her feet, the toe of her tiny boot turning over the pebbles; while her companion, his eyes fixed full upon the stony orbs of the giant king opposite, sunk into a deep, motionless revery.

And the voiceless spirit of the dead past seemed to brood over its shattered temple, and sink down upon those intruders of to-day in an enveloping and almost palpable hush. Suddenly, sharp and clear, cut through the heavy stillness the man's voice; and this time he spoke as if he had made up his mind and knew precisely what he meant to say.

"I doubt not that both you and your friends,'' he said, "have looked upon me as a careless, reckless, eccentric creature, without feeling or sentiment; without even much depth of character. You were but just in so judging, for such was the impression I sought to convey. Am I right in my belief?''

Edith still examined the pebbles at her feet, and,

without lifting her eyes, murmured some reply, almost inaudible, but seeming to imply dissent.

"My position and prospects as a younger son," the other resumed, steadily, "with only my commission and career in the Indian service, were not such as to justify me in forming any plans for the future. I therefore sought only to live in the present. But my philosophy was not strong enough to protect me against myself! For some time past I have thought only and always of another. Need I tell you that that other is yourself?"

Still the girl responded not a word, nor looked up from the ground, though the flush on her face grew deeper, and the small foot nervously tapped the sand, still faster than before. The Englishman rose from the stone at her side, and stood before her with a mien of mingled dignity and dread, while his voice was still steady, but with a thrill of longing, yearning entreaty in it, as he asked:

"Does my avowal offend you? Are you wounded that he you deemed an idle jester, to whom you gave no encouragement to justify his speaking thus, should dare declare that he admires you — that he *loves* you?"

Once more the quick, sharp thrill passed through the frame of the young girl; the flush upon her cheek deepened to a crimson flood that swept over brow, neck, and bosom; the little foot ceased its beat upon the sand, and once more she raised her hand with a warning — almost imploring — gesture.

But the man saw it not; for the mighty torrent of his pent-up passion had broken the barriers of habit, of convention, and of race, and now swept him on like the flood of the mighty river near, when its rushing tide sends it downward with resistless rush toward the sea.

"Yes, who *loves* you!" he cried; "loves you with the wild passion of a heart that never loved before! with the deep, strong passion of a man who is no trifler; whose very soul feels, a thousand times more than words can tell, those nameless charms of person, mind, and heart, that have linked his every thought to you forever! I have seen, though I cannot tell, how pure, how good, how beautiful you are! I have seen your thousand priceless gifts of mind and heart, and have been mad enough, selfish enough, to dream of securing all these for myself! Oh, Edith, will you share the title and the rank soon to be mine? — worthless without you — whose possession alone permits me to reveal the secret I else had carried to my grave — the secret of my deep, devoted love for you!" And, throwing himself once more by the young girl's side, he sought to seize her hand and press it in his own.

Edith withdrew her hand, but very gently, from the ardent clasp of her lover's, and, for the first time, looked up. The hot flush had given place to deadly paleness, the eyes were suffused with tears, and she showed painful agitation in her face and manner, as well as the broken voice in which she answered :

"This is so unexpected, so agitating, I really know not how to answer without wounding you, for I never dreamt that you cherished such feelings for me, and I have never once thought of the subject you speak of so seriously. Oh, Sir Charles! let us still be friends"— he made a quick, impatient gesture at the word — "for, indeed, I *do not* look on you as a stranger. I esteem you, and — and admire you more than any man I ever met before. I mean," she added, blushing brightly at her own words, "of course, *as a friend.*"

Once more he made the impatient gesture of denial, and again he rose and stood before her.

"We can never be *friends!*" he said, quietly.

"We shall meet again in Europe," she said, more in continuation than in answer, "and shall, perhaps, even make another tour together. Then, after knowing each other longer — after studying each other's characters better — we might determine if — if — whether we are really suited to each other. For you know," she added, hastily, to cover her confusion, "our educations and associations have all been so different!"

The light faded from the eyes of the young man, and the glow of passion passed from his cheek, as the girl spoke thus in an almost pleading tone, and he answered sadly:

"I understand you now. You seek to spare me the bitterness of a direct refusal, which your kind heart would be pained to give. My folly in supposing I could win a virgin heart like yours, without proving myself worthy of it, is rightly punished. This is your meaning?"

She made a faint gesture of dissent, but he caught it, and the embers of hope, almost dying in his heart, glowed under it into a fresh blaze.

"You will give me at least some hope? Oh, Edith, tell me, if you do not love me, that at least you love no other! For I confess I had my doubts, and that is one reason I have hastened this precipitate avowal."

"Your question is an unfair, and might be an indelicate one," the girl replied promptly, and with some spirit; "but I do not hesitate to tell you that such is not the case. I do not hesitate to accept your affection because of a warmer feeling for any one else, nor can I explain the sentiments I really feel for you. For until the last few moments, I have never asked my own heart the question, and now I feel too bewildered even to think." Then she blushed brightly, and cast down the candid eyes, until now bent upon him, as she added softly: "But tell me whom you thought your rival."

Sir Charles hesitated but a moment, ere he answered: "Your candor merits the truth from me. When the *caïque* overturned you into the Nile, for the first time my own heart stood revealed to me in my agony at your danger, and, I must add, my jealousy of your rescuer. That young Egyptian has much in his favor to win a maiden's heart — rare personal beauty, courage, honor, and high intelligence. He has, besides, the romance of his life and habits, and I feared your fancy might have been captivated by these; but, above all, he has twice saved your life at the risk of his own! Hence I was, and am, jealous of the Egyptian — not for my own sake, but because I do not believe so incongruous an alliance would insure your happiness."

The shifting color of Edith betrayed some emotion while Sir Charles said these words, but she soon recovered herself, and when she answered, there was no tremor in her voice, her clear blue eyes sought his fearlessly, and spoke the soul of truth, but on her lip there was a curl of scorn.

"Sir Charles," she said, calmly, "you may dismiss your fears for me, and your jealousy on your own account; for Askaros is not, and can never be a rival of yours with me, and that he knows, I am quite sure, as well as I. That my girlish fancy was taken captive for a time by the graces of this young Haroun el Reschid may be true; that my heart or my judgment have ever been

14

influenced by him, is not so. I owe him a debt of gratitude; but I have never dreamt of paying him such a price for it as to unite my destiny with that of one of different race — to renounce my country for a barbarous land like this. Believe me, an American girl, however young, has too much common sense to turn her dreams into realities.''

It was strange to see how the *rôle* of the two speakers was reversed as the interview proceeded; how the strong, intrepid, reckless man became more confused, and the timid, gentle girl calmer and more self-possessed. For Sir Charles answered her almost indignantly:

''Oh, Edith, you are calm and cold as a marble statue! It almost maddens me to hear words of caution from your lips! What has caution to do with love — with affection? which converts even me — the worthless idler — into the earnest man whose whole happiness or misery hangs upon your lips! God never gave you beauty, and soul, and tenderness, to be wasted on the barren pursuits of fashionable life! to wither and fade without ripening into affection for some congenial heart! Trust yourself to me. Let mine be the task to warm into life those softer feelings that change the girl into the woman. For truly has a woman said, 'We pass not over the threshold of childhood until led by love.' Let mine be the hand to lead you over that threshold; and my life shall be one long effort to secure your pleasure and your happiness.''

He paused for a moment, but the girl only looked fixedly upon the ground, and his lips trembled with the strong passion that rent and mastered him, as he resumed:

''I can offer you now rank, wealth, high social position. These, others can offer you, too; but I can give you, besides, the devotion of a heart that has never throbbed for woman before. In you I see the fulfilment of my boyhood's dream, my manhood's search — a perfect woman! Oh, Edith! send me not back into the dreary desert of indifference, whence you rescued me; reject not a love such as is seldom laid at woman's feet twice in a life! Do not give me your answer now. Reflect upon it; look well into your heart, and see if the electric thrill of mine has not reached it. And then, at least, give me hope! tell me that I am not quite indifferent to you! that my devotion may yet win you to be my bride — the mistress of my destiny!"

Speaking thus, he stooped down and pressed his lips upon the passive hand of the young girl, who sat still and mute, as though overwhelmed by the rushing torrent of his passion.

Then, rising, he strode rapidly away.

CHAPTER XIII.

A NEW FRIEND WITH AN OLD FACE.

EDITH did not offer to detain her lover by word, look, or gesture. She remained sitting at the foot of one of the huge and ancient kings, with statue-like immobility; the shifting color in her cheek, and the unequal heaving of her bosom, alone showing that she possessed more life or motion than they. Towering up to the height of sixty feet, those massive monarchs of the past sat upon great thrones hewn from the immemorial rock, ranged at equal distances around the hall.

The contrast between the fair, fresh beauty of the young girl — as she sat there with the framework of ruins behind her, the grotesque sculpture of Egyptian antiquity upon the walls, where were mingled ox-headed and ape-headed human figures with other fantastic devices of that dead time, and the passionless faces of the stone Colossi gazing down upon her — was very striking. It looked, as it was, a reunion of the present with the past — the new with the old — the living with the dead — the connecting link which, in all ages and forever, must bind all humanity and its works in the great chain of creation, which stretches to earth from God.

Left thus entirely alone — for the others were now exploring a distant chamber of the ruin — the young girl leaned her head upon her hand, striving to collect her wandering thoughts and analyze her feelings. The task was a more difficult one than she had imagined, for the thoughts were rebellious, and in her mind and heart a confused chaos of feelings and fancies struggled for the mastery.

Was she indifferent to Sir Charles? or did she love him enough to accept his offer?

She could not answer even to herself, so suddenly had the question been presented to her decision.

In the ordinary course of social life, seeing so much of a young man, and being thrown so much into his society — even without coquetry, or her vulgar sister, flirtation — the idea might have suggested itself to her. But in this Eastern tour, with its strange phases of daily life, seeming more like dreams than realities, she had forgotten the usual formalities of intercourse, and restraints of society. She had accepted the constant society and intercourse of Sir Charles, almost as she had that of her brother, forgetting for the time that he was a stranger, and she an attractive young girl.

She knew she liked and admired him, as she had so frankly avowed to him, more than any man she had ever met; but was this love? Did she really love him? She was unable to solve the question to her own satisfaction; and she recalled with a strange thrill the sensations she had experienced in her intercourse with the young Egyptian — at first sight — during his wild avowal of his burning passion — after her rescue from the river. And this, she confessed to herself, had been, for the moment, a much warmer and more engrossing feeling than she now experienced for Sir Charles; though he

14 *   L

was certainly more congenial to her in thought and feeling than his unacknowledged rival.

She had scornfully repudiated the idea that Askaros could ever be anything to her; but at that moment her heart belied her lips, and she clenched her small hand and stamped her foot impatiently, in sudden anger at the consciousness. Was he not, as she had said, alien to her in every particular of birth, blood, breeding, and association? Was he not — although as a Copt he boasted his descent from the old Egyptians, to whom her race was but a thing of yesterday — was he not the countryman of those squalid and ignorant natives she saw around her, scarcely elevated above the brute creation in comfort, condition, or culture? What was this boasted descent, then, from the mighty people of that past which bequeathed to the world its poetry, its science, its prophecy — even the forms of its religion?

Impatient at her own thoughts, and tired of the conflict in her own heart, she raised her eyes and fixed them, to distract her thoughts, upon one of the colossal sculptured kings, which had sat immovable in his niche for thousands of years — the giant hands resting on the massive knees, and passionless and godlike calm stamped upon the still features of the grand, beardless face.

Was she haunted by one thought? For as she looked, she seemed to trace in the features of the granite giant a shadowy resemblance to those of the young Copt of whom she had been thinking; and the more closely she scrutinized, the stronger the likeness grew.

She rose impatiently to seek her companions, half terrified by the strange coincidence — still distrusting her own senses.

"This is indeed the land of marvels and of mystery,"

she said, aloud. " Will I ever be able to get back to real life and common sense again?"

That night Edith confided to her father the offer of the Englishman, as well as the uncertain state of her own feelings. She admitted that she did not feel inclined either definitely to accept, or to reject him ; but made no allusion to her strange fancies concerning the Egyptian.

Mr. Van Camp, who was devoted to his daughter, and would have been pleased at no offer which could possibly take her from him, was thoughtful enough of her welfare to see how advantageous such an alliance would be in all respects ; and, besides, he entertained the highest respect and regard for the Englishman personally, irrespective of his newly acquired wealth and title.

He proposed calling Miss Primmins into consultation : "For," he said, "although Priscilla is very eccentric in some respects, still she is a strong - minded woman in worldly matters, and has a vast deal of common sense and shrewd observation. And, my dear, you know marriage is a serious thing, and not to be contracted without proper prudence and reflection. Let us consult your aunt, therefore, and see what her opinion is."

Edith consented, although not exactly considering the spinster the proper arbiter of affairs of the heart. When the matter was unfolded to the chaste Priscilla, the surprise of that ancient maiden was only equalled by her delight. ˙

" Who would have expected it ! " she exclaimed, with a look of beaming approval cast upon her niece. " What a sly little puss you are ! and what a knowing fellow Sir Charles is ! Where could my eyes have been ? Ah ! you artful little minx, to keep so demure, and pretend to be so unconscious ! just as if any woman can have love made to her a month without finding it out! Thank heaven! *I* never was bothered that way. The men knew better than to talk nonsense to *me!* But it suits Edith very well. And, of course, you accepted him, my dear; and I will soon call you Lady Aylmer. It sounds very nice, don't it?—'Lady Aylmer's carriage stops the way!'

"I think now I can see you coming from the Queen's reception-room, for you will go into the *best* society in London. You must make Lord Charles get a foreign embassy. It gives one the *entrée* into the best circles abroad, and he can get a secretary who can do all the diplomacy, except the dining-out and reception business. When is it to be? Very soon, of course; and I suppose we shall have to hurry back to Europe now. And goodness knows *I* am sick enough of fleas, and bugs, and beetles, and crocodiles, and broken-nosed statues, and mummies, and undressed men! I shall be glad enough to breathe pure air, and sleep in clean sheets again!"

Here the spinster paused, from sheer want of breath, allowing Edith to say:

"But, aunt, you run on too fast. I have not even accepted him yet."

Miss Priscilla's lower jaw dropped, in her astonishment—her eye glazed—she gasped for breath.

"Not accepted him! A real lord! with heaven knows how many thousands a-year, and a house in London and another in the country! A member of *Parliament*, too; and as fine a young man, besides, as could be found even in Boston! Is the girl mad? Brother, what does this mean? Surely *you* will not encourage such folly!"

"But, aunt, I am not sure I love him enough to accept him."

"Love him!—fiddlesticks!" retorted the exasperated Primmins. "Who expected you would, or ought to, before he asked you? The very idea is highly indelicate and immodest! But now that he has proposed to you, you have a right to esteem him; and in time, I do not doubt, you will learn to do your duty as a wife—love, honor, and obey him—after you have made that promise at the altar. I hope those silly romances you are so fond of reading have not turned your head, and made you believe you are going to find knights and heroes in real life, and devoted love, and all that sort of stuff; or we may expect, some day, to see you running away with that good-looking Egyptian, living in a stone barrack without furniture, being bitten by snakes, and drowned in a river, in this horrible country!"

This unforeseen echo to her own thoughts did more to convince the girl of the folly of her fancies than greater eloquence could possibly have done. Her native common sense came to the aid of regard for the Englishman, and her wavering will was decided.

After much more conversation it was decided that, when Sir Charles renewed his suit the next morning—as he certainly would do—he should be referred to her father, who would consent to a provisional engagement for the term of one year, that they might better study each other's characters and dispositions before entering into an irrevocable bond. Kissing his daughter fervently, and giving her his blessing, Mr. Van Camp dismissed her to the most restless and uneasy slumbers her unclouded life had ever known.

Next day, Sir Charles renewed his proposals, accepted

gladly the terms imposed, and took his leave of the party, whom he was to rejoin in a month's time at Venice, a proud and happy man. But he left Edith scarcely knowing whether she felt most happy or miserable; but, on the whole, rather dazzled by the bright visions of the future, which her lover painted for her in vivid language, and with an ardor not to be mistaken.

Let us now accompany the successful suitor down the Nile, and, leaving him at Cairo, see how it has fared with his less favored rival in the interval.

CHAPTER XIV.

THE COPT AND THE HEBREW.

THE day succeeding the disappearance of the younger Askaros — whose absence did not alarm the household, as it was his habit occasionally to absent himself for short periods — was marked by another menace of danger to his family.

His father received a formal summons to attend the Grand Council within ten days' time, to undergo a formal examination of his accounts as Khasnadar under Mehemet Ali; a summons which he knew boded him no good, that council being composed of the creatures of Abbas, and only the instrument of his oppressions and confiscations under form of law. The old man, conscious as he was of his own rectitude, was greatly troubled in mind, and apprehensive of danger; and he regretted the absence of his son, whose counsel he needed, and on whom he depended in all matters of doubt and trouble.

Feverishly impatient, he could not remain in his house, and went forth to visit the young Syrian, on whose testimony, together with the duplicate vouchers and receipts, which, as Wakeel, he had made out and retained in his possession, he relied to acquit him.

The visit was not a reassuring one: for Daoud, while

expressing the greatest devotion and readiness to serve his patron, increased his apprehensions by the evident anxiety he manifested, and the seriousness with which he treated the subject; both plainly intimating his belief that it was a plot to despoil the old man of the great wealth he was supposed to have accumulated.   It, moreover, led him on to talk, with the garrulity of age, of the investments he had recently made, and the precautions he had taken to place large sums out of the reach of the rapacious Viceroy; and to his chagrin Daoud discovered that very considerable sums — in fact sufficient for a competence for his son — had been placed in the English funds, in anticipation of the attempt to plunder him, which he had dreaded ever since the accession of Abbas.

The Syrian made a note in his mind of these investments, however, which, in event of the death of both father and son, would fall to El Warda — the old man informing him that such were the provisions of his will: so cupidity came to the aid of hate and jealousy in the heart of the traitor.

From the Syrian's dwelling the old man passed down through the *Mooskie*, where the shops of the foreigners were situated, across the Turkish quarter, and ambled easily on his donkey down into a neighborhood where the streets were narrower still, the houses more mean and squalid, and the filth and garbage more offensive to sight and other senses.

It was the Jewish quarter into which he had penetrated; each nationality at Cairo having its own distinct district, closed with a gate at night, and under its own *sheik el belled*, or prefect, responsible for its quiet and good conduct; an office of great responsibility and power, as well as of great plunder.

Pausing before one of the largest of the dismantled-looking stone houses of this quarter — the entrance and courtyard of which indicated squalid poverty on the part of its owner, as did the dilapidated door and external appearance of the building — the old man dismounted from his donkey, put the bridle behind the saddle, and left the beast, who arched his neck, stretched out his legs, as if to take firmer position, and then stood still as a statue.

Passing up the steps, a dirty dismal interior, composed of long low galleries with an infinite number of unfurnished rooms, presented itself; and the old man, clambering up another narrower flight of steps, like one who knew the way, traversed a long low gallery, and reached a strong wooden door studded with iron nails. Upon this he knocked thrice with his staff in a peculiar manner. The door opened, and a withered old woman, dirty and ragged, appeared and answered to his inquiry in a shrill, cracked voice.

"*Moosh foke!*"—(He is not at home.)

"He will be at home to me," responded the old man. "Tell him Askaros the Khasnadar has come to see his old friend Ben Moussa, the Israelite. He will be at home to me."

The old crone muttered between her teeth, "*Moosh Yahudi!*" (He is no Jew) glanced suspiciously at him, slammed the door in his face, and hobbled off. The old man laughed quietly in his white beard, but remained standing, as if he were sure of the return of the ancient and uncourteous handmaiden.

"Cautious as ever," he muttered to himself. "Well, I suppose there is cause. All hunted animals learn suspi-

15

cion, and old Moussa's experience has not been such to inspire confidence in Turk, Arab, or Christian — 'Gentiles' as his people call them. But he will see *me*, and not where he receives the outside world either.'' And again the old man chuckled as though at some good joke, and waited patiently.

Presently the shuffling feet of the old woman scraped along the floor; the door opened wide this time, and the withered finger beckoned him to enter; but the filmy eye gazed with curiosity, not unmixed with discontent, upon the stranger admitted within those carefully closed portals, where precaution seemed so useless and so absurd. The old man put her gently aside, as though he knew the way, and entered a small room, bare of all furniture save some dirty divans and boxes, apparently containing papers, in niches in the wall. Passing through two or three similar apartments to where a winding stair led to the upper rooms, he stepped up to what appeared to be the outer wall of the house, and tapped three times — as he had upon the door — on a particular spot, where hung a ragged curtain.

Opening noiselessly was disclosed an entrance to a narrow passage, scarce high enough for a tall man to stand upright, which wound downward into the obscurity. Stooping his tall form, the old man entered this, and groped his way through the darkness till he felt what seemed to be a velvet curtain, which he pushed aside. Then stood revealed a scene so dissimilar to the surroundings, that one not in the secret would have believed himself dreaming, or the victim of some trick: for the apartment beyond was fitted up in a style of regal luxury surpassing the barbaric splendor of the palaces even of Abbas himself. Good taste combined with lavish wealth

in the decorations of the chamber, as well as in its sumpt-
uous appointments.

The finest fabrics of Damascus and of Broussa, stiff
with gold embroidery, covered the divans, the carpets
were the most costly Turkish rugs, while cashmere shawls
of fabulous value were strewn over the seats and cushions.
The room — for it had no windows to admit light from
without — was lit by large, richly chased silver lamps
hanging from the ceiling; the floor was tessellated mosaic,
inlaid with squares of wood and mother-of-pearl; objects
of European art in pictures, statues and bronzes, were
hung upon the walls or standing upon pedestals. Immense
wealth, and its lavish and tasteful expenditure were apparent in this chamber, and its contrast to the poverty
and squalor of the outer apartments was startling indeed.

Rising from his divan, the owner of the house advanced
to meet his guest, with even more than the usual Eastern
warmth and hospitality.

Like his visitor, he too was an aged man, with a full
and snowy beard, and a large frame, bent and bowed as
much by sedentary labors as by years. He was thin and
wiry, but not muscular, and wore the dress of the Barbary Jew. A long loose wrapper of dark silk, a red mo-
rocco belt round the waist, and an undershirt of striped
silk with silver buttons .

As he raised his head, with its ample white turban, from
the bowed position habitual to it, the face was unmistakably that of the Israelite of high type, such as we see it in the
pictures of the old masters, or in the cities of the East
and West to-day. There were the high aquiline nose,
curved like an eagle's beak; the broad thoughtful brow;
the large, inscrutable eyes, like black fathomless wells,
into whose depths it was impossible to penetrate, reveal-

ing nothing of thought or feeling except at will. The perfect oval of the face, with its olive tint and its full, mobile lips, even with this aged man, indicated sensuality checked by indomitable will.

When he sat down, the long, snowy beard, as fine as silk, fell even to his knees ; and when he rose, it swept over his breast, like the mane of an old lion, imparting a dignity to him that made him the living image of the Patriarchs of his ancient people, in the days when Jerusalem was still the chosen city, and its people the people of God.   He looked the type of what the genius of Michael Angelo has made living marble, in the statue of Moses in the Church of San Pietro in Vinculis — so solemn, sad and majestic were his face and mien.

" In the name of the Patriarch Abraham ! the common father of Copt and Israelite, thou art welcome to this house, into which few Gentiles enter," said the host, with a gesture of greeting.   " The sight of a friend so long absent is as a balm to mine eyes.   This house and all it contains is thine."

He led his guest to the seat of honor on the divan, and clapping his hands thrice, called "Zillah!"

Then there glided into the room a young Jewish maiden, richly dressed, and with her wealth of raven hair wound like a coronet over her broad, low brow, and thickly studded with precious stones.   In her hand she bore a small silver salver, with sweetmeats and wine of Cyprus, which she timidly offered the guest and her grandfather. Then, taking up and kissing the hand of Askaros, she retired as silently as she had come.

Then a *chibouque-ghi* brought in the inevitable nargileh and coffee, and, for a time, the two old men smoked in a silence broken only by the bubbling of their water-pipes. The Israelite spoke first.

"The face of my friend is troubled," he said. "The shadow of some sorrow, past or to come, obscures the sunshine of his contentment. Let him unburden his heart to Moussa-ben-Israel, who is willing to share the load with him, how heavy soever it may be."

"Rightly hast thou judged, O son of the Patriarchs!" replied the Copt. "The dark shadow of a sorrow is spread over my soul. I come to thee for counsel and for help; for well does Askaros know, from times of old, that he will never call in vain on Moussa-ben-Israel, even when those of his own faith he dare not trust."

"*Peki!*" returned his host. "But how can the perse-cuted son of a despised race — who has to burrow like a fox in his hole to baffle the Moslem spoiler; to hide away from the light of day all evidence of comfort, that he may not be robbed and maltreated — how can he, placed so low, stretch forth the hand of help to one placed so high as the powerful and wealthy Khasnadar, to whom both Turk and Nazarene pay reverence? I fear my lord is but jesting with the poor Israelite he has hon-ored with his friendship."

"Not so, O Moussa!" was the answer. "For none is safe in Egypt from the prowling tiger, who has suc-ceeded to the lair, but not to the nature of that lion of Islam — Mehemet Ali! My soul is dark within me, for I see the signs of coming danger; and I seek thee in whom I confide more than in living man, although thou wilt still cling to thine ancient superstition, and reject the incarnate God, in the person of His Son!" and he crossed himself. "But that is a matter between thy God and thee. In matters of this world I know I may trust

15 *

thee. Hearken, then, closely to what I have to tell thee.''

And he proceeded to unfold to the old Israelite his doubts and fears, giving him full details of all matters connected with them.

Moussa-ben-Israel sat motionless while the other spoke, his shaggy eyebrows drawn down over his sombre eyes, into which there crept a deeper shadow; occasionally stroking his beard with his right hand, but never interrupting the long recital.

When it was concluded, he said briefly:

''Thou hast reason to take precaution. There is danger to thee and thine in this thing. But tell me one thing more: canst thou trust the young Syrian, Daoud-ben-Youssouf, thy former Wakeel? Thou knowest, him I never fancied. I always deemed him far too old for his years — a dangerous thing in youth — and as slippery as smooth. Beware, O my brother! of that frozen snake; else may he sting the bosom that warmed him. He is far too old for his years, believe me. Zillah tells me thy daughter hath been here of late, and she distrusts thy former Wakeel. This she hath told Zillah; for the young women have but one heart, and keep nothing the one from the other.''

''Truly, I suspected not that!'' cried the old man, startled. ''And I have been foolishly indiscreet in telling the young man my plans and purposes. But I have come to thee, O Moussa! as I said before, for counsel and for aid; and what I now do, I shall tell none, not even my son. I seek, firstly, through thy aid, to place in the land of the *Frangi* the proceeds of these jewels. This thou well canst do through thy kindred in

Holland and elsewhere, and from thy knowledge of those countries where thou didst so long sojourn.''

As he spoke he took from within his girdle a small chamois-skin bag, and opening it, disclosed a number of rare and precious stones — diamonds, emeralds and rubies — into which he had, in the Eastern fashion, concentrated much wealth.

''These thou wilt take and deposit in the name of my son, and, failing him, of my adopted daughter, El Warda, in the hands of some of thy people abroad, keeping thyself only a memorandum of the same, and sending one to thy kindred. I dare not keep one; but thee I know I may trust now, even as I have done so often before, ere our beards had become snow, and our hearts water! The second favor I shall crave of thee will be even a greater one. It is that, in case the danger may descend upon me, and El Warda shall be deprived of myself and of my son, that thou wilt take her under the shadow of thy roof, until she can be sent out of this wicked and this weary land. Here thou canst conceal her, and in Zillah she will find a comforter and a sister. Swear this to me, O Moussa! for my heart groweth sick with a strange presentiment of evil for the poor child. For thou knowest she is beautiful, and the lust of Abbas is only equalled by his cruelty and his avarice.''

The Israelite rose, placed his hand beneath the right thigh of the Copt, and said, solemnly:

''By the God of Abraham, Isaac and Jacob! I swear to thee thy wishes shall be as laws unto Moussa-ben-Israel in those things which thou hast spoken. And may God so deal with me as I keep this oath!''

Then, after a moment's pause, he resumed, in a less serious tone:

"But I trust we may both be over anxious regarding these matters. Age, like evening, lengthens the shadows of all things, until they grow far greater than the substance. So may it be with us!"

The Copt shook his head.

"Neither thou nor I are children, O Moussa," he said, "nor yet over timid. But we both agree in the danger that menaces from the cruelty and calculating avarice of Abbas. But thou hast taken a great weight off my heart by thy promise, which I know thou wilt keep."

"So help me the Lord of Israel!" was the solemn response.

Then, satisfied with the pledge, and, after mutual benedictions, the two old men — so dissimilar in faith and life, character and creed, yet brethren in native truth and nobleness of soul — parted, never again to meet this side of the Great Judgment-Seat.

A painful gloom depressed the heart of each; and, as the Copt, accompanied by his host to the outer door, passed into the open *house*, the old Israelite's hitherto calm face worked with emotion, and he clutched angrily at his white beard as he muttered:

"Why did he trust that slippery Syrian! I fear evil may come of it! — I fear evil!"

CHAPTER XV.

THE WILD DOGS.

THE exultation and regrets of Princess Nezlé Khanum had both been premature. The young Copt had escaped one peril only to fall a victim to another.

A practised swimmer, when he plunged into the swollen tide and sunk deep under its waters, he did not rise immediately to the surface, fearing treachery on the part of the vindictive woman, who might order her slaves to fire at his head as soon as it appeared over the water, but floated on the undercurrent, which swept him rapidly out of range of vision, in the gray dim obscurity of the early morning.

Then he rose to the surface, the point below Boulak making a bend in the river, that of itself would hide him from any one in the palace. Still he floated down a further distance of a mile, then striking out for the shore, reached it in safety, though chilled through by his long immersion, and exhausted by his sleepless night and the exciting scenes through which he passed. He felt worn, jaded, miserable in mind and body; but, at the same time, thankful for deliverance from the peril he had so narrowly escaped, he breathed an inward vow

M 177

that he would profit by his lesson, and lead a new and better life thenceforward.

He could scarcely believe the incidents of the past night realities, and not the creation of a fevered dream, so strange and unreal did they seem in the cheerful light of day, and under the splendid sunlight which now began to gild the fresh and rising morn. Weary, worn, with his wounded arm beginning to grow stiff and painful, he dragged himself along the paths through the fields that skirted the river, over the soft, adhesive mud, still damp from its recent inundation. He was several miles from Cairo, having drifted some miles below Boulak, and having to make a detour to avoid her palace, lest some of the Khanum's people might be prowling in search of him.

He well knew she was a woman who would spare no precautions, and take nothing for granted, and that she would never believe him dead until she heard of the discovery of his corpse. He, therefore, determined to make a wide detour; but soon fatigue and languor overcame him, and he lay down under a palm-tree, on the thick grass, and fell into a deep, refreshing slumber. It was past noon when he awoke, and, feeling the need of refreshment, went to a coffee-house on the roadside and took some *kibabs* of roasted meat and brown bread, with a handful of dates. Then he resumed his walk; and unwilling to pass through the city of Cairo in his present attire, lest some one should recognize him, struck out for the *Shoubra* road, which would lead him by the desert to the *Bab-el-Nazr*, or Gate of Victory, by the famous tombs of the Memlook kings.

This was a circuit of several miles, and he was already beginning to feel severely the pain of his wound, but he trudged on, full of shame and regret for the past, and of good resolves for the future, mingled with thanks for his deliverance forever from the wicked Circe, who had so nearly imperiled both his body and his soul.

It was near twilight of the short winter's day when the young Copt, worn and weary, reached those wonderful structures known as the Tombs of the Caliphs, or of the Memlook Sultans, which rise out of the bare bald desert near the *Bab-el-Nazr*, or Gate of Victory, which leads into the Turkish quarter of Cairo. These buildings, combining the character of mosque and palace, are the best specimens of Saracenic architecture remaining in Egypt; and, though crumbling to ruin and much dilapi-dated, still present a most imposing appearance, with their great domes, their high minarets, and their tessel-lated walls — relics of by-gone splendor. Formerly the centre of a great city, with the residences of the court favorites grouped around them, in the days of these Caliphs — now they stand as the memorials of an almost unknown and forgotten age, in a clime and country even where everything seems to belong to that past — even the present. Like the Pyramids — which the father of history, Herodotus, declares to have been, even in his ·day, the property of tradition — these more modern memorials of man's vanity and pride are now left to crumble into dust, useless and uninhabited by man, with their only tenants the prowling wild beasts and the birds of the air.

High up against the clear blue of the evening sky, rose battlemented towers, airy minaret and rounded cupola, quaintly designed and carved with all the intricate deli-cacy of Moorish architecture. But from those silent balconies of the high minarets came no voice of Muezzin

now, proclaiming the greatness of God, and calling the
faithful to His worship. The foul vulture, folding his
heavy flapping wings, sullenly settled down to perch
upon them, screaming his obscene cry; and the fox
looked out of the windows over the dreary desert, where
the eyes of kings and conquerors had proudly gazed upon
a great city, when armies with banners filed in and out
of the Bab-el-Nazr, where now only the laden camel and
the patient donkey with his panniers pass. The unrelent-
ing Past had devoured her children, even to their tombs.

As though in mockery of fallen grandeur, and in scorn
of the crumbling but still majestic ruins, near these old
palaces of fórgotten Sultans, on a sort of mound, was
cast all the refuse of the city. There, too, were thrown
all the dead animals, and, though in that dry and burning climate these rapidly turned to dust, still the air
around was infected by the heavy, loathsome odor of
putrescence from rotting vegetable and decaying animal
life. Here, too, in the midst of this festering garbage
and corruption, the Egyptian wild dogs had burrowed
into the hillside, and raised their progeny, never entering the city, nor mingling with the tamer animals of the
same species that inhabited the different quarters of the
city, by some arrangement understood among themselves.
For in Egypt, the dog, being considered an unclean animal, is not domesticated, as with us; though Eastern
humanity, or religious feeling, forbids the destruction of
animal life unless for food, or from necessity. Therefore, the dogs increase and multiply in immense numbers,
but live and die homeless and masterless, subsisting upon
the offal thrown into the streets, and constituting themselves the scavengers of the city.

They go in packs, patrolling certain quarters or streets,

and the interloper, not belonging to that quarter, is sure
to be severely punished, if not killed, when he ventures
out of his own beat. But these city dogs are partially
tamed. Accustomed to his presence, though not made
the associate of man, they skulk away at his approach.
Not so those, desert born and bred, which partake more
of the nature and habits of the wild beast — gaunt, grim
and wolfish in appearance, with long lean, almost hair-
less bodies, wild, eager eyes, and long sharp teeth, displayed and used for slightest provocation on man and
beast. Cowardly, too, as ferocious, they never attack
but in packs, howling — not barking — with a whine like
that of the jackal. During the day they sleep in their
hillside burrows, awaking and prowling out for prey as
the sun sets, gorging themselves on garbage, or offal,
during the night.

This peculiar spot was known to be particularly dangerous from the ferocity of its troop of wild dogs : and
Askaros quickened his steps as he saw the sun declining,
to get out of a neighborhood so unsavory and unpleasant
in all respects.

Heedless of these inconveniences, however, seemed
the Bedouin Arabs of the desert, whose low, black tents
he saw stretched fan-like on the ground a hundred paces
off, their small, wiry horses picketed motionless on the
sand, each with his nose in a bag of oats, tied round his
head, as an impromptu manger.

The Copt strode rapidly on, loosening in his belt the
dagger which he had borne away as a trophy from the
harem, turning his head occasionally for a quick glance
around, but seeing or hearing nothing which could dis-
compose him. The Bab-el-Nazr was now in sight — his
road leading to it — when, suddenly turning one of the
16

little hillocks to get a shorter cut to it, he stumbled into the very midst of a pack of wild dogs, gorging and grumbling over the almost clean-stripped carcass of a horse.

The savage brutes, whose foul jaws were dripping with blood, and whose bristling hair and angry eyes showed their hunger as yet unsated, while they snarled and snapped and tore at each other, as one would secure a morsel coveted by the rest, suddenly ceased their strife. They heard the step and saw the form of the intruder, and fifty glowing eyes glared with mingled rage and fear upon him.

In the dead stillness that ensued, Askaros could distinctly hear the loud beating of his own heart. He stood motionless; for he knew flight would be the signal for a chase, in which there would be no hope of escape, since, even in his full freshness and vigor, he could not outstrip the pursuit of those fell hunters, who would rend him limb from limb. His very soul sickened within him, as it would have done at no ordinary peril, before this hideous and revolting shape of danger and of possible death. But he stole his hand to his poniard, braced every nerve and muscle, and, watching warily what next the dogs might do, made no movement to provoke them. Motionless he stood as an inanimate object, in the hope they might resume their feast, and permit him to steal away from their dangerous vicinity.

The wild dogs seemed almost as startled and perplexed as the man. They suspended their meal and their conflict among themselves, stared stupidly at their enemy, then, abandoning the carcass, broke into small groups, and turned inquiringly toward each other, to take counsel together. But they ever turned their long wolfish heads and gleaming eyes upon their new and living quarry. A

suspense of some minutes, which seemed ages to Askaros,
ensued ; and then one gaunt, grim dog, whose grizzled
muzzle, and wrinkled, brown skin denoted great age, and
who seemed the leader of the troop, advanced stealthily
a few paces in advance of the rest, and, crouching low,
turned his head, uttering a long, low howl. This seemed
the signal for the pack to group themselves in solid mass
behind him. Turning its head once more toward its
human foe and possible prey, the hideous thing, to whose
protruding tongue and grisly jaws the remnants of its foul
repast still clung, crouched again almost on its belly,
and dragged itself, step by step, forward, its blazing,
yellow eyes, with tawny iris, fixed on the man's. Slowly
the rest of the pack, like well-trained hounds in view of
the deer, followed in his wake.

The blood of the Egyptian crept chilly through his
veins, and his heart almost stood still, as hope deserted
him, and a doom more dreadful and more hideous than
that he had just escaped now confronted him. But still,
even in this terrible emergency, his courage did not
desert him. Flight was impossible : he must front and
meet the danger.

Quickly he glanced around, to see if any chance could
offer a stick or stone among the rubbish ; but the desert
pebbles were too small for useful weapons, and the stony
surface of the sand presented not a switch or shrub.
Griping hard his dagger, he raised his head, threw up
his arm in a menacing gesture, and made a step forward
toward the dogs. As he did so he shouted desperately
a call for help, in hopes of calling the attention of the
Bedouins, whose dusky forms he saw flitting among their
tents, scarce a hundred yards away—in the hope, too,

of terrifying the savage dogs, still crouching for their spring.

In the one hope he knew not whether he had succeeded. In the other he had certainly failed! Whether the sound of his voice and the meaning of his call had reached the Bedouin camp he knew not, and had no time to watch. His other hope, of terrifying his assailants, he saw, at a glance, had failed, and that his voice and gesture had accelerated the catastrophe he had sought to avert. For, at the sound of the human voice, the gaunt leader of the grisly pack rose from his crouching posture, every hair in his hide bristling with rage, his eyes aglow with hungry hate, and snarling till his sharp, white fangs were fully displayed.

Then, with a low howl, he dashed forward to assail the daring stranger, followed by the whole pack in serried column, none daring to pass their leader.

With a brief inward prayer to the Virgin for mercy on his soul, Askaros sunk on one knee to meet the upward bound of his assailant, as he sprang like a panther on his prey. Catching him full in the throat with his dagger from below, he drove in the sharp steel up to the hilt, hurling the beast backward, with the blood streaming from the half-severed head and foaming jaws! The sight of his blood seemed to infuriate his followers; and with their savage instinct they fell fiercely upon him, rending and tearing till his quivering limbs were still. Then they fought and struggled for his scattered fragments, which they greedily devoured, forgetting for the moment their human foe.

With straining eyeballs fixed upon the foul things, snarling at his very feet, Askaros stood still as death; for he knew the slightest movement would turn their rage upon him, and his very soul sickened at the thought, that he saw his horrid doom shadowed in that of his recent victim. Still resting upon his knee, and still griping the dagger, as his only earthly hope, he waited till their fearful repast was done.

It was soon over, and with it the respite accorded him. For the wild dogs, still unsated and made more savage by the taste of fresh blood, again ranged themselves in column, and with a low howl, that to his excited ear seemed his death-knell, once more rushed upon their victim!

At that second flashed past his swimming vision what seemed a white apparition — then another — and another! as with a wild yell three Bedouins bore down upon them. Their white bournous fluttering in the wind created by the arrowy rush of their fleet mares — the sharp points of their long lances glittering like stars — they charged right into the midst of the wild pack — trampling, spearing, and scattering them in all directions!

The howls and wails of terror from the stricken brutes succeeded fast upon the ominous growl that had but now preceded their attack; and Askaros — recovering from his surprise at the unexpected deliverance — saw his late assailants now dispersed in headlong flight, now writhing on the spear-points of his new-found friends.

"Thanks to the Virgin!" he cried; "my prayer has been heard, and I have been spared this fearful doom! And now I must thank the human instruments she sent for my deliverance." And he turned his steps toward the tents, there to await the return of his rescuers.

A few moments later he was sitting smoking with the Sheik of the tribe, under his low black tent, in the middle

16*

of which only could one stand erect. His wounded arm
had been cared for, and submitted to the skilful surgery
of these children of the desert — learned only in Nature's
lore.   No prince in his costly palace could have displayed more courtly dignity and courtesy than did the
swarthy Sheik, sitting under his black tent, his camel's-
hair bournous almost his sole garment, and the cushions
on which they sat almost his only furniture.

" We are of the tribe of Abou-Gosh," he had replied
to the other's inquiries; "and come from Syria.   Our
presence here is accidental — Allah surely sent us," he
added with grave courtesy, "to be your rescuers. *Allah
Kerim!"*   (God is great.)

" Abou-Gosh!" answered the young man; "well do
I know that name.   He is the Bedouin chieftain whom
men call King of Syria; who owes allegiance to neither
Sultan nor Viceroy, and levies his tribute on all strangers
passing from Joppa to El Khuds, the Holy City.   He is
my father's old friend.   But where are my deliverers,
that I may thank them?"

The Bedouins were sent for by the Sheik, entered and
stood waiting with all the impassive quiet that characterizes the every movement of the children of the desert.
When Askaros offered them a liberal *backschisch* (present,) they put it aside and shook their heads.

" The children of Ishmael who dwell in tents," the
Sheik answered for them, "have no use for gold.   Their
wants are few — steel heads to their lances, a handful of
dates to eat, and a horse to ride.   They need nothing
more; far less would they be paid for the small service
they rendered you.   We are all the children of Allah,
whether we dwell in tents or in cities; and we are all

bound to aid each other. *Bismillah!*" (God be with you.)

The young Copt rose to depart, after bidding a courteous farewell to his host, who commanded two of the Bedouins to conduct him to the Bab-el-Nazr, lest he were again attacked; for he saw his guest was weary and faint from loss of blood.

In silence did Askaros pass to the gate, with his wild escort, where he again vainly strove to press a reward upon them. Then he wearily dragged himself along until he reached the outer wall of the garden of his father's house. He rested for a moment in the narrow street, vainly searching for the key; apparently he had lost it during his wanderings; so, striking upon the gate, he called aloud: "Ferraj! Ferraj!"

"Home, and safe at last!" he murmured, gratefully. "Did Haroun himself go through more adventures in twenty-four hours than I have done? God be praised for my safety — I scarce deserve it."

As he spoke he turned quickly; he heard the sound of stealthy feet moving behind him. As he did so, he felt himself seized by strong hands, his arms pinioned to his side, and a cloak thrown over his head, almost stifling him, and preventing the utterance of a sound or cry. Then he was lifted up, thrown across a horse in front of a rider, and slowly and stealthily borne away through the dark and deserted streets.

Through his brain there flashed one thought:

"I have not escaped the Khanum! She will now complete her work. Oh! why was I saved from the wild dog, to glut the maw of the tigress?"

But powerless to act or move, the young man made no struggle, and was borne along unresistingly.

As the seizure was effected, and the captors — joined
by a company of armed and mounted men, who had
lurked at the corner of the next street — moved off with
the prize — a dusky, shadowy shape, which seemed to
spring out of the very wall, glided cautiously after the
retreating band.   It followed swiftly and stealthily upon
their track ; the shades of night soon swallowing up captors and spy, who dogged their steps — as they hurried —
whither ?

CHAPTER XVI.

THE TIGER-TAMER.

ABBAS PASHA, Viceroy of Egypt, sat on his divan in his desert palace of *Abbassieh*, which in one of his freaks, he, like a new Aladdin, had caused to spring up, in the midst of the sterile sea of sand. Far as the eye could reach, from the upper windows of the palace, naught was to be seen but the desert; and the lofty pile of stone, with its wide wings, large enough for the accommodation of the court of an European king, occupied the centre of a square, surrounded by barracks, in which were quartered several regiments of soldiers, as a guard to the palace and person of the suspicious tyrant.

The whole fabric seemed to rise like an exhalation out of the dreary desert which environed it.

The barracks were long, low buildings, two stories high, over which rose high in the air the towers and cupolas of the lofty palace. But they entirely surrounded the square, and ingress or egress from the palace was through one of their gates, a wall of solid masonry shutting out other entrance.

There was a heavy cloud on the Viceroy's brow, and his ill-humor was so evident, that his cringing courtiers

kept at a distance, preserving a respectful silence, and a
stillness like that of death reigned in the apartment.

Abbas beckoned to Mahmoud Bey — long since reinstated and in high favor — and, at the sign, the obsequious chamberlain glided forward, kissed the hem of
his robe, and awaited his master's orders.

"Did you tell the consul-general," said Abbas, "that
I was ill and could not see him?"

"Effendina, I did.   I repeated the words as given,
which were engraved on the memory of thy slave."

"What said the infidel in reply?" asked the Viceroy.

"He replied, O Effendina! that 'it grieved him much
to hear of thy failing health, but that the matter on which
he wished to speak was most pressing.   If, therefore, ill
health incapacitated my lord from the public affairs, he
would be compelled to transfer the consideration of the
matter to Stamboul, as it concerned the honor of his
nation.   So spoke the insolent Giaour!"

A blacker frown darkened the brow of Abbas, and he
muttered: "May his father's grave be defiled!   What
then didst thou answer?"

"I replied, O lord of my life! that although thine illness had been serious, yet was I charged to say, that in
the event of the actual necessity of the visit, my lord the
Viceroy would, in defiance of the order of his Hakeem,
allow the consul-general to visit him.   He could not
come into the city, but would receive him here at the
Abbassieh."

"*Peki!*" (it is well), said the Viceroy: "thy face is
white in my presence.   Thou hast fulfilled my orders
with discretion.   And so the dog said he would come
to-day?"

"Highness, yes! and the hour has now come when he should arrive."

"*Peki!* he shall be received. Give the necessary orders for his admittance."

As he spoke, a noise in the outer court, in which the rolling of wheels, the trampling of horses, and the clattering of sabres, as the guard turned out to meet some visitor, announced an arrival.

"The son of *Sheitan* (Satan) is not only pressing, but punctual," muttered the Viceroy. "What can he know, and what does he want? *Bakaloum*, we shall see!"

Steps were now heard reverberating through the long galleries which led to the reception-room, the curtain was pushed aside, and the obsequious chamberlain entered, ushering in the same consul-general, whose presentation has already been described, followed by his suite.

The Viceroy rose, advanced a few steps to meet him, and motioned him to the seat of honor by his side, which he took.

After a few preliminary compliments had been exchanged, a chibouque smoked, and a cup of coffee sipped, the consul-general, still holding in his hand the long pipe with its amber mouthpiece encircled with jewels, turned gravely to his host and said:

"Highness! I must apologize for insisting on an interview, after learning the delicate state of your health; but my business was so pressing I could not defer it; so hope you will excuse me."

"You are welcome!" answered Abbas; "and your visit is better for my health than that of a Hakeem. Already I feel strong enough to hear what you have to say."

This polite speech was contradicted by the covert sneer which lurked in the corners of the sensual mouth.

The consul-general did not seem to have perceived the covert irony, but answered promptly:

"Then, Highness! not to fatigue you too long, I will tell you what brings me here. Your people — I am sure without your orders — have done wrong and injury to mine; and, at the same time, have insulted the government I represent by so doing. It is for this I come to-day, to demand reparation of the wrong, and the punishment of the wrongdoers."

"The consul-general knows I respect him, and his government also. It is only necessary to prove the wrong done him or them, to insure its reparation. Of what has he to complain?"

"Highness! I have to complain that the translator of my consulate-general, Askaros Kassis by name, has been forcibly abducted, and is now a prisoner in the citadel of Cairo, in contempt of my protection, and in violation of the rights of foreign agents in Egypt, as recognized by your predecessors and yourself."

With all his self-control, Abbas could not prevent a red flush rising to his cheek at the mention of the name of the man he hated, and the bold utterances of the consul-general; but his manner continued as calm and unruffled as ever, as he said:

"Since we are to discuss matters of business, let us do so without all these witnesses. I had flattered myself your visit was one of courtesy, or, at least, touching some grave public affair! Since, however, you propose converting my palace into a *meglis* (council-room) for petty personal affairs, more fit for my minister of correctional police than for you or I! we had much better conduct our discussion alone! Mahmoud Bey! and you Hussein Pasha, our minister of foreign affairs, together with Zacchi Bey, our chief interpreter, remain — the rest may retire!''

His commands were promptly obeyed. Then turning to the consul-general, who smoked his chibouque gravely and placidly in the interval, he said:

"Now, I am ready to hear your complaint. My ears are open.''

"Highness! I repeat what I have already said, and ask of you an order to Elfy Bey, Governor of Cairo, and commanding at the citadel, for the release of my *protégé*, Askaros Kassis, and the punishment of those who have dared seize on and imprison him by violence.''

"You talk strange things," said Abbas, coldly. "How know you, in the first place, that the man of whom you speak, and whom you claim as a *protégé*, is a prisoner at the place you mention? Have you any proof, or is it mere suspicion?''

"Highness! I assert only what I know, and can prove. The proof I can produce, if necessary, as your Highness, as I supposed, seems ignorant of this outrage.''

"How and when was the man imprisoned?''

"Highness! he was seized by treachery, in the night-time, at his own gate, by the servants of Elfy Bey, taken thence, and secretly immured in the dungeons of the citadel.''

"How know you this, if, as you say, the thing was done secretly?''

"Highness! it is enough to say I know it, and can prove it.''

"Doubtless, enough to satisfy myself; but I must have positive proof before taking steps against one of the most

17   N

faithful of my servants; for such is Elfy Bey, Governor of Cairo."

"Know then, Highness! that when the capture was effected, the Nubian slave of Askaros, Ferraj by name, concealed by the shadow of the wall, witnessed the act, and, following on the track of the captors, recognized the face of the captain of the guard of Elfy Bey. Furthermore, he followed them until they entered the gates of the citadel with their prisoner, and the gates were closed upon them. Then he came to me, three days since, and revealed what he had seen and knew."

The lip of the Viceroy curled with a contemptuous smile, as he replied:

"Thou art yet new in this country, O *Elchee!* (ambassador!) and knowest not how these slaves will lie. Thinkest thou I would weigh, for an instant, the oath of a wretched Nubian slave against the word of the *Governor* of Cairo, should he, as is most probable, deny the truth of this wild story?"

"Highness! there is yet further proof; for the faithful Nubian lurked under the wall of the citadel, made the cry of a bird, which his master knew, and shortly afterward there fell a scroll, written in his blood on a piece of linen, and tied to a stone, which the father of Askaros declares to be the writing of his son. Highness! behold the scroll."

He unrolled a small parcel, which he took from his pocket, containing a piece of linen, on which was traced in red letters with some sharp instrument, in Arabic characters, the words, "I am imprisoned in the citadel," with the signature of his signet-ring stamped upon it on black wax, in Egyptian fashion.

"Highness! does that satisfy you that the Nubian spoke truly?"

For a few moments Abbas did not reply, revolving in his subtle mind how to meet this unexpected difficulty, which frustrated all his plans. He glanced from under his bushy eyebrows at the face of the consul-general, which was still as serene and calm as when he had entered — not a sign of impatience or irritation visible upon it — and adopted his line of policy.

"Thou art newly arrived in this country, O Elchee!" he said, "and hast no conception of the trickery and frauds perpetrated under the shields of consuls here by designing knaves who win their confidence, and seek their protection to defeat the ends of justice. I know the family of this man Askaros well; and they are among the most cunning and disreputable of that most knavish people, the Copts — who are neither Mussulman, Jew, nor Christian—but a compound of the worst qualities of all. Both he and his father were born my subjects, and still are so, and have many matters unadjusted with my government. It is doubtless to avoid the detection of his villanies, or the punishment of his crimes, that this man hath sought the puissant protection of thy consulate-general. It may be that Elfy Bey, not knowing thy claim to him, to avoid scandal, arrested him in this quiet way, without meaning any disrespect to thee or the great nation of which thou art the honored representative. Therefore, even if all thou tellest me be true, had we not better arrange it amicably?

"Come," he added, laying his hand familiarly on the consul-general's knee, like one asking a favor. "Let justice take its course with this man, who is unworthy of thy protection, and who really is not entitled to it under our laws, since at the time he applied for it he had still unsettled affairs with the Egyptian government. Take no further notice of, or trouble about this thing, and there is no request thou canst make of Abbas Pasha for thyself or friends — no valuable concession of privileges thou canst ask, which shall not be granted — and thy influence and power in Egypt shall be second only to my own. Shouldst thou wish to make *protégés* of fifty other Copts, do so, and no complaint shall be made. But this one I cannot give you. Reasons of State, as well as private ones, forbid it. And if thou shouldst persist in pressing this matter, we might cease to be friends! Is it agreed, O Elchee?"

The consul-general to whom this tempting offer was made — the value of which he well knew — did not pause for a moment's reflection, but answered as soon as the Viceroy had ceased speaking.

"Highness! had you known me longer you would not have made such an offer to me, which, under the guise of a compliment, conceals an insult. You may be able to buy your slaves for house or harem here, but you cannot purchase me, neither by flattery nor by appeals to avarice. I only ask my rights. More, I do not claim — less, I will not accept. It is for you to decide whether you will give me these, and we remain friends, or refuse them, and compel me to act in a way that will displease you."

From under the contracted brows of Abbas there gleamed a glance of mortal hate upon the bold representative of the infidel, who thus bearded him in his own stronghold, and disdainfully rejected equally his proffered friendship and his favors. Had he dared, he would have summoned his guards, and ordered the immediate punishment of his insulter. He half rose from his divan, the fingers of his right hand convulsively clutching at the hilt of the jewelled dagger he wore in his breast, as though to strike him dead. But the next instant his mood seemed to change. He threw himself back on the cushions of the divan, with an expression of utter weariness in face and form, and drawled out to his interpreter in a languid voice:

"Tell him I am weary of all this talk. If he wants to discuss such trivial matters as this about a wretched Copt, let him go to my ministry of foreign affairs. Let him go now, for I am weary."

And raising his hand, as though to brush away some intrusive insect, he sunk back on his divan, as though giving *congé*, and finishing the audience.

The consul-general did not understand Turkish; but the manner and gesture of Abbas were too significant to be misunderstood. He saw they meant insult. Rising suddenly from his seat before the interpreter could render the words, he flung down the chibouque he held in his hand, which fell against the divan, almost striking the Viceroy — and confronted Abbas with folded arms and knitted brow — indignation and scorn written on every feature of his usually composed and smiling countenance.

"Tell your master," he said, sternly, to the interpreter, "that he forgets he is not speaking to one of his slaves, but to his equal — who represents a country to which Egypt is but a petty province, against which, should he provoke its anger, he is more powerless than the meanest of his subjects before him. I shall not remain here to be insulted, but demand immediate satisfaction here and now, before I go."

17 *

"*Enta magnoon?*" (is he mad?) asked Abbas, fiercely, roused from his assumed apathy into mingled astonishment and rage at the unexpected demonstration of the consul-general, whose attitude and looks explained the purport of his words. "What does the madman say?"

"Effendina!" said the terrified and cowering interpreter — abject fear stamped on his face, and trembling from head to foot — "I dare not repeat his words, which are unfit for your highness to hear!"

"Ass! and son of a line of asses! Repeat them to me instantly," growled Abbas, "or I shall take a way of finding thy tongue, which shall never after utter words again."

Thus reassured, the shrinking interpreter explained the purport of the consul-general's speech, as mildly as he might, softening down the offensive expressions.

"False dog!" said Abbas; "I know that he said more and worse than thou hast told me! But it matters not. I know his meaning. Tell him there has been some mistake. Ask him to sit down again, and take his chibouque, and we can explain it."

The consul-general, still standing in the same attitude, replied, coldly:

"Tell the Viceroy the mistake, then, is on his part, not on mine. I will neither sit nor smoke with him, until he assures me he meant no insult, by manner, gesture, and speech, which seemed to imply it."

"*Bakaloum!*" answered Abbas, impressed by the resolute bearing of his guest, which had greatly disquieted him, and excited a vague fear in his breast.

"Tell him I was seized with a sudden return of my illness, and that what he mistook for discourtesy was the effect of a severe spasm of pain. In Allah's name! tell him not to stand there all day like a *Fakeer* on penance ; but to sit down again like a reasonable being!''

The consul-general, accepting the apology, resumed his seat and his chibouque, then said:

"Highness! it grieves me much that this unpleasant mistake should have occurred, which I shall forget at once — trusting you also may do the same. But, disagreeable as my duty may be, I must perform it, and request an immediate investigation into the affair of which I spoke to you.''

"Do you know," said the Viceroy, "that the appointment of the man you speak of, was never confirmed by my Government, and is therefore invalid?''

"Highness, I do not deny that question is still in controversy ; but pending its settlement, I must insist on the man's liberation. Show me good reason for not retaining him in the position, and I shall not insist upon it ; but it is an insult to my authority to imprison him thus, and at this time.''

"*Peki!*" (so let it be,) said Abbas ; "I have no reason to refuse your request. If, as you say, the man has really been seized, through the officious zeal of the Governor, who, for aught I know, may have some other charges against him, we will not quarrel over so wretched a creature. He is not worthy of it. He shall be liberated — if now in prison — to await the examination of his claim for protection, already instituted. In the meantime, I must ask the favor of you, not to employ him actively in your business with my Government.''

"Highness, your wishes shall be complied with. May I ask, to avoid further misapprehension, that your Highness may cause to be prepared and given to me the formal order for his liberation, addressed to the Governor of Cairo?''

Abbas frowned darkly, and his swarthy face grew suddenly red, for he saw the distrust implied in the request. But he only spoke a few words to the interpreter, who retired, returning a few moments afterward with a written slip of paper, to which the Viceroy affixed his seal with his signet-ring.

"If it be as thou sayest," he said to the consul-general, as he handed the paper to him, "this order will liberate the man, on whatever charge he may have been arrested. But recollect thy promise concerning him, for the matter is one which touches the dignity of my Government, as well as thine. Let us now converse on other and less disagreeable subjects."

Smoothing his brow with ready dissimulation, and making himself as agreeable as possible, the Viceroy then passed to other topics, confiding many apparent secrets to his guest, as though to a trusted friend, dismissing him with almost affectionate fervor.

No sooner had he left, however, than a trusty messenger was dispatched on a fleet horse with a message to Elfy Bey, immediately to liberate the prisoner before the formal order came, and to degrade the captain of the guard who had seized him, explaining to Askaros that the arrest had been made without the knowledge or order of the Governor. The disgraced captain was to be sent to a post on the Upper Nile, and bribed to silence by a good *backschisch.*

"That son of *Sheitan,*" said Abbas, with a fearful malediction launched after the departing consul-general, "seems born to be my plague; and his Government is too strong to quarrel with, if I would secure the succession to my son El Hami. But what fools these Franks are! I would have made his fortune, and he throws it away, out of pure vanity. I wish I could venture to give him a cup of coffee — for I hate him worse than any of his infidel brethren, who will roast in Gehenna. But I am wearied, and must seek solace and sympathy, where alone on this earth I can find it.''

He rose, and passing through several suites of apartments, reached at last a door, before which was seated the Kislar Aga, or head eunuch, a grisly black, magnificently attired, his dress glittering with gold embroidery and precious stones. He was armed with a crooked Damascus scimitar, the hilt of unicorn's horn, encrusted with precious stones, the scabbard of silver washed with gold. The guardian of the harem rose, with a profound reverence, at the approach of his master, in whose presence alone he stood up, ranking all the other functionaries of the palace, and prostrated himself at his feet.

The Viceroy permitted him to kiss the hem of his robe, and, leaving him groveling on the floor, entered the harem, where he found her whom he sought. It was no young and lovely Georgian or Circassian, with skin of snow, auburn hair, eyes of azure, and form of voluptuous mould; nor the more dusky beauty of Egypt, with its supple graces of form, eyes of gazelle, hair of night, and teeth of pearl, that rose to greet and meet the cruel and jaded voluptuary, as he entered those sacred precincts.

It was an aged woman, brown, wrinkled, withered, haglike, with bowed and stooping form, tottering as she shuffled toward him, her worn face lighting up with pleasure as her bleared vision recognized him.

Between the pair there might be detected enough resemblance to show that they were of the same blood: and the face of the man softened into human sympathy, even into fondness, as he said:

"I trust thou art in health, and happy, O my mother! for thy son hath come to pass in the light of thy presence a few hours—the happiest he knows—his only relief from his many cares and troubles."

"*Bismillah!* (God be praised) I am well in health, my son, and thy coming is as sunshine to my old heart! O my best beloved! Come! I have prepared thy food, and thou must eat, and I will listen to all thou hast to tell."

She clapped her hands, and slaves entered, who arranged upon a table the repast, of which Abbas voraciously partook, for so suspicious was he of poison, that he ate nothing which was not prepared by those withered hands, or under her eye, habitually, whenever at the same palace with her.

To his jaded senses and ulcerated soul, the love of woman or the friendship of man, now appealed in vain. Even the most revolting vices — fouler than those practised at Caprera by the tyrant Tiberius — palled upon his debauched appetite.

His son appealed only to his ambition, as continuing his line, and perpetuating the power and the wealth he had ceased to enjoy. But the sentiment of affection for his mother was the sole green oasis left in the arid desert of his soul — the small remaining link which bound him still to humanity, and proved him not utterly a monster. In her society he forgot his cares and the disgusts of the day, and when, replete with food, after a long confidential conversation, he fell into a heavy slumber on the divan, his mother sitting by to watch his repose, his face seemed to have regained the freshness and frankness of his early youth before unrestrained passions and unlimited power had erased from it the signs that this man too, tyrant, debauchee, human-tiger as he had become, had been created like all men, by God, "in His own image."

Let us drop the curtain over a scene too sacred for intrusion, which displays the only redeeming trait of one, whose life, otherwise, seemed all evil, and whose death a judgment for sins, against which both earth and heaven cried aloud.

CHAPTER XVII.

THE WARNING AND THE FLIGHT.

TO his infinite surprise, on the day that witnessed the interview between the Viceroy and consul-general, Askaros was summoned from his prison to the presence of Elfy Bey, the governor, who received him with cordiality, even with kindness, and insisted on his seating himself on the divan beside him, to partake of pipes and coffee.

He then proceeded to apologize to his bewildered prisoner, expressing the great regret he experienced at the blunder his stupid servants had made in arresting Askaros, mistaking him for a totally different person, whom they had been sent to apprehend, which error he himself had just discovered. Glancing at the common soiled and torn dress which the young man still wore, he accounted for the mistake by that masquerade, and announced to the astonished captive that he was at liberty. He also kindly tendered him a change of raiment and a horse to ride, that he might return home in proper dress and style.

The governor then summoned the captain of the guard, and went through the farce of degrading and dismissing him, as pre-arranged by the Viceroy.

The late prisoner and present guest of the governor had to reassure himself he was not dreaming, when, bathed, well dressed, and refreshed, mounted on a charger of Elfy Bey's, he sallied out of the citadel gates, by rubbing his eyes and pinching his own flesh, to convince himself of the waking reality. An upward glance at the frowning walls of the citadel, whence Emin Bey took his headlong leap on horseback, on the night of the slaughter of his Mamelook brethren by Mehemet Ali, reassured him; and he turned his head toward home with that rejoicing feeling of renewed liberty, only felt by a newly-freed prisoner, or one who has just risen from a bed of long illness.

He was more mystified than ever, for it was now evident that they were not the emissaries of the princess who had ensnared him; nor could he comprehend why, when once safely under the tiger-claws of Abbas in the citadel, he should have been so mysteriously set free. He knew too well the country and its ways to believe for an instant the truth of the governor's statement: but was all in the dark as to the real solution of the puzzle.

As he was revolving these things in his mind, allowing the horse's rein to drop loosely on his neck, as he walked along slowly, picking his way through the crowded street of the Mooskie, he felt some one pluck at his sleeve, and looking down, saw a vailed woman, enveloped in a silk cloak, who motioned him, with an imperious gesture, to pass under a porch, where the street was less crowded, she turning to that spot and awaiting his coming.

Instinctively he obeyed the summons, and soon his horse stood by the side of the shrouded figure, and lifting the vail, she disclosed the familiar face of the old Frenchwoman, dropping it immediately again after revealing herself.

18

She clutched his arm so hard again that he writhed with pain — for it was his wounded arm she grasped — and hissed out in low but distinct accents:

"I know all that has happened to you — more than you know yourself — and so does the Khanum.

"You have provoked the wrath of the tiger and the tigress, and have just escaped the jaws of one to fall under the claws of the other.

"Return not to your home, for her emissaries will soon be on your track, and dog your steps, until in some moment of imprudence you will be seized or assassinated. Neither will the tiger fail to spring again, though now he is compelled to crouch by a hand stronger than his own.

"Be warned in time, and fly — now, on the moment — for every hour's delay brings you nearer your doom."

"But," said the young man, bewildered by this warning, and the knowledge she seemed to have of his affairs, "how have I been freed? and where can I fly? Why should I skulk away like a felon, when I have committed no crime?"

"You ask as many questions as a woman," she replied, impatiently, "and you will talk while you should be acting. Your liberation is due to the consul-general, who was notified of your seizure and place of confinement by your faithful Nubian Ferraj. His arm is strong, but it is not so long as that of Abbas, nor can reach so far. You should fly, because danger and death dog your steps from one against whom you have committed a crime she never pardons.

"Where should you fly? Over the desert to Syria, where the arm of Abbas, long as it is, cannot reach you, nor even that of the great lady. From thence the whole world is open to you, and you may make terms soon to return. For I know one of your enemies is falling into disgrace, and will soon be banished from this country."

"You are sure you do not deceive me?" asked the young man.

"Why should I?" responded she, laughing scornfully. "Ask, rather, why I trouble myself, and take the risk of provoking the wrath of the great, for the safety of thy baby face, and I will tell thee. It is not so much through love for you — although I owe a debt of gratitude to all your house — as for the sake of my lamb, El Warda, whom I love as a daughter, having none left of my own, whose foolish heart would break if aught of evil befell you. Stay to ask no further questions, but hurry on to the gate of Bab-el-Nazr, which leads to the desert. There secrete thyself until Ferraj comes with thine own Arab horse, Selim, and provisions for the journey. If thou wilt do so, give me a word for El Warda, that she may be sure of thy safety, and send Ferraj to thee."

Askaros felt there was too much force in what the woman said, to neglect the warning.

He was satisfied by her look and manner that she was sincere, and felt the weight of her advice. He therefore took off one of his rings, and gave it to the Frenchwoman, in lieu of a letter, which he had no materials to write, which would serve as a sign to his father and sister that the woman came from him.

She seized upon it, made him a hurried gesture of farewell, and disappeared in the crowd.

Half doubting the wisdom of having so implicitly relied upon a woman whose character he knew to be worse than equivocal, Askaros, however, deemed it best to proceed on the path he had agreed to take.

He turned his horse's head toward Bab-el-Nazr, which
he reached in safety; and looking out, saw the low,
black tents of the Bedouins, with many camels and
horses grouped around them, still dotting the edge of
the desert.   The thought flashed upon him that there
might be his refuge until Ferraj came; so he rode up,
passing, not without a shudder, the spot now marked by
the bleaching bones of several of his assailants, where
the wild dogs had well-nigh made him their prey.

Dismounting, he was hospitably received by the Sheik
at the door of his tent, who gave him welcome, and after
partaking of his hospitality, asked shelter and counsel.
The Sheik listened in silence to the young man's explanation of his peril and meditated flight, and then replied:

" Thou hast shared the bread and the salt of the sons
of Beni-Hassan, and thou art as safe beneath their tents,
even from the search of the Grand Padishah, (Sultan,)
himself, as though thou wert, even now, sitting under
the tents of Abou-Gosh, King of Syria, the Great Sheik
of all the children of Beni-Hassan, who own no other
lord.

" Rest there, and I will send one of my people to
watch at the Bab-el-Nazr for the Nubian on the white
horse, and to bring him hither. *Mashallah !* I have
said it ! "

The Sheik then informed Askaros that he and his tribe
proposed striking their tents the ensuing day; but as
their caravan, with its laden camels, would travel but
slowly, and as he was in haste to escape over the border
into Syria, out of the jurisdiction of Abbas Pasha, he
advised him to start without delay, and await the arrival
of the caravan on the other side.   He offered to send a

Bedouin guide with him, who knew the whole route, and where to rejoin them.

These arrangements having been understood, Askaros awaited anxiously the arrival of Ferraj, entertained in the interval by his host with strange experiences of the desert, on which his life had been chiefly spent, and which he seemed to love, as the sailor loves the sea.

The Nubian at length arrived, and testified his joy in a lively manner at once again beholding his master — kissing the hem of his garments and his hand, and showing the same devoted affection a spaniel might have done. To his surprise, his master saw he had not only brought the white horse, Selim, but another, also, and that each had a bag strapped upon his back.

"How is this, Ferraj?" he asked; "do you suppose I will take a baggage-horse with me on such a journey, like a woman on her wedding procession?"

"*Moosh wahed, etnain,*" (not one, but two,) answered Ferraj, pointing first to his master and then to himself. "*Ana ra!*" (I go, too!)

"Impossible!" said Askaros; but relenting, as he saw the big tears start into the eyes of the faithful slave, he added!

"Well, as you will! But this horse of the Governor's must be returned to him. I will ask the Sheik to send him back for me."

What was the surprise of Askaros at finding the Sheik unwilling to do so.

"The horse is a good horse!" he said, sententiously, scanning his points with the eye of a connoisseur, "and my brother has got him now where his former owner can never reclaim him. Why should he not keep him?"

The young man was surprised at this strange notion of

18 *   O

honesty, among a people so punctilious in other things, not knowing at the time, that the theft of an Arab horse is considered as great a feat among the children of the desert as any warlike exploit, and fully as much courage and cunning displayed in the one case as in the other, the renown of success being commensurate.

He evidently lowered himself in the Sheik's good opinion by insisting on the restoration of the Governor's property, which was finally led away for the purpose, after an animated discussion.

But at a later period, in Syria, Askaros saw the Sheik riding an animal very like him, only with closely cropped mane and tail, and did not venture to ask any impertinent questions of the Sheik as to its identity. Neither did he ever see Elfy Bey again, to learn of him whether his steed had been returned, and afterward stolen by those adroit robbers, as was more than probable, in consonance with Bedouin etiquette in such cases.

That night Askaros and his two attendants rode away from the hospitable tents of the Beni-Hassan, and plunged into the trackless waste of the desert, to seek the safer refuge of the Holy Land.

CHAPTER XVIII.

THE OLD COPT'S SIESTA.

WHEN the old Frenchwoman performed her mission, and announced to El Warda the peril of him who was at once her brother, and more than brother, the conflict in the girl's soul was very great. Rejected affection, wounded pride, keen jealousy, strong passion, and a sense of having been made a dupe by the artful princess — all struggled for mastery in her young soul, and converted her at once from a child into a woman.

She immediately sought the old man, and explained to him, in general terms, the peril of his son, without entering into all the particulars revealed to her by the Frenchwoman, suppressing also the real cause of the wrath of Nezlé Khanum, as to which she had been bound to secrecy.

The old Askaros, who looked worn and haggard, and on whom his late apprehensions and troubles had wrought strongly, making him appear far more aged and feeble than before, listened in silence to her story, and signified his assent to his son's flight, a gleam of pleasure lighting up his face, when Ferraj declared his intention of accompanying his master.

He took the young girl's head between his withered
hands, and stroked down the rich curls of her raven hair,
gazing fondly and wistfully into her face.

"Thou wast my comfort and consolation," he said,
"when my son left me once before, and I know thou wilt
be so again. I feel very sad this evening, and a presentiment of evil weighs heavily on my spirit. Thou
knowest I received another and more pressing summons
from the Grand Meglis to-day, and have had besides a
secret message from Zoulfikar Pasha, that they rely on the
testimony of my former *Wakeel*, Daoud-ben-Youssouf, to
prove me a large defaulter to the Government. If that
young man prove false, then am I lost indeed. And my
son is not here to protect me!" cried the old man, with
a sudden burst of anguish. "O *Sitta Mariam* (Virgin
Mary,) have mercy upon me, a sinner! and make me
not desolate in mine old age, like Job!"

Touched and afflicted by this burst of passion from one
habitually so calm and self-composed, the young girl
knelt at his feet, and by a thousand little endearments
sought to console him. She partially succeeded, for he
grew more calm, and an air of resignation settled down
over his features, as he looked tenderly down upon her.

"Oh, my dove! my sweet child! aptly named 'the
rose,' how does thy love bring balm to this sore-stricken
heart? Yet another terror assails me! Moussa-ben-
Israel is wise beyond most of the children of men, and
seldom have I known his judgment prove false. He mis-
doubts Daoud, and suspects a plot between him and
Abbas, in which you are to be the prize of that boy's
selling me to the Viceroy. If this be so, there is thy
danger, the same as mine; but what are the few sands of
my worn-out life to the fresh spring of thine? Hearken

unto me, therefore, and heed me well. I have made a pact with the Israelite, whom many Christians might well imitate in truth and honor, that if aught happens to me, he will protect and conceal thee from the spoilers, and send thee abroad to his kindred. With him have I placed the bulk of my fortune, and full provision hath been made for thee. Therefore, should Abbas, as is possible, come like a thief in the night, and take me away, repair thou forthwith to the house of the Hebrew, and be guided by his counsel. His daughter Zillah loveth thee well, though, unhappily, she shares her father's delusion, and rejects the true faith ; yet otherwise is she fit friend and companion for thee. Once I had hoped these aged eyes might have seen the fulfilment of the secret wish of my heart, that he whom thou hast known only as thy brother might be the protector and sharer of thy life. But now, the blackness of a great darkness hangs over this fated house. My son is a fugitive, my own life is in peril, and more than thine, trembling in the balance also. But God is just, and we must put our trust in Him. Now go, my child, for body and mind are both very weary, and I would repose ; but let me give thee my blessing first, thou angel of my house ! "

Dismissing the tearful girl with a solemn benediction, the old man, whose venerable aspect and snowy beard gave a patriarchal dignity to his face and mien, reclined on his divan, and sought solace in his nargileh from his sad forebodings.

It was early spring, but the heat was equal to that of summer in more temperate climes. The great fountain in the centre of the apartment was in full play, and threw up its jets of silvery spray high into the air, bubbling and murmuring with a soothing sound, as the water fell back

with a splash into the marble basin below. The high
latticed windows were open, and through them came
whispering, laden with the sweet scents of the garden, the
perfumed breath of spring. The sunbeams stole slant-
ingly into the apartment, some of the rays resting above
the head of the old patriarch like the halo above a saint.
Blended with the soothing sounds of the whispering
breeze and plashing water came the regular measured
murmurs of the nargileh, as the pale-blue smoke floated
upward like incense from its silvery bowl.

The influence of the place, the time, the season, seemed to subdue the feverish excitement of the old man.
Gradually his face grew more composed, the deep lines
softened down, the knitted brow grew smoother, and the
compressed lips unclosed, until a faint smile relaxed their
rigid outline. Pleasant thoughts or memories appeared
to have succeeded the painful ones which had so recently
been tormenting him.

The smoke, at first rising in quick, dense clouds from
his nargileh, came more regularly and slowly, until at
length it ceased to rise, and the bubbling sound succeeding each long-drawn breath ceased also. The long
coil of the flexible tube glided serpent-like on the tassel-
lated floor, as the amber mouthpiece dropped from the
relaxing hand; his head fell forward on his breast, as he
seemed to sink into a peaceful slumber.

The fountain still kept on its ceaseless play; the
buzzing bees flew in and out of the latticed windows
from the gardens, whence still stole in at intervals the
whispering breeze with its rifled sweets, but no other
sounds disturbed the stillness of the vaulted chamber.
The shadows lengthened as afternoon passed into evening, and the sunbeams withdrew from the chamber as

dusk came down, heralding the approach of night. But still the old man stirred not, and seemed placidly to slumber, his face as calm as that of a sleeping infant, with an expression as though of renewed youth, strangely out of keeping with his snowy beard, stamped upon it.

Thrice did El Warda steal on tiptoe into the chamber, and twice retire, from reluctance to awaken the sleeper from what seemed so pleasant a repose. The third time she called softly to rouse him for the evening meal. Receiving no answer, she made a louder call. This, too, being unheeded, she stole nearer to him, and touched his hand, which was hanging down from the divan, but started back with a strange flutter at her heart — it was icy cold.

Closer she crept, and peered anxiously in his face, the features of which were locked in a repose stiller and deeper than that of sleep.

Terrified, she scarce knew why, with gasping breath she ventured to place her hand on the forehead — and then the dreadful truth flashed upon her, and her wild shriek rang through the building, summoning the domestics, who rushed in haste toward the sound, to find her fainting on the floor, with the face of the dead man bent down over her, wearing the same look of love for her it had ever done in life.

A greater King than he of Egypt had summoned the old patriarch into his presence; and the craft and cruelty of the living despot stood baffled in the presence, and through the power of a monarch, before whom all mortals must bow down.

Death had entered the house of Askaros, and silently stolen him away from the hate and the avarice of Abbas.

CHAPTER XIX.

A RACE WITH THE KHAMSEEN WIND.

DAWN on the desert! A gray glimmer first breaking out in streaks on the eastern sky, followed by a rosy flush, as spears of light seem to shoot athwart the veil of darkness; for the night had been black and starless, and the gloom more impenetrable than ever, just preceding the daylight. All was still and silent as the grave, save the sighing of the wind, which swept with a sobbing sound over the wide wastes of sand, which the growing light disclosed. For ever, over the desert, night and day, blows a strong wind; never ceasing, except as the prelude to a storm, or the terrible hot blast the Arabs call *Khamseen;* Europeans the Sirocco, whose burning breath often brings death, or whelms whole caravans beneath the billows of fiery sand it sweeps over them, and which thus become their graves.

Suddenly the shrill neigh of a horse broke the sepulchral stillness, followed by a grunt of disapproval in Arabic, as the Bedouin guide accosted Ferraj, reproaching him for not having brought a mare, which never neighs or gives warning of its approach; since, on the desert, each stranger is regarded as an enemy, and secrecy, silence, and swiftness, often the price of life.

216

Three horses were picketed, their feet hobbled with ropes, and munching at their provender, tied to the nose of each in a canvas bag.

Three forms of men, wrapped in blankets or woollen bournous, were also dimly discernible, stretched upon the hard, gritty ground, whom the horse's neigh had awakened. All three rose — two of them making their prostrations toward Mecca, and going through the Mussulman formula of prayer. The third stood erect, looking out with curious and inquiring gaze over the desert, as the growing light revealed its bare, bald surface, in a way which indicated it was a novel sight to him.

Even as he looked, the gazer could see the curtaincloud of darkness lifted, and, like the glittering shafts of Hyperion, shot down the arrows of sunlight from that great orb, which suddenly rose large, round, and fiery red in the eastern sky, with no lingering prelude of rosy flushings to announce his coming, flooding at once earth, air, and sky with his full effulgence. At a short distance from him the gazer saw the airy and graceful forms of a troop of gazelles, standing motionless, sharply defined against the background of sky and distant horizon, looming up gigantic in the haze; the next moment, with heads tossed erect, snuffing the morning air, tainted to their delicate nostrils by human presence, the herd was bounding away, with a fleetness which more resembled the flight of birds than the movement of wingless creatures, until, dipping behind a small sand-hillock, the graceful creatures were lost to view.

Askaros — for it was he — looked around, and could see neither on earth nor in the sky the presence of any other living thing; beast or bird there was none in view, and he felt that even the sight of the vulture, sailing in

19

mid-air, would be welcome to break this lonely and life-less prospect. Before, behind, all around stretched out the sandy wastes of the desert, bounded only by the dim and distant horizon; without a shrub or blade of grass for the aching eye to rest upon and refresh itself. But though the man seemed saddened by the view, the horses seemed to enjoy it, for they tossed their heads exultingly in air, and with expanded nostrils, seemed drinking in exhilaration with the breath of the desert, testifying their delight by a low whinnying, and pawing the earth as though anxious to break into a mad gallop, racing against the wind.

To break the silence which oppressed him, Askaros raised his voice to a shout, hoping possibly to scare up some living thing. But his cry fell flat and almost echo-less on the wild waste, sounding muffled and dull even in his own ears — like that of a man shouting in a vault — while the rarity of the desert-air shortened his breath and constricted his lungs, as on some lofty mountain-top.

The morning prayers of the Nubian and Bedouin hav-ing been concluded, each took from the breast of his shirt his pipe, and proceeded to smoke in satisfied silence; then, rising up, took a small bag containing dried camel's dung for fuel, with which they kindled a fire and pre-pared coffee. This, with brown bread and a handful of fresh dates, composed their morning meal.

Askaros partook also of this simple fare, smoking his pipe after, instead of before his meal, according to Euro-pean habit. This ceremony concluded, all three again remounted, and, led by the Bedouin, traversed the desert in a particular direction, there being no path or any other indication which would seem to show the road; the in-stinct of the Bedouin, and his familiarity with the level plain alone, serving to guide them. Rapidly rose the sun; soon fiercely asserting his sole supremacy over the desert, where his beams met no obstacle, and were relieved by no shade. By midday so fervid and overpowering was the heat, that Askaros, hardy as he was, felt almost fainting and dizzy with the glare, his eyes not being protected like those of the others by the projecting cowl of the bornous, which they drew over their heads in the fashion of a hood. Several times he stooped and dismounted, interposing the body of his horse between himself and the sun, as the only shade he could find, crouching down in the hot sand, which almost blistered his feet, and reflected a heat like an oven.

Welcome indeed was the sight of an oasis, which gladdened his eyes, apparently about a mile distant, the waving of whose palm-trees he certainly could distinguish, and even the sparkling waters of a pool he was almost sure he could see rippling to its bank.

With outstretched hand pointing eagerly in the direction of this welcome sight, he cried out eagerly to the Bedouin:

" How far is it to yonder water? We shall stop there."

The white teeth of the dusky Arab suddenly shone through his dark skin, as he answered with a grin the young man's anxious inquiry.

" *Moosh moia—saba* (not water—sand:) it is the Mirage."

As the young man, doubting still the delusion of his senses, strained his eyes upon the spot, he was still more convinced that he was right and the Bedouin wrong; for not only did he see the clear pool and the shady palm-trees now, but could even detect human forms and camels moving along the banks, as well as the huts of an Arab village, crowned by the dome of the usual mosque, with its minarets, in the midst.

As still gazing intently, he was about reproving the Bedouin for jesting with and deceiving him, another sudden change took place, which staggered and silenced him; for the pool seemed suddenly to enlarge into a wide lake — the trees rose to gigantic height — and the huts expanded into stately buildings of Moorish architecture — while the mosque became the counterfeit presentment of one of the palaces of the Memlook Sultans, its turrets and pinnacles glittering and gleaming, like those of a fairy palace, under the rays of the sun.

"Sitta Mariam protect us! it is enchantment!" muttered the Copt, in whom education had not entirely eradicated native superstition.

"Allah preserve us! it is the work of *Jinns!*" (evil Genii) exclaimed the Bedouin, prostrating himself, and striking the sand with his head, as he went through his *namaz*, or prayers.

The Nubian, the whites of his eyes rolling wildly in his black face, was too startled or amazed to say or do anything — but stared, like his master, at the strange sight, equally new to him.

Even as they gazed, however, palaces, lake, temple, palm-trees, men, and camels, all became more and more indistinct, like a dissolving view in a magic mirror, then faded utterly away, leaving again nothing visible to the aching eyes that strained after it, but the bare desert and distant horizon.

Askaros breathed a deep sigh when the pageant passed away, and turning to the Bedouin said:

"It is natural that we who have never seen this strange sight before, should be astonished at it; but how does it happen that you — to whom it must be so familiar — should show such terror? For it is a harmless vision — though it juggles with the eyesight, and mocks the hopes of men.''

"Effendi!" answered the Bedouin, gravely, "we who live on the desert, in the full sight of Allah — not hidden in towns — learn many things unknown to you men of the cities! Many times, indeed, as many almost as the years of my life, have I seen the mirage, and cared not for it; but only twice before have I seen the palaces of the great King Solomon, built by the Genii, whom he controlled, and with the sight of which those evil spirits sometimes mock the eyes of men — as they did but now. Each time was the sight followed by the wrath of those evil Genii — which is a consuming fire — when Sheitan sends them from the pit of Eblis to roam this desert — once the site of their great and glorious cities, before the anger of Allah visited it and them. Each time before, after mocking us thus with the sight of shade, and water, and great cities, have those Genii ridden down upon us, with the fiery wind of the desert, and destroyed almost the whole of our caravan, with many of my kindred. Therefore it was, I prayed to Allah to crush the power, and restrain the vengeance of those wicked spirits — for in His hand alone is the power, on the earth, as in the air, over Sheitan and his host.''

There was something in the tone and look, as well as in the speech of this unlettered child of the desert, with his simple but sublime trust in God, which thrilled to the heart of the young Copt, and made him feel how inferior he was in faith to this rude Bedouin. Yet he smiled to himself at these superstitious fears, which reflected no corresponding dread in his own breast — trained as he

19 *

had been in the polite skepticism of an English university.

So he permitted the subject to drop, without discussion, and they plodded wearily on for an hour more, until they reached a small clump of trees, where they made their mid-day halt, and rested until the noonday heats were over, resuming their journey with the setting of the sun, and only resting from midnight to sunrise again.

About noon the next day, while they were experiencing a repetition of their sufferings of the previous one, Askaros impatiently called out to the Bedouin to know when they would reach the next oasis, and what it was called.

"It is called The Diamond of the Desert," replied the Bedouin, "and we may reach it in three hours' time. We are not travelling fast to-day, for the horses all seem languid and unwilling to go on — mine as well as yours — and anxious to go back rather than forward. I scarcely can keep my mare straight! Yet Desert Star knows the road as well as her master!" he added, patting the neck of his horse, which turned its head, and gazed with almost human appeal upon its rider.

"Perhaps," said Askaros, scoffingly, "the horses covet the hospitalities of the Genii, proffered us yesterday, and wish to turn back to enjoy them. For my own part, I confess, I should feel inclined to accept them, if they were tendered again!"

The Bedouin, with a terror-stricken face, raised his hand in deprecation, and was about to speak; but ere any words could issue from his lips, a moaning sound swept down to them on the wind, as though in answer to the rash speaker's challenge, and a column of fire seemed to tower up into the air, blood-red against the sky, in advance of them.

Rearing straight up, and plunging until she shook the powerful bit loose from her tongue, the Desert Star wheeled short round in her tracks, and bounded away with the fleetness of a gazelle over the ground they had just traversed.

As though in imitation of her example, Selim and the steed of the Nubian followed her lead, and pressed in a mad race on the flying footsteps of the fleet mare. Wrenching himself round in his saddle, the Bedouin, instead of checking his mare, dug his sharp shovel stirrups into her flanks, to urge her onward, shouting back:

"Follow for your lives! It is the Khamseen wind. We may escape it by flight! to meet it is death!"

No other words were exchanged between them as they rushed along in their wild race for life, in the seemingly desperate hope of out-stripping the whirlwind, whose rising moan grew louder; and as Askaros turned his head and looked back, he saw the fiery pillar whirling on faster and nearer to them. Stronger and more fleet than the mare — though she was of the purest Aneyzeh blood — the white Selim soon bore his master to the Bedouin's side, and the two swept on like the wind together — the Nubian dropping behind in the race.

Then, with laboring breath Askaros addressed his companion:

"What is our hope of escape? Can we hope to outstrip the wind? and if not, why defer our doom, if it be inevitable? Tell me, O son of the desert — for I would know the truth, and front my fate like a man!"

"*Allah Kerim!*" (God is great) responded the Bedouin; "in His hands are life and death. When his

Kismet comes, man must submit.   But there is a chance of escape left us yet.   See yonder palm-trees!'' and he pointed to what looked like a hillock in the distance. ''If we can only reach that shelter, we can avoid being buried under the column of fiery sand you see sweeping down upon us, and which else will scorch and consume us, and under which we shall else soon be buried from sight of man or vulture, until the next Khamseen shall disinter our bones!''

No other words were spoken, but they swept on, Ferraj toiling in the rear, the red pillar looming up nearer and broader, and more fiery, as it pursued them.

A cry, as of human agony, smote sharply on the ear of Askaros.   He turned his head, and, to the surprise of his companion, checked his fleet steed and wheeled him round, against his will, after a short, sharp struggle, and galloped back — toward death!

The Bedouin glanced back over his shoulder, sharply checked his mare an instant — shook his head as though in doubt — then goring her bleeding sides with the cruel stirrups, and shaking free her rein with a cry of encouragement, darted again like a bird on his forward course.

''*Magnoon!*'' (mad), he muttered; ''better one die than all three !''

The abrupt movement of Askaros had been occasioned (as the Bedouin saw) by the sight of Ferraj, standing over his fallen horse, which he strove in vain to drag up to its feet; and the cry had been the last farewell of the faithful soul to his master, so well beloved.

But a sharp pang seemed to rend him, when he saw that master rushing back to succor him, at the peril of his own life; and as Askaros approached him, with a piteous cry he shouted:

"Save yourself! my Kismet is accomplished! This horse can go no further! Fly yourself while it is yet time!" for even as he spoke the first faint puffs of hot wind, like a furnace-blast, mingled with heated sand, struck upon the faces of both — the *avant-couriers* of the advancing Khamseen, whose mighty pillar of flame was marching down swiftly upon them.

"Mount behind me quickly!" said Askaros, "Selim will carry both."

"No! no!" said the Nubian. "I will not peril your life. If it is the will of Allah, I shall live, or I shall die. Leave me and save yourself. Selim cannot carry both."

"You are risking two lives by your obstinacy," cried Askaros, impatiently, "for I swear I will not leave you! So jump up behind me without more words!"

The Nubian's habit of blind obedience to his master's orders conquered his reluctance; he leaped up behind, and the gallant horse, with his double burden, again strained every sinew in renewed flight—following the track of the Bedouin, whose white bornous was still visible in the distance.

But the pace of Selim was sensibly slackened by the weight of his double burden; though the Nubian's spare figure did not greatly increase the weight, yet it was enough to tell heavily in addition.

The foam upon the bit of the straining steed began to be streaked with blood: and the laboring chest and heaving flanks to indicate coming exhaustion.

Still he bore on gallantly, without touch of scourge or spur, until, at last, they were on the very verge of the clump of palms—their ark of safety—where they could see the Bedouin as he sat on his mare on the outskirts, his

P

hand over his eyes, peering into the desert, while louder yet, like the shrieks of the angry Genii, came the rushing sound of the fatal wind, and fiercer and more frequent the fiery breath of the giant-shape now sweeping down upon them.

Just then, the noble horse, that bore them so gallantly, tripped, stumbled and fell heavily forward. He staggered to his feet as both his riders sprung off, looked with glazing eyes upon his master, into whose hand he thrust his nozzle, licking his hand as a favorite dog might have done, and then reeled and fell a second time, a slight shudder convulsing his whole frame—stretched out his graceful limbs with a low moan—and died.

As Askaros, overpowered with grief at the death of the friend to whom he owed his life, stood over him in stupefied sorrow, the Nubian seized him in his strong arms, as though he were a child, with the strength of desperation, and rushed to the copse, into which he stumbled and fell—just in time.

For when they rose to their feet, and looked out into the place they had just left, the fiery cloud had passed over it, and they saw it rushing on beyond: the spot where the noble steed had fallen being marked by a mound of heated sand, which rose in billowy undulations over the whole surface of the plain, smoking like a lime-kiln, and exhaling a stifling odor, even in the sheltered spot where they stood in safety.

"Sitta Mariam!" ejaculated the Copt, fervently; "I vow an offering to thee for this miraculous preservation!"

"Allah Kerim!" (God is great), echoed the Nubian.

"The Genii have been propitiated by the sacrifice of the steeds which belonged not to the desert," said the

Bedouin, stroking fondly the neck of his mare, which laid its graceful deer-like head against his breast, as though understanding him; "but to Allah be the praise and glory nevertheless! Thy Kismet, O youth!" he said, turning to Askaros, "will be a fortunate one! Here let us await in peace and safety the coming of the caravan, which passes this way. Within three days we shall rest under the tents of our great Sheik, Abou-Gosh, for we are already in Syria, and no hawk, Turkish, Egyptian or Frank, can hunt its game here, without permission from the Sheik, our master."

CHAPTER XX.

A MODERN FAUST.

WHEN the tidings of the young man's flight and the old man's death were brought to Abbas Pasha, he at first disbelieved the intelligence, suspecting some trick. But when the news was fully confirmed, he sent for Daoud-ben-Youssouf, who promptly obeyed the summons, and stood for a second time in the Viceroy's presence.

"What means all this?" growled Abbas. "Canst thou give any clue to the place where the younger of these dogs is hidden? For they tell me the old one is dead, and steps must now be taken for regulating his succession. Knowest thou, as thou hast boasted, where his great wealth is placed, and how invested?"

"Effendina! the affairs of the Khasnadar are better known to me than to any other man — both his public and his private — and I am prepared to prove my assertion. Of the hiding-place of the young man I know nothing, for I have not seen him for a long time, and the people of his household only know that two days since, his Nubian slave, Ferraj, disappeared, taking with him the favorite horse of Askaros and another, and had not returned. Hence, they suppose both have fled away together."

"Why should he fly?" asked Abbas; "he had just been set free, and had no cause for fear."

"Effendina! that is a mystery which, as yet, I cannot solve. But give me a little time, and I hope to do so."

Abbas Pasha mused a few moments; then, fixing his dull but penetrating eye on the young Syrian, said:

"Thou hast the wisdom of the serpent: what now dost thou propose to do, to earn the reward I promised thee, for thy first plan hath failed, and thy testimony is useless against a dead man — so also thy treachery?"

"Effendina! if the humblest of thy servants might be allowed to speak, he would say that, though the man is dead, yet the succession lives still, and that is of more importance than the man. The natural heir dead, or fled away, no one knows where, and no near blood-relations left, it is the duty of the government to take charge of the estate for the benefit of the heirs, as well as to regulate its accounts with the treasury. Hence the road is easier now to travel than heretofore."

"Verily thou art a young Sheitan," said Abbas, admiringly; "though thou speakest truly in this matter, which Sheitan, thy father, generally doth not. But I see thou hast something further to say; so be not over-modest, but speak out. What is it?"

"Effendina! the mind of thy servant, reflected in his face to an eye which sees everything, was troubled on this point. To secure the management of that estate which will meet the views of your Highness, it is necessary it should be committed to the hands of some one who could be trusted, and with sufficient capacity to settle it satisfactorily."

Abbas threw himself back on his divan with a roar of laughter.

20

"Ho! ho!" he cried; "this is too good. So our modest young scribe thinks the proper person to administer that estate is the late Wakeel of the late Khasnadar, now gone to his rest in the bosom of his Father Abraham; or, what is more likely, roasting now in Gehenna. Is it not so, O youth! whose bashfulness equals thy discretion? Thou crowest loudly, indeed, for a cock whose spurs are yet ungrown, and whose beard would never betray thee under a woman's veil." Then, relapsing into seriousness, he added. "What thou dreamest of is impossible. Great indeed would be the scandal, were so important a trust placed in hands like thine; and plain to the eyes of all men would be the price of thy treachery to thy patron. No, no! Go home, and dash water on thy head to cool thy fevered brain, which makes thee fancy thou art more than a tool in the hands of thy superiors, and canst claim thy reward before thou hast earned it. No! I shall name a well-known friend of the late Khasnadar — Zoulfikar Pasha — to take charge of the estate for the benefit of the family and kindred of the dead man, and to regulate his accounts with my government, that all men may see and admire the justice of the Viceroy, even toward those whom it is known he loves not. Then, through the agency of the Grand Meglis, with the aid of thy testimony, and the proofs thou hast promised, we can confiscate that property, and take it into our possession, for the ends of public justice. Thy vanity and grasping avarice must have clouded the usual clearness of thy vision, if thou canst not see how incongruous would be thy double duty, or should dream of mounting the top round of the ladder before planting foot on the lowest."

Despite his habitual dissimulation, the face of the

Syrian, while the Viceroy sneeringly spoke, eying him over the while, like some small reptile striving to climb — underwent many changes ; and though he bent his angry eyes, full of evil fire, toward the ground, as if too abashed to raise them, the flush on his pale cheek betrayed the emotion in his soul.

Abbas marked it with his cold, cruel eye, but made no comment, for he regarded Daoud merely as an instrument he could use and cast aside as it pleased him, and his malign spirit enjoyed the infliction of torture on one so callous, and so little troubled with scruples of conscience. So, with the tiger instinct natural to him, he prolonged the cruel sport, and played with the writhing victim anxious to escape.

"Thou hast forgotten one thing," said the Viceroy. " If the old man be dead, and the young one an outlaw by his own act, the girl of whom thou hast spoken to me becomes the heiress to these great possessions, and will not lack for suitors. It may be that Zoulfikar Pasha himself, who is the handsomest man in my domains, might like to take charge of her, as well as of the estate.   With all the best intentions toward thee, how can I decently restrain her choice, should she choose to marry before our plans are completed, and she is known to be a pauper, and fit bride only for a lover so disinterested as thyself."

Through the base, yet not utterly degraded spirit of the Syrian there shot a pang, keen almost as the death-agony — a fierce thirst for the blood of the man who thus taunted him, coupled with a sickening sense of his own ineffable baseness, in being a thing which merited such scorn even from the evil creature who entertained it. He dared not trust himself to reply, lest he should betray himself. He only bowed his head yet lower, as though in self-abasement, that he might hide the glare of his eyes, which might excite the distrust of the tyrant: for he felt that the hell in his heart was blazing out through those windows of the soul, and could not be hidden were he to raise them.

Abbas gloated over his confusion and shame, and sought to increase them.

"Thou art silent," he said. "Art thou convinced, and wilt thou then be content with the two hundred purses of gold as thy reward, relinquishing all thought of the maiden, as a prize now far too great for one in thy low station to aspire to? Answer."

Mastering himself by a mighty effort, while he registered in his soul a secret vow of vengeance against the smiling despot, the Syrian raised his head, wrath no longer burning in the eyes, now encircled with two livid rings, and sunken deep in their orbits, like those of one just recovering from almost mortal illness. In truth, the whole face seemed to have aged suddenly, and his voice sounded harsh and hollow when he spoke.

"Effendina!" he said, "I am not so blind or so silly as you deem; neither am I aspiring higher than I ought. I freely admit the force of what your Highness says as to the succession, and the choice made proves the wisdom of my lord's far-seeing mind. But as regards the girl, Effendina, she cannot inherit these estates, for she bears not the name, and is not of the blood of Askaros, but only, like myself, one of the children of his bounty. This thing will explain to my high lord, and justify what he deemed the presumption of his servant, who knows his own place too well to aspire above it!"

Surprise succeeded scorn upon the face of Abbas.

"Explain this riddle to me," he said, sharply. "Canst thou prove this statement?"

"Effendina, the fact is well known to all the friends of Askaros, for of near kindred he has none, and probably the girl herself, of all the household, is the only person ignorant of it."

"*Peki!*" said Abbas; "so much the better, then. In that case thou mayest fear no rivalry, and doubtless the girl will gladly seek the shelter of thy hareem when she finds herself friendless and poor. Unless," he added, with a sinister glance, "some one tells her of thy faithful services to me, which she might not appreciate. Women are so wrong-headed! But fear nothing. If thou dealest faithfully with me, thou shalt have both girl and gold. Now go, and prepare carefully thy papers for the Grand Meglis, for that intermeddling *homar* (ass) of a consul-general cannot now annoy me further."

With hate in his heart, but with respectful deference in his manner, Daoud knelt down and prostrated himself with lowly reverence before the Viceroy, who seemed to have utterly forgotten his presence, and retired backward from the room; but no sooner had the curtain dropped behind him, than the mask he had worn fell from his face, which grew fiendish and fell in its fixed resolve.

"Ay," he muttered, grinding his teeth, "truly shalt thou pay my price, and with usury too! And then — and then? — another perhaps thou wottest not of!"

He was startled from his reverie by a shrill cry seeming to come from high in air, and glancing through a window by which he was passing, saw one of the desert hawks — a small, fierce bird — pounce down upon and strike a vulture twice its size, whose torn plumes and blood-bedabbled crest attested the severity of the stroke,

20*

as it flew fast away, dropping its prey as it fled, on which the hawk settled down.

"An omen! an omen!" gasped the Syrian, "sent by the master whose servants we both are. I accept it, and woe to thee, foul vulture!" he hissed, shaking his clenched hand in the direction of the chamber wherein Abbas sat, "when the appointed hour shall come for the hawk to strike!"

With head once more proudly erect, and with the step of a conqueror, the Syrian, pausing a moment on the threshold to shake the dust from his feet as he passed over it, muttering to himself, strode rapidly away, like one possessed of an evil demon.

Two hours later, as Daoud-ben-Youssouf sat in his upper room, looking out over the Ezbekieh in the dim twilight, his lamp not yet lighted, his old Arab servant, a withered crone — cook, housekeeper and drudge — shuffled into the room, and announced, with a mysterious air, that two veiled women — an old and a young one — demanded to see the master of the house. The leer in the old woman's eye indicated her belief in the purport of the visit, and the Syrian, indignantly hurling an Arab malediction at her, sternly commanded her to bring no such messages to him, on pain of instant dismissal from his service, and to send the women away. For, in the thorough absorption of his soul, he had no time or taste for the usual frivolities or vices of youth, and lived the life of an anchorite, so far as mortification of the flesh in every way was concerned.

As the old woman, grumbling, was withdrawing to fulfil his orders, she was pushed aside by the unwelcome visitors, who walked into the room unannounced, the elder woman standing in the doorway, which she entirely filled up with her bulky person and spreading dress, dropped the curtain down so as to leave only Daoud and the younger woman in the room alone.

As the angry Syrian was about to repeat the uncomplimentary remarks he had just made his servant, the woman advanced and threw back her veil. As she did so, amazement succeeded anger on the young man's face, and so great was his agitation that he supported himself by clutching at the window-sill.

The woman spoke first.

"Daoud-ben-Youssouf," she said, "you know me too well to doubt for an instant the purpose of my visit, unmaidenly and immodest as my presence here may seem, alone in the night-time, with unveiled face, in your house. But I come on matters of life and death — from the feet of a dead father to search for a lost brother! from a house of mourning to see whether El Warda has yet one friend left? Where is my brother? If living man in this city know, thou art the man!"

"Sit down," gasped the Syrian, whose face had grown ashy pale, and whose lips quivered. "Call in your companion, and we can talk in French, for it is not meet for your maiden reputation to be left alone in a room with a man. That reputation is dearer to me than my life."

The girl did not take the offered seat, nor summon her companion. She smiled a sad, wan smile, and shook her head.

"Daoud," she said, "trouble not yourself with such trifles. I was a girl this morning — I am a woman now — and, like yourself, have had enough of Frank training, to care little for foolish forms. What I have to say to you, and hear from you, must be said and heard alone. Listen to me! The day before he died, my father was

warned by one in whom he trusted, to beware of you —
for you meditated treachery — and I believe the shock
of that revelation, joined to other griefs, caused his death.
I come now to prove whether you are false or true this
night; for, in your hands now, I know, will rest the
fortunes and the fate of my brother and myself. Thus
much I know. Now, tell me first, where has my brother
gone?"

Over the face of the Syrian, as she spoke, there swept
many changing emotions; but the predominating expression was one of hungry, craving admiration — his eyes
strained upon her countenance, and his ear eagerly drinking in the sound of her voice. When she ceased, repeating again her closing question, which he seemed not
to have heard — he answered vaguely, like a man talking
in his sleep:

"Where has he gone? I do not know!"

"You know, and will not tell, Daoud! Why will you
not tell me — his sister? Are you truly then our enemy?"

"Your enemy?" gasped the Syrian, recovering at
once all his faculties, and speaking almost with indignation. "O El Warda! star of my boyhood! sunlight of
my manhood! sole hope of my heart! there runs not a
drop of blood in these veins that I would not pour out
in your service. You have no slave you can command
more absolutely than Daoud-ben-Youssouf, whose greatest
sin has been only loving you too well! It grieves me,
indeed, to hear that my old friend and benefactor should
have listened to the lying tongues that defamed me. For
how could I meditate treachery to him, and hope to fulfil the cherished wish of my heart? And you know well,
O El Warda!" he added, dropping his voice, "what
that wish ever has been."

The girl looked bewildered and perplexed — passed her hand over her brow, as though to clear away a mist gathering over her sight, and said softly :

"Indeed, Daoud, I did not doubt you, for I remembered the days when we were as brother and sister — eating of the same bread — drinking of the same cup — and studying out of the same book ; and that is not so very long ago, although years seem to me to have been crowded into the last few weeks. But my father is dead — my brother has gone I know not whither — or whether he will return — and the desperate hope came to me, that you might know and tell me, and give me counsel what to do, though my father warned me not to trust you, even with his almost dying breath. Surely, you could not be so base and cruel as to deceive me, or betray the friends of your childhood?"

"The suspicion itself is an insult," said Daoud, with an air of wounded pride. "That is a question I cannot discuss, even with you. If you still regard me as worthy of your confidence, tell me what I can do to serve you — and yours," he added, with hesitation.

"Find where my brother is, and let him know all that has happened and is happening here. Give him advice what is the safest and best for him to do ; for you have a ready wit, and can find out better than most men. Do this, and I will pray for you to Sitta Mariam, and be for ever grateful ! "

"Gratitude is but a chilly recompense," said the young man, gloomily. "I need more."

"Well, then, I will regard you as my second brother!" said the girl, pleadingly.

"Mine is not a brother's love for you," responded Daoud, almost fiercely ; "it is a frantic, frenzied passion

—a certainty that you must be mine only—mine wholly, or I shall die—a dream that visits my nights and haunts my waking hours—that curses and blesses my existence equally—and that finally will drive me mad or desperate, if it meets no requital. O, El Warda! whose step is lighter than the gazelle's; whose voice is sweeter than music; whose face and form is more lovely than those of Houris—and whose presence alone in this chamber makes it a heaven to me—smile upon me! Make me the happiest of living men, by telling me that I may have hope—that you will not condemn me to sit for ever, like the lost Jinns, gnashing my teeth in darkness, with the glories of the opening heaven shining within my sight, though shut and barred out forever to me, as to them!''

As he closed this impassioned appeal, he sought to seize the girl's hand, and throw himself at her feet in an agony of impassioned supplication.

But El Warda gently, but firmly, repulsed him, re-proachfully saying:

''O Daoud! Is this a time or a place to speak thus to a poor, weak girl, who comes to throw herself on a brother's friendship? Can I think of love, with my dear old father lying dead on his divan, and but a few moments since having passed from the house of mourning? While my brother, Askaros, is now a fugitive—perhaps a corpse on the desert; for the horrible Khamseen has been blowing all day, and thither he fled but two days since. Or, if escaped that peril, dead perhaps for ever to me; since he never would have left his father and his home had it been safe for him to stay in Egypt. How can you expect me to trust, or even to respect you, if you are so selfish, and abuse my confidence in you thus?'' And the soft dark eyes were suffused with tears she could no longer suppress.

A wild joy flashed through the heart of the Syrian, not only at the hope conveyed by her words, but on learning the route which Askaros had taken, as well. In his vivid imaginings, he already saw the bones of the man he regarded as his only rival, bleaching on the sands of the desert. But he only bowed his head, as in contrition, and excused the ardor of his language by the warmth of his passion, pleading for forgiveness, and promising to sin thus no more ; and the girl, like most of her sex, was willing to pardon the fault, in view of its cause.

But, although her distrust was removed, she was mindful of that parting injunction of the elder Askaros, and did not inform the Syrian of her meditated removal, after the burial of her father, to the dwelling of Moussa-ben-Israel.

Therefore, after receiving many promises from Daoud as to the efforts he would make to discover and communicate with her brother, the young girl summoned her companion — her favorite servant and guardian from childhood — and retraced her steps to the home once so happy, but now only the tomb of her affections ; leaving the Syrian in a frame of mind he himself would have found it difficult to analyze — the wildest hope and joy conflicting with the blackest grief and despair.

All that night he rested not ; and the belated reveller or intriguer, skulking homeward through the Ezbekieh, late in the night or at early dawn, looking up at his window, where still shone the light of his lamp, and seeing his light figure rapidly moving to and fro, would smile and say to himself :

"What a student, truly, is Daoud-ben-Youssouf!"

And a student he was ! but, like Faust, of things unholy ; and his "familiar," Mephistopheles, who led him on blindfold over the path that leads to perdition, was not at his side, but seated within his own soul.

CHAPTER XXI.

UNDER THE TENTS OF THE BENI-HASSAN.

THE long, low, black tents of the Bedouins of the tribe of Beni-Hassan were pitched in the fertile valley near Jericho, of which once famous city the name now only remains — not a trace even of its walls, which fell before the blasts of Joshua's trumpets, being perceptible.

The ruins of the ancient aqueducts, which formerly conveyed water from Jericho to Jerusalem, alone attest the fact of the existence of a city on that site, now covered by the mud huts of a small Arab village. Squatting among the ruins of an old fort constructed during the Crusades, may be found the Sheik of this village, who appropriated it to his use, and made it his residence.

The valley is one of great fertility, and under careful cultivation; and the rich verdure which clothes it contrasts strongly with the iron mountains which shut it in on one side, and the sterile desert which leads to the Dead Sea and Jordan on the other.

In the very heart of this fertile valley the wandering tribe of the Beni-Hassan were encamped for a time — the tent of their great Sheik, Abou-Gosh, being only distinguishable from that of the others by its superior size,

and his long spear, with its pennon, sticking upright in
the ground in front of it, in token of his remaining some
time at that spot.

Flocks and herds of goats, sheep and cattle, browsed
around, tended by a few wild-looking Bedouins, easily
distinguishable from the common Fellah, or peasant, by
their dress, and wild untamed look.

At the door of his tent, smoking his nargileh, sat the
great chief himself, like another Abraham — to the pictures of whom, in the old editions of the Bible, he presented a striking likeness. So grave and patriarchal was
his aspect, with his long, white beard, stately figure, and
calm, composed countenance, that no one would have
dreamed him to be the great robber chief, at whose name
travellers grew pale, and who levied tribute on all passing from Joppa to Jerusalem, or from the Holy City to
Damascus. His face and mien, however, indicated the
habit of command — for his sway over his own people
was as absolute as that of the ancient patriarch to whom
he had been likened; and neither to the Sultan, nor to
the Turkish Governor of Syria, did he own any allegiance, or pay any tribute, except to the former, as chief
of "the Faith" and spiritual head of Islam.

As he looked over the green valley clad in the bright
livery of spring, and his eyes roved over the countless
flocks and herds, an expression of contentment was on his
face, and he seemed in good humor with himself, and
with the world. No care appeared to disturb his serenity,
as he slowly inhaled the perfumed smoke, which rose in
vapory clouds in the still air. A light step behind him,
as the curtain of the tent was pushed aside; and the
slight graceful form of a young Arab girl, whose unveiled
face was sweet in expression and regular in features.

though of a pale copper color, stood still in the opening, and with arms meekly crossed over her bosom, awaited his notice.

The grand old face of Abou-Gosh lit up with pleasure at the sight of the girl, to whom he spoke in tones as soft and gentle as those of a woman.

"How is our guest to-day, O my daughter? Has Azrael ceased to flap his black wings over his head? What saith thy mother, O Amina? for well skilled is she in the illness that kills, and the herb that heals."

"The stranger in our tents is greatly better, O my father!" replied the girl, in a voice melodious as her face was sweet; "and my mother says the danger is now past; the fever is gone, and the sick man may now rise from his bed and breathe the fresh air again. This came I to tell you."

"Thy voice is ever to me like that of one bringing glad tidings," responded the Sheik, "and it is doubly so to-day. For this youth is the son of one of my oldest friends, a good man, though a Nazarene, and the boy's own looks please me much. Do they please thee, my daughter?"

The girl blushed through her dusky skin at the question, and bent her head in maidenly modesty, but she answered with the frankness of her training:

"I have sat by the bedside of the young Frank, O my father, for many days past; and I cannot but feel an interest in the stranger, who is truly very handsome, and whose voice is like music—very unlike those of our own people!"

The old Sheik laughed gently under his beard, but only said:

"Now go my child, and tell thy mother, if she thinks

it will do him good, to bid him clothe himself and sit here by my side; for this fresh air will do him more good than all the drugs of the Hakeem! or even the herbs that she is so cunning to compound." And the girl disappeared again within the tent.

Shortly afterward, while the great Sheik still sat smoking, apparently meditating over some serious thought, the curtain of the tent was again pushed back, and Askaros appeared. The Sheik, rising from his cushions with grave dignity, welcomed him, and motioned for him to take a seat beside him, proffering the mouth-piece of the nargileh to him, from which, after having taken a few inhalations, the young man returned the tube to his host.

"I trust thou art again well," was the Sheik's salutation; "and that the breath of the evil Genii, who chased thee across the desert, now no longer poisons thy veins. My wife, who is well skilled in the lore of the Hakeems, tells me that thou needest now only rest and pure air to regain thy lost strength, and that all peril to life hath passed."

The young man briefly declared his convalescence, and made his acknowledgments to his host, for the kindness and care to which he owed his life.

But the Sheik checked the expression of them, briefly saying:

"As much would I have done for any passing stranger, and thou art not a stranger to me; for the son of thy father hath many claims on Abou-Gosh, who never hath failed friend or foe. It hath been a great pleasure to me to do any service to the son of one I love so well."

Three weeks had passed since Askaros bad been brought to the tents of the Bedouins, upon a camel, stretched in a state of utter unconsciousness by a fever, which seemed to dry up all the springs of life.

During that period he was at first ignorant of all that was passing around him ; but, as his convalescence commenced, he became conscious of the presence of a light airy female form, flitting near his couch, felt occasionally the timid touch of a soft, cool hand upon his fevered brow, and heard the music of a low, sweet voice chanting the plaintive melodies of the children of the desert. As he grew better, and his eyes could bear the glare of daylight, he saw the face and figure of the young Bedouin girl just described ; and it afforded him a dreamy enjoyment to watch her flitting around him, and through the tent, half closing his eyes, that she might not know he was watching her.

At length he ventured to accost her, and had short conversations with her and her mother, a comely matron of middle age, who was always there, but in whose movements and conversation the young man did not take so deep an interest. From them he learned that the caravan, when it reached the shelter to which their guide had conducted himself and Ferraj, had found him delirious and stricken with fever, and had borne him across the desert to the safe refuge where he now was, as the guest of the Great Sheik Abou-Gosh.

Inquiring for the faithful Nubian, he was told he too was safe, and in the tents ; on hearing which the young man, with sigh of deep relief, breathed a short prayer to the Virgin for all her mercies, and sunk again into peaceful slumber.

Now, although the crisis of his disease was over, the young man still felt himself incapable of much exertion of body or mind, so worn and wasted was he by his illness: and his host, perceiving it, forbore to excite him, and forbade his talking of himself, or of his affairs, until he was stronger, with that absence of curiosity and true hospitality which characterizes the Oriental in his dealings with the stranger who shares his salt.

Another week passed, and Askaros in the interval had been so far restored to his usual vigor, as to have mounted a horse and accompanied the Bedouins on an excursion to the Dead Sea and the Jordan, which was the limit of Abou-Gosh's authority, the opposite bank being under the dominion of a rival chieftain, with whose people the Beni-Hassan were ever in a state of quasi war.

With them, too, he witnessed the chase of the gazelle over the desert, where they hunted with trained hawks, much after the fashion of the knights and ladies in the Middle Ages, only for different game, the manner of which was thus: mounted on their Arab horses, and accompanied by the fleet Syrian greyhounds, with their long feathery tails, they would start up the gazelle from its hiding-place, which would soon outstrip the pursuit of the fastest horse and fleetest dog among them.

Then with a peculiar cry, launching the hawk into the air, he would circle up until lost into a mere speck hanging in blue ether, then swoop down like a lightning-flash on the head of the quarry, buffeting its face, and blinding its eyes with its strong wings. The gazelle would soon rid itself of its feathered assailant, by striking its head upon the ground, and then resume its flight. But the pertinacious foe would come down upon its head again and again, repeating its assault, until at length, blinded and wearied by the incessant attacks, and confused by the cries of the huntsmen and chase of the dogs,

21 *

the exhausted gazelle would be caught by the greyhounds, or speared by the Bedouins.

Partaking in this chase, he soon won the admiration of the Arabs for his perfect horsemanship, an accomplishment they prize above all others; and his reputation soon reached the gratified ears of Abou-Gosh and his women, who felt a pride that the young man was worthy of their care and hospitality.

So matters went on, until one morning, when, sitting in front of the tents with his host, Askaros, after telling him his story and his present plight, announced his intention of trespassing no longer on his hospitality, and of taking his departure.

Abou-Gosh did not immediately respond. He seemed to reflect seriously for some minutes, as though revolving in his mind the tale which had been told him, then raising his head, and looking him full in the face with his bright dark eye, as untamed as that of an eagle, yet not without a certain softness lurking in its depths, said:

"Poor boy! hard is thy fate! — sad thy past, and gloomy thy present and future! I know Abbas Pasha well. Thou hast provoked the hate of no common enemy. But where dost thou propose to go, on leaving those friendly tents?"

"I scarcely know," replied Askaros sadly; "all the earth is a place of exile to me now. But I shall go first to Joppa on the sea, and there I will decide whither to direct my steps. Possibly I may go to the land of the Franks."

"Why shouldst thou leave thy birthplace, and the home of thine own race, to go among the Frank strangers, whose ways of life and whose religion is so different — ay, more widely apart from thine than ours are?

"Why needest thou leave at all!" he added, fixing his bright eye full on the young man's; "already our people love thee, and praise thy skill in all manly sports, as equal to that of any born Bedouin. Stay, then, with us under our tents. Rude as they are, they are better than the Egyptian prisons, or the homes of the infidel Franks, for one born and bred in the East. For I have seen enough of them travelling here in Syria to know, as I said before, that their ways, and even their religion, which they call the same as thine, are as different as their costumes and their speech."

Ere the young man, in his speechless surprise at this unexpected proposition, could collect himself sufficiently to reply, the old Sheik still more gravely resumed, laying as he spoke his swarthy right hand, on which the sinews stood out like cords, on the shoulder of Askaros, as a father might on a son's.

"Hearken unto my words," be said, gravely, "and reflect before you decide. My sway over the Beni-Hassan, as thou knowest, is great: and my will their law. I have no son to succeed me, and I am growing old. If thou wilt consent, I will adopt thee as my son, and as the heir to my wealth, which is great in flocks and herds, and to my rule over this tribe. To confirm this more strongly, and to please my people, I will give thee in marriage the daughter of my old age, Amina. who is fair to look upon, and a woman any man might love, who hath helped to bring thee out of the valley of the shadow of death by her gentle ministering.

"And I am the more tempted to make thee this offer, because I suspect that the young girl loveth thee, even as Rachel loved Jacob, though possibly she knoweth it not fully herself. But a father's eye cannot be deceived.

Say! wilt thou be the son of Abou-Gosh, and his successor, and find rest and peace under the tents of the Beni-
Hassan? Reflect well upon it, and give me an answer
at sundown!"

And, gathering his robes about him, Abou-Gosh rose
from his cushions and passed beneath his tent, leaving
the young man sitting alone, too much overpowered by
the strangeness of the offer to utter a syllable in reply.

Yet the offer, wild as it seemed—that he, with his
Frank culture and civilized tastes, should relapse into the
primitive existence of the Bedouin—half shepherd, half
robber—was not without its temptations, making an appeal to the romantic side of his character. From the
midst of a confused turmoil of plots, stratagems and intrigues, he had passed suddenly, as through the valley
of the shadow of death, into the repose of this new and
primitive existence, a reflection of the days of the ancient
patriarchs, when Lot and Abraham divided their flocks
and herds, and parcelled out the domain of their world
between them. Here, at least, the wearied brain could
find repose, the wearied body rest, and the anxious spirit
steep itself in oblivion, and find nepenthe.

The lotus-eaters of the days of Ulysses might have led
more torpid lives, but never could have enjoyed more
immunity from mere worldly cares, than the Sheik of this
pastoral tribe, who was absolute master of the smiling
and fertile valleys, hemmed in by the high mountain
ranges from all foreign intrusion, stretching down, with
interspaces of arid desert, to the sea on one side, and the
hill country of Judea on the other.

Then, too, the girl who was offered to him in marriage
was passing fair! and pure as the snowflakes which
crested Mount Lebanon, in mind and heart.

True, she was only a savage! a child of the wilderness! born and bred under tents, with no mental culture, and not the most vague conception of the civilization which he had seen abroad, and set up as his ideal, and which he saw personified fully, for the first time, in the person of the American maiden.

True! but *she* had repudiated the warm outgush of his affection and admiration, with words and gestures of wondering scorn, when he dared shadow it out to her, on that memorable day when he had avenged himself by afterward saving her life; and never since had his eyes looked upon her—most probably in this life never would again, for he was now a fugitive, and her presence in Egypt was as evanescent and fleeting as the mirage which had mocked his vision on the desert. Why should he pursue a phantom, when he might grasp a warm, living, glowing, substantial reality, now so near him? for he doubted not that the great Sheik, so wary and so wise, had not spoken without knowing the real state of his daughter's heart! He might also be King of Syria, if he chose! Should he abandon that certainty, to chase a flying phantom over the world, which his reason told him he would never clasp!

Absorbed in these reveries, he closed his eyes, and before him came the vision, as in a panoramic view, of the first time he had seen the fair American girl, standing framed in the rude stone window of the Hotel d'Orient; her blonde tresses floating over her brow of snow and blushing cheeks, her large blue eyes shooting down rays of mingled wonder and admiration on the Egyptian cavalier and his white charger, contending for the mastery beneath her casement.

And at that view of past rapture, faded at once and

forever from his soul the mirage vision of the pastoral
Bedouin existence, with its simple cares and barren
hopes; and the image of the Arab girl, in contrast with
that apparition of true womanhood, seemed something
scarce above the animal creation, or the brutes that
perish.   He unclosed his eyes with a start, for the
familiar voice of Ferraj sounded in his ears, and looking
up, he beheld the faithful Nubian, his dress disarranged
and splashed with mud and soil, as though from hard
riding, the beads of sweat dripping from his brow, standing before him.   In his hand he held a scroll, sealed
like an Eastern letter, which he extended to his master.

"What is the meaning of this, Ferraj, and whence
came you?"

"From *El Khuds*, (the Holy City,) and this is a
writing for the Effendi, entrusted to his slave by the
consul, to whom it was given by Jona-dab-bar-Elias, the
Hebrew, who had it from Egypt."

Wondering from whom the letter might be, Askaros
tore open the envelope, and found on a slip of paper the
words which follow, in Arabic characters:

"Moussa-ben-Israel, of Cairo, sends greeting to
Askaros Kassis, who, he learns from one of his own
people at Jerusalem, is now the guest of the Great Sheik
of the Beni-Hassan, Abou-Gosh, with whom may peace
abide! It imports him to know that his sister, El Warda,
is now safe under the humble roof of the writer, her
father's oldest friend, and cannot be found by any who
seek to do her wrong. Of this be sure. It grieves me
to tell Askaros that he is now sole living bearer of that
name; his father, and my friend, went to his rest on the
11th day of Sciawal, at peace with himself and all men.
He died without pain, going out quietly, even as the

nargileh he was inhaling when the death-angel summoned him. Grieve not overmuch, for he died full of
years and honors, a just man made perfect. The earth
is for the living, not the dead, therefore, let Askaros look
to his own needs. Let him take warning, and confide
nothing to him he has heretofore considered his best
friend at Cairo, and his father's also, for he is even as
was Joab, who, while taking Amasa by the hand, and
asking, 'Art thou in health, my brother?' smote him
with his left hand under the ribs, so that his bowels
gushed out and he died!

"Let him take warning from that example of friendship! I say no more; for, though a young man, he to
whom this is written is wise for his years.

"A letter sent through the same channel as this cometh, will reach the sister and living friends of Askaros,
whom may the God of Abraham, Isaac, and Jacob, (who
is the God of the Nazarene as well as of the Hebrew,)
guide and guard, and have in His Holy keeping! *Selah!*"

Signed in black wax to this scroll was the seal of
Moussa-ben-Israel, in Hebrew characters. A postscript
had also been added, which ran as follows:

"Also am I charged by the consul-general, his protector, to tell Askaros, that in whatever land he may seek
refuge, there will he find a representative of his nation,
through whom he may confer with home and friends,
and with himself. He further promises to spare no pains
or influence to secure the safety and speedy return of
Askaros to his native land."

The receipt of this seemed to awaken the young man
from his day-dreams, and cause a complete revulsion in
his thoughts and feelings.

It roused him to the recollection that he had duties

toward others to perform, apart from his own ease and comfort, which he could not honorably renounce for the tranquil existence, of which he had been dreaming a few moments before.

His father's fair fame, and his sister's safety, both called trumpet-tongued upon him to shake off both sloth and sensual selfishness, and act like a man.

And over and above all these considerations, blending with, as though part and parcel of them, shone the fair face of the American girl, like that he had often prostrated himself before in worship at Cairo, in the solemn niche of the old Coptish Church of the Virgin, in those days of sunshine never to be his again.

The spell was broken. The lotus-eater rose from his bed of asphodel, where he had been soothed to slumber by the murmuring music of drowsy fountains and droning voices, an awakened and energetic man; once more ready to act, to dare, to suffer, as a man must in a world of strife and struggle, where the wrestler, like Antæus of old, should grow the stronger after every fall, and spring up re-invigorated after touching his mother earth. Rising up, it may be, with some stains of that earth upon him, but staining not his inner man; for, with such soiling of the body, in such strife, often comes purification of the soul.

So, at the appointed hour, the young Copt met the Great Sheik, with a calm and composed countenance, on which the resolve of his soul was written, and while thanking him for all his kindness, and for the last and greatest favor of all which he meditated, courteously declined it, explaining and pleading his own duties. He also announced his intention of departing on the ensuing morning for Joppa, with his faithful Nubian, there to determine his future course.

With the stoicism of the Indian savage, whom indeed, the Bedouin much resembles in many points of appearance, life, and character, Abou-Gosh accepted the decision as final, wasting no words in useless argument or expostulation, and seemed to forget the subject. But there were moist eyes under the tents that night, when the speedy departure of the stranger was announced : and one woman's heart beat high with indignation, the other's throbbing with a dull aching pain, and vain longing, at the news. For both mother and daughter had hoped that the proposal of the Great Sheik to their guest — on which he had consulted them — would have been thankfully accepted.

So, at the first gray glimmer of dawn, on the next day, Askaros bade farewell to Abou-Gosh, and to the tents of the Beni-Hassan, unwitting that the tearful eyes of the Arab maiden strained after his receding form with a long, wistful gaze, from a rent in the canvas of the tent, and that a fond, forgiving heart sent a benison after him.

His own heart was heavy and sad enough, as over the still and sterile mountains of the hill country of Judea he took his way back to Jerusalem and Joppa, on his return to what men call civilization — the simple patriarchal life, like the black tents, fading away from his view as he left that peaceful valley — never again to return.

22

CHAPTER XXII.

THE BRIDE OF THE SEA.

BEAUTIFUL art thou still, O sad city! that sittest by the sea, like another Niobe, weeping for thy children and for thy glories, which have vanished and return not.

Lovely in thy weeds of widowhood, with thy marble palaces crumbling to decay; thy black hearse-like gondolas gliding over slimy and almost deserted waters: thy women all in mourning; the best and bravest of thy sons eating the bitter bread of exile, or vainly striving to break the chains which fetter limbs and soul; lovely in spite of these, in thy hectic glow of decline, like a fair consumptive, art thou still, O Venice!

The scene shifts from the sands of the desert and the black tents of the Bedouins, to the old city of the Doges, where the lion of St. Mark's crouches under the Austrian eagle, and the steeds of brass, glittering in the sun, have succumbed to a stronger than Doria, and are bridled at last.

It was at a period when the Austrian rule seemed more firmly fastened on Venice than ever; and when her government seemed crushed out of nationality into a military district upheld by the bayonets of a foreign soldiery; while her people, broken in fortune and bankrupt of hope, sullenly and sadly submitted to a doom they were powerless to avert. Saddest spectacle under the sun is such a contrast; where the gifts of Nature and the prodigal profusion with which she has endowed both place and people — bathed in the brightest sunlight under the bluest of skies — are all rendered sources not of pleasure, but of pain, by the cruelty of a conqueror.

Such was Venice in the early winter of 1854, when a party of foreigners, lodging in one of the palaces overlooking the grand lagoon, were passing a season there; gliding over her silent canals in the noiseless gondola, and visiting her sad, old churches and the palaces of her doges and princes, with their rare wealth of pictures by the old masters, still the attraction and the charm, which invite and keep the stranger spell-bound in that city of the dead.

They are old friends of ours, these foreigners, whom we have met in Cairo and up the Nile; and few changes have taken place in their appearance or outward seeming, drifting as they have all been upon the smooth tides of a summer sea, and only seeking pleasure in novel excitements, as they have rambled leisurely from place to place.

Old Van Camp looks as rotund and as ruddy and placid as ever; the chaste Priscilla as angular in face and form, and equally dissatisfied. The younger Van Camp is fearfully and wonderfully arrayed in the most exaggerated of English travelling costumes, made of the coarsest tweed stuff, of the loudest pattern; the short shooting-jacket with the innumerable pockets, the tightest of pantaloons, and the most complicated straps of leather cross-

ing and recrossing themselves over his manly chest; with
a small Scotch cap with silver thistle in its side, not shel-
tering a nose grown ruddy and swollen from exposure to
the sun.

Sir Charles is with the party, and to an observant eye,
there is a change in him, slight perhaps, but perceptible.
The reckless carelessness of his manner, and the abrupt
oddity of his speech, have been succeeded by a measured
formality of carriage and address.   He is stiffer and
colder than formerly, and talks less.   His old humor
seems to have deserted him, with his accession to his new
title — for his father was dead, and he is now a peer of
Great Britain.   There is a look almost of anxiety or
trouble on his brow, which destroys the frank, open expression it used to wear.   Upon the whole, he looks
like a man who has some secret care weighing upon his
mind, which he cannot, or will not divulge, and which
gnaws him secretly, as the concealed fox did the Spartan
in the old story.

Over Edith, too, there has come a change somewhat
similar to that observable in her affianced; though she
looks almost as fresh and fair as when we last saw her.
She has apparently, at one step, passed from a careless
laughing girl into a quiet serious woman, and her smile
has lost its great charm, of irradiating the whole face like
a sunbeam when it broke forth.   She looks *blasé* and
careless prematurely, and the eager interest she formerly
manifested at all novel sights, has been succeeded by a
polite indifference which does not seem natural to her.
She has become in those few months a more thoughtful
and more elegant woman, and the most fastidious critic
could find nothing to cavil at, in her cold, calm manner
and speech; but the gush of youthful impulse which had

seemed to bubble up from her fresh nature before, as from a pure well-spring, has vanished entirely, and her manner is as composed as that of a woman of middle age. Whether this change was agreeable or acceptable to her affianced lover was impossible to say, for their intercourse was as constrained and guarded now as the most rigid spinster or dowager could have desired. But the pleasure of Sir Charles in her presence did not seem so great, nor his own manner so enthusiastic, as it had been on that memorable evening among the ruins of Luxor, when he declared his passion, nor after their first re-union in Europe. The cloud had risen so imperceptibly and so gradually, that, until it hung like a chilly veil between them, neither of them could have explained how or whence it first arose.

They were both painfully conscious of it, however, though each strove to hide that consciousness from the other and from themselves, for the conditional engagement was now understood to be a positive one, to be consummated the ensuing winter, with the approval of all parties.

Miss Priscilla Primmins was much pleased with what she deemed the great improvement in the manners both of Sir Charles and her niece ; and was loud in her eulogiums thereupon, very little to the satisfaction of the latter, to whom she confided her opinions.

"Did you ever see such an improvement, my dear, in any man's manner as in Sir Charles's !" she would cry out enthusiastically, after he had been especially serious and silent during the visit he seemed to think it his daily duty to make' formally — having some near relatives, stopping at another hotel, where he was quartered.

"I can scarcely believe he is the same rattle-cap who

22 *   R

used to talk so much nonsense, and be actually so rude to me sometimes at Cairo! Why, he is as sedate now, and as sensible as your father. It is wonderful how travelling does improve one! Don't you think so, Edith?"

The girl, thus appealed to, would vaguely murmur out her assent, and the spinster would continue:

"And I notice the same thing in you too, my dear. You used to be a tiresome little chit, as full of frolic and fun as a kitten, and quite as mischievous, but now you really look and act as Lady Aylmer ought to do! and one would suppose from your dignified manner you had passed a season in London already, been presented at Court, and lived among lords and ladies all your life. I never did see so great a change in so short a time! But I begin to fear, my child, that your new rank will turn your head, and you will be ashamed of your untitled relations, and very naturally too! Perhaps I would feel the same were I in your place; for I am not a fashionable woman, and your brother is certainly not presentable in high circles. He does 'get himself up,' as he calls it, in such a wonderful way — looking for all the world like a gentleman's groom, or a sporting character."

"Oh! aunt, how can you talk so?" replied Edith, tears of vexation rising up into her blue eyes. "Indeed you make a very great mistake. I have none of those feelings, but quite the reverse. I do wish," she added, vehemently, "there were no such thing as lords, and ladies, and titles, and fashion in the world! for while they seem of vital importance to others, my poor republican head cannot be taught to put any value upon them, outside of their owner's merits. For I believe with Burns:

'The rank is but the guinea's stamp,
A man's the gowd for a' that!"

"Hoity toity! what nonsense," said Miss Priscilla.
"Is the girl distracted? Suppose Sir Charles were to
hear you uttering such vulgar sentiments? They will do
very well in America, my dear, where, by-the-by, we
never practice them in our best society; but here in
Europe they are low, absolutely low!" and the spinster
made a wry face, as though compelled to swallow some
nauseous mixture. "My dearest Edith, pray do not
talk in that wild way. I say again, suppose Sir Charles
were to hear you, what would he think?"

"Well," said Edith with some spirit, for her temper
was unequal now, not even as formerly — "well! suppose
Sir Charles should? what then? Is a woman supposed
to sacrifice utterly all her own thoughts and feelings to
the man she marries — or rather, that her friends marry
her to — and become a mere echo of his ideas and opinions? Sir Charles knows I was neither born nor bred an
aristrocrat; and there are many points on which our views
and feelings are totally dissimilar, I might almost say discordant. He has been educated in one school, and I in
another."

"Very true, my child; but you will very soon adapt
yourself to your new sphere, for you have quite the '*air-
noble*' already. How do you like Lady Jane Hoauton-
ville and her daughter, his cousins, who are staying at
Danieli Hotel with him?"

"Not at all!" said Edith, promptly; "I think them
both very impertinent: and I do not know which I dis-
like most, the patronizing condescension of the mother
or the frigid insolence of the daughter! If they are a

fair sample of Sir Charles's relations, I fear we shall not agree very well.   He seems to think them perfection, and was speaking only yesterday of Lady Jane as a perfect model for imitation, and how fortunate it was for a daughter to have such a mother.   I had to bite my lips, for fear of saying something rude."

"Well, my dear, we *should* call her 'stuck up' in Boston, that is a fact ; but she is a woman of title, you know — grand-daughter of Lord Bareacres and niece of Lord Squander ; so, being so highly connected, she is naturally proud, and puts on airs, as everybody would. She never seems to see me at all, and has never uttered a syllable to me since we first met ; but she is a *very* lady-like person — when she chooses to be," added Miss Priscilla, *sotto voce*, determined not to encourage her niece in the ideas she saw fermenting in her mind.

For Miss Priscilla had made up her mind that the match with Sir Charles was a great thing ; and obstinately closed her eyes, and sought also to shut Edith's, to everything which was not "*couleur de rose*" in regard to it.

This conversation, which was only one of many similar ones, will show the nature of the cloud which had been gradually rising between the two affianced ; composed, it is true, of light, floating vapors, and small discordancies, yet gradually gaining shape and consistency, until it opposed a veil between them, and made their intercourse far more awkward and constrained than it should have been under the circumstances.   In fact, the first romance subsiding into a less bewildering sentiment, Sir Charles soon saw, that on many points, not only of taste but of feeling, his ideas and those of the American girl were not congenial, especially in the matter of social distinction, and the deference to be paid to rank and position, on which he laid great stress. Edith differed entirely from him, and seemed to take a pleasure in asserting that difference, both by word and action, toward the titled relatives with whom he was travelling, and whom he relied on to introduce and pioneer the future Lady Aylmer on her introduction into "society," by which both he and they meant the *élite* of the London world only. The rest of mankind, resting outside of the charmed circle, being regarded as "people nobody knows."

Matters stood in this uneasy condition, when an excursion was proposed, one day, to visit some of the famous glass-factories on the opposite side of the lagoons, which Sir Charles volunteered to accompany, without his female relatives.

They took a gondola on the Grand Canal; and the two gondoliers in their picturesque costumes — one standing just on the front of the cabin, the other at the sharp stern of the boat — rowed swiftly on past marble palaces, crumbling to decay, untenanted now, many of them, save by bats or owls, and others serving as barracks for Austrian soldiers, whose white uniforms were hung out, in lieu of draperies, from the wide windows, and who sat smoking their short pipes at the doorways, or on the window-sills of palaces once tenanted by the Doges and Senators of Venice, the Dorias, Falieros, and others whose names are historical.

Yet the beauty of the site, and of the marble edifices which covered it, could not be wholly obscured by the brutalities of man, and the clear blue sky reflected in the rippling water, as they glided out into the lagoons, en-

hanced the pictorial loveliness of the scene, when looking back upon it.

The party comprised only Mr. Van Camp and his
sister-in-law, Edith and Sir Charles.

Twilight was setting in as they swung round in the
gondola to return to the distant city, now dimly visible
through the evening haze, as its lights began to twinkle
like dim stars.

The sun had rushed to his rest, an orb of burning red,
suddenly dipping down and disappearing behind the
horizon—casting no lingering glances behind, but ushering in the evening all at once ; the moon, with its round
silvery shield, shedding its soft rays over water and sky,
which alone were visible from the gondola.

The two elders of the party, complaining of the chilliness of the evening air, withdrew into the cabin, leaving
Sir Charles and Edith alone together—the gondoliers at
each end of the boat keeping time to their oars in a low,
measured chant, in the musical Italian tongue.

The softening influences of the scene and hour were
not unfelt by the two young hearts, soon to be united in
so close a tie, and both seemed under the spell of their
witchery.   Instinctively they drew nearer to each other,
all their late coolness and reserve melting away.   And
as Sir Charles took the small hand that hung listlessly by
the fair girl's side, he pressed it warmly in his own, and
gazed fondly in her face, with all the fervor of a devoted
lover.   A chill shot through his heart as, with the unerring instinct of true affection, he felt that there was no
reciprocal ardor in the heart which seemed to flutter so
wildly in the young girl's bosom, and that the pressure
was not returned — nay, even the small soft hand half
withdrawn from his own, by an impulse she could not

control. The bright blue eyes were not turned toward his, under the silvery sheen of the moonlight, but cast down upon the rippling water; and her thoughts seemed wandering far away from him, who stood by her side, living and breathing at that moment for her alone.

"Edith!" he said, with tears in his voice; "dear Edith! for God's sake tell me what this means! How have I offended you, and what has wrought this change in your heart, that you treat me like a stranger — yes, more coldly than a stranger — and seem to recoil from my very touch? I have seen and felt this for some time past, and only forgot it for one brief, rapturous moment now, soon to be recalled more painfully to the truth. Have I, then, grown repulsive to you? for God's sake tell me, before it is too late!"

The impassioned and earnest tone in which her companion spoke, roused the young girl from her reverie. She breathed a deep sigh, as though suddenly recalled to the fact of her lover's presence, and tears rose to her eyes as she answered:

"Indeed, Sir Charles, you do me and yourself an injustice. You are very far indeed from being repulsive to me, for I respect and admire you as much as ever, and would not wound you for the world! I am indignant with myself that I cannot make a warmer return for your affection; but I begin to fear it is my nature — for I *must* tell you the truth — that I do not and cannot love you as I know you deserve to be loved, and as my heart tells me I ought to love you! It would be dishonorable in me to deceive a heart so noble, and so loyal as yours; and I tell you, with mortification, and pain, and shame for my own cold heart, that what I have dreamed of love, but never felt, is far different from the feeling entertained for you. I honor, esteem, respect you! I look up to you for guidance, and entrust my future fearlessly to your keeping; but I would deceive you, did I tell you that my love for you is the same as yours for me. Why this should be so I cannot tell; I only know such is the truth."

Over the fair, smooth brow of the Englishman there seemed to pass a spasm of deadly pain; and she felt a shuddering thrill shake the strong hand that still held hers. Then that hand closed convulsively on hers with a clasp which was painful, and turning his face toward her, he pleaded his cause, with all the fervor of a strong nature habitually kept under control, but sweeping every-thing before it when once unchained.

"Edith!" he said, "when I unsealed my heart to you, sitting amidst those ruins at Luxor, and obtained from your virgin lips the confession that you were not in-different to me, I felt that it was all, and more, than I had the right to ask, on the first avowal of my passion! But now, after long months of intimate acquaintance, when we know each other better — when our troth is plighted — such cold, measured words as those you have just uttered, cut me to the heart. They prove that the love I feel for you is not shared — that my affection is not re-turned — and that, rich as I have grown in worldly goods, I am a pauper in what I prize more — and that you can give me your esteem, but not the love which alone is life to me!

"Oh Edith! think well ere you reject the priceless wealth of such an affection as mine, and cause it to wither and die for the want of the sunshine of a look or word of yours. Not twice in a lifetime is a love, so deep and devoted as mine, tendered to any woman: and I know you too well, to believe that you would be the wife of any

man you did not love. What is my fault? Tell me,
that I may amend it. In what have I been wanting, that
you have cooled thus in your treatment of me? Tell me,
that I may repair it. But, oh, Edith! dear to me now
as ever, in spite of this mortal chill which strikes to my
heart at your avowal — be not so cruel, so pitiless! No
longer be an image of snow, but a woman; and recipro-
cate an affection which will make the happiness of two
lives perfect."

To this impassioned pleading of her lover Edith knew
not what to reply. She felt the force and truth of what
he had said; and she felt also keenly, the ingratitude she
manifested toward this heart, so noble, so loyal, so generous, even in its pain. She felt her own heart softening
toward him, more than it had done for many months,
and mistook the sentiment of sympathy, or of pity, for
that of love, which it no more resembles than the moonlight does the sunlight. So she replied in a softer and
more sympathetic tone to her lover's appeal and recant-
ed more of her avowals than the truth warranted, under
that impulse: leaving him, although not completely satisfied, yet partially convinced that she had spoken more
coldly than she felt, and that the affection she entertained
for him, though not so fervent as he might desire, yet
could be warmed into a greater glow by the fire of his
own.

Half in pity, half in gratified vanity, she was listening
with a pleased and attentive ear to his fervent protestations, and glowing plans for their future, when the gondola was suddenly arrested, and she looked up to see
what the impediment might be, which had interrupted
the smooth motion of the barge, and their whispered
conversation at the same time.

23

The gondola had passed out of the open lagoon and entered the Grand Canal. The moonlight was as bright as day, and every object on the canal distinctly visible along its whole length — the black shadows of the marble palace on its banks, the column, and winged lion of St. Mark's reflected in the clear mirror of the limpid waters — producing the effect of a double Venice — while from time to time floated on the air snatches of melodies of Tasso's verse breathed by the lips of the gondoliers, coming mellowed by distance over the waters, like echoes from pleasant memories of the past.

Edith looked up suddenly, as the gondoliers backed water with their oars, and after a slight shock — as though the gondola had grazed another — the bark floated like a swan on the water, and she saw the face and form she least expected to see at that place and time, but which she had often seen in her sleeping and waking dreams.

For as she looked up, there shot out of the small canal spanned by the Bridge of Sighs, with its palace and prison on either hand, which runs at right angles to the Grand Canal, a small gondola, so rapidly propelled by its careless gondolier, that its sharp prow seemed threatening to cut right into the broadside of the one in which the young maiden was listening to a love-tale, newer and fresher, if not so rhythmical as those of Tasso — and told in another tongue.

The rapid backward movement of the gondoliers alone saved the collision; and as the smaller gondola shot across the Grand Canal, just grazing the prow of the larger, a form rose from the seat outside of the cabin, and gazed eagerly into the other boat. And the eyes of Edith and of Askaros met once more! those of the former full of wonder and surprise — those of the other filling their dark lustrous orbs with a light more difficult to define, in which rapture and pain seemed strangely blended.

It was but an instantaneous flash of recognition; and the light gondola, propelled by the vigorous arm of the single gondolier, shot with arrowy speed down the canal, in the direction from which the larger had just come, and turning into another small canal, was lost to view.

The quick eye of Sir Charles had also recognized an acquaintance, and he turned in surprise to Edith:

"Why, there is our young Egyptian prince!" he said, "or his ghost; although he wears the European dress now, and devilish well he looks in it too; though thinner than in his bags. Who would have expected to meet *him* here, after so unceremoniously cutting us all in Cairo, as he did. You know I tried my best to fish him up when we came down the Nile: but the old house was empty when I went there—all the family away—and our dragoman told us they had all gone away somewhere. By Jove! I must fish him up to-morrow; for he really is the most civilized Eastern I have ever met. He came pretty near giving us another upset with that careless gondolier of his, though!"

Edith murmured something in reply, but complained of the chilliness of the night air, and joined her father and aunt in the cabin, whither Sir Charles reluctantly followed; and the interrupted conversation was not resumed, as they soon reached their residence in the Palazzo, which was their temporary home, and spent the evening at the theatre of San Felice.

Edith retired to her rest that night with a troubled brow, and a more agitated heart. As she disrobed herself, and laid aside the jewels she had worn at the opera-house, she murmured to herself:

"Does it not seem like a fatality, the perpetual apparition of that man! as though he *did* possess the magic carpet of the Persian prince, and could transport himself at will, as I once jestingly declared he might. How strangely does he seem wound up with the thread of my life! And how wan and worn he looked in the moonlight! like one who had suffered much in mind and body since we met, so many months ago, in that mysterious land of his, where everything seems supernatural."

Smiling at her own fancies, she stepped to the window overlooking the Grand Canal, through which the bright moonlight streamed with a brightness like that of day, and waving her hand theatrically, exclaimed, laughingly:

"If truly thou art Haroun-el-Reschid, I summon thee by this spell to appear!"

As though in answer to the invocation, round the corner of the palace, from the small canal, there shot out a light gondola; and standing on the deck, leaning against the cabin, in the full light of the moon, she saw again the face and form of him she had summoned! But he saw her not; his eyes were fixed on the distant stars, and the gondola glided so swiftly past that she had scarcely seen him ere he had vanished again. With a superstitious thrill of terror, the maiden shivered as though with cold, and she withdrew from the casement, and with a troubled mind and heart sought her couch, to be haunted with the wildest dreams, in which she could trace only one actual figure — that of the mysterious and omnipresent Egyptian.

CHAPTER XXIII.

MOUSSA-BEN-ISRAEL.

A FEW weeks after the interview between the Viceroy and Daoud-ben-Youssouf, when the farce of a judicial investigation into the accounts of the late Khasnadar, Askaros Effendi, had been gone into, and through the garbled accounts of his former Wakeel, Daoud, judgment had been rendered in favor of the Egyptian Government for several thousand purses, with heavy arrearages of interest — amounting to a confiscation of the estate — the Syrian was again summoned into the Viceroy's presence.

He naturally supposed it was to receive the thanks, and the promised reward from the Viceroy; for the sessions of the Grand Meglis were secret, and his treachery to his former patron had been so adroitly veiled under the feigned fear and reluctance with which he had testified, having also made apparently so desperate an effort to conceal the account-books which compromised the Khasnadar, as to deceive all not in the secret. Those forged books, by an understanding with Mahmoud Bey, were stolen from the place where he had secreted them, by the old crone, his servant, and delivered up to the Meglis; so he considered himself safe from detection. He had even allowed himself to be imprisoned for several days, for refusing to divulge where those account-books were : and was only liberated when they had been found, as stated above.

For the sole restraint, the sole fear left to this subtle and reckless intriguer, who played with life and soul as a child with its toys — prized one moment, thrown away the next — was the dread of El Warda's discovery of his treachery; which he well knew she never would forgive. With that fear lost, like Satan, went all his fear.   Great as was his avarice, vaulting as was his ambition, implacable as was his hate, the master-passion of his soul, perverted as it was, could be found in his affection for this gentle girl.   So strange are the diversities of human character! so mysterious and inscrutable the workings of the human soul!   If, on the earth's wide surface there existed two beings, more utterly dissimilar in mind, heart and soul, than El Warda and Daoud — the one all light, the other all darkness — hard, indeed, would they be to find.   Yet the strange attraction of opposites manifested itself here : overpoweringly in the case of the man, fitfully and feebly in that of the woman, whose purer nature recoiled instinctively from the occasional exhibitions of the darker soul of the Syrian.

With the haunting fear of detection set at rest, he cared for naught else ; and it was, therefore, with a light heart and a serene brow that he mounted his donkey, and set out for the Abassieh, to obey the Viceroy's summons.

While he was still on his way there, another had been ushered into the presence of the Viceroy, in secret audience : and that other was the venerable Israelite, Moussa-ben-Israel, who had also been peremptorily sum-

moned to the palace of the Pasha, by an order he dared
not disobey.

The old man, as he stood before Abbas, after prostrating himself in Oriental fashion, was not clad in the
costly garments he had worn in his own house, when he
had received the elder Askaros in his secret chamber.

He now wore the yellow cap and gabardine, distinctive
of the Jew, and squalid poverty and misery were stamped
upon his external man. Long years of pitiless persecution and ruthless cruelty had taught his people to counteract the greed and grasping avarice of the Turk, by
concealment of the wealth they coveted, and by a courage
which, though passive, was none the less unflinching and
heroic in its contempt of danger, torture and death. In
the East that mysterious race — sole living link between
Deity and man, through whom the rich heritage of salvation and the promises of God to man have been revealed in all ages — still present their peculiar characteristics; which, in the West, by the attrition of intercourse and marriage with other races, are rapidly being
obliterated.

Moussa-ben-Israel, as he rose up from his prostration
before the Viceroy, presented that type of his tribe,
when they sought to eke out the lion's skin with the fox's,
and to oppose craft to cruelty; and his appearance and
manner were by no means so prepossessing as when, in
his own house, he had welcomed his friend, and his true
nature was free to exhibit itself. Then, his port and
mien had been erect and fearless; now, the head was
bowed, and he seemed like one bending under the burden of many years, as he stood with downcast eyes, and
arms dropping nervelessly by his side, before the Viceroy, whose countenance wore its blackest aspect.

"Dog of a Yahudi!" was the Viceroy's salutation; "son of the stiff-necked race, whom Turk, Nazarene, and Gentile equally hate and despise! I have permitted thy presence to pollute my palace, because I have some questions to ask of thee! Answer me truly, though thy tongue be so skilled in lying as to make it difficult, or I shall cause it to be plucked with red-hot pincers from thy blaspheming jaws. They tell me that if living man knows, thou knowest where the treasures of Askaros Khasnadar are concealed; and he was a defaulter to my Government, and seems to have taken all his wealth to the pit of Eblis with him when he died, for my people cannot find it. Thou alone knowest where it is hidden, and if thou wilt tell me," said the Viceroy, suddenly changing his manner into one of patronizing kindness, "my gratitude shall richly recompense thee for the public service thou wilt have conferred." And he leaned forward on his divan, almost caressingly, toward the old man.

"Effendina!" replied the Jew, apparently much confused and astonished, and plucking nervously at his long snowy beard as he spoke, "you surely must be jesting with your poor servant. Does he look like a man"— and he glanced at his soiled and worn gabardine—"apt to know of State secrets, or to be entrusted with the hiding-place of concealed treasures? Surely my great lord amuses himself by mocking at the poor Hebrew, who served his grand-sire!"

"Pig! Swine! Offspring of the thrice accursed race, which not only denies the true Prophet, but slew its own God!" shrieked Abbas, in a frenzy of rage. "It is *thou* that laughest at the beard of thy king and master. Answer my question, and answer it truly; or, by the tomb of the Prophet, I will cause each separate hair of thy beard to be plucked out by pincers, and thine eyeballs to be seared with hot irons. Answer, dog! or prepare to meet the wrath of Abbas Pasha, for well do I know thou liest, and that the secret conveyance of the wealth of Askaros is well known to thee, as well as the place to which his son and daughter have fled!" And he clapped his hands sharply together.

"Send the man with the bowstring," he said to the attendant who came at the call. And a moment after, a grim, black Nubian, hideous in face and figure, with a knotted cord in his hand, entered, and, after prostrating himself, passed silently to the side of the old Hebrew, watching a signal from his master, then and there to strangle him.

But, instead of inspiring fear or abject humiliation, the insulting words of Abbas, and the presence of the hideous executioner of the will of the tyrant, seemed only to have infused new vigor and courage in the breast of the dauntless old man, whose manhood seemed to rekindle under the ashes of years at this trial.

The stubborn obduracy, the unflinching fortitude of his long-enduring race, seemed all concentrated in his person, in this crisis. He raised his head, and the grand old Jewish face, with its bold outline — nose curved like the eagle's beak; firm, full lips, massive jaw, from which flowed, like floss silk, the snowy beard, falling upon the chest, and with the full bright eye, like an eagle's, too, undimmed by age — elevated itself to a level with the cruel countenance of Abbas, as he sat on his divan, and thus the Hebrew spoke:

"Grandson of Mehemet Ali! who art now, by the will of God, Viceroy of Egypt, the sands of my life have

S

already ran too low, and the time of my departure is
already too near, in the course of nature, for thy threats
to terrify me, or to extort aught from my lips, which I
wish not to tell. I am older than thy grandsire would
have been were he now alive! Respect that age, if thou
respectest naught else. Speak to me like a human being, and not as to a dog, and I may tell thee, not all
thou askest, for I cannot tell what I do not know, but
much which it may profit thee to hear. Now, dismiss
that creature with the cord, for only cowards speak under
such compulsion, and lie when they speak. From the
lips of Moussa-ben-Israel a lie never came, nor fear to
his soul, except of Jehovah Jireh alone! While that
Nubian stands there this tongue is mute. Thou canst
cause it to be torn with pincers from this mouth, but thou
canst not compel it to speak. I swear to thee, O Abbas!
by the great Jehovah whom alone I worship, that thou
never shalt learn from me what alone I know, except on
the conditions I have named, and one other condition:
that I shall be permitted to depart in peace, when I have
spoken. Swear this to me by the tomb of the Prophet,
or work thy will, and see me die in silence, my secret
unrevealed. I have spoken!"

The old man ceased — his bent form erect for the
moment with the vigor of youth; his dark eye flashing;
his breast heaving — confronting Abbas with a pride
greater than his own.

The first emotion of the Viceroy at seeing one whom
he considered, with the prejudice of his bigoted nature,
as utterly destitute of courage or principle, rise to the
full majesty of outraged manhood, and defy death, torture, and his wrath, which all his subjects knew was
deadly, was one of utter amazement. He listened in

mute surprise, which was converted into reluctant admiration as the old man proceeded.

When his voice ceased, Abbas drew a long breath, and spoke, as to himself:

"And this man is a Yahudi!"

"Ay! Effendina! a Hebrew of the Hebrews! by blood, faith, and training! One of that race thou hast been taught to despise; but who are men, even as are Mussulman and Nazarene, and in whom persecution, like a furnace seven times heated, for generation after generation, hath developed a strength of will, a quickness of intellect, and a pertinacity of purpose, which a softer training would never have produced, and which have made that scattered race—a nation no longer—a power over the whole earth.

"Hearken unto me! O Viceroy! In that great book of faith which thy Prophet reverenced, and from which he drew many of his precepts and his laws for Islam, thou mayst read how Jehovah never failed to protect His chosen people against the Pharaohs, and other kings of Egypt, who sought to harm them. Effendina, thou hast drank of the waters of the *Ain-el-Moussa* (Well of Moses), near Suez, and the Mollahs have told thee the story of that persecution of my people, and how it ended. *Thotmas* was a mighty king, and *Moussa* but a poor Hebrew; yet look how Jehovah weighed the one against the other? Effendina, I have spoken!"

"What he saith is true!" muttered Abbas. "The Mollahs at Suez have told me that tale! Sheitan protects his own! This old man is stubborn, I see, and I cannot frighten his secret out of him, so must try coaxing! for I must have it. Slave!" he said aloud to the grim Nubian, who stood like an ebony statue. "Retire!"

and making another prostration, the executioner retired as noiselessly as he had entered.

"Now," said Abbas, turning toward the Hebrew, "that I have humored thy whim, I presume those stubborn lips of thine will unclose, to sing something other than the glories of the race of which thou art so proud! But stay!" he added. "Thou art old and feeble, and to prove how much of my favor thou hast earned by thy plain speaking, thou shalt sit down in my presence — a privilege, as thou knowest, accorded to few of my subjects;" and he pointed to a pile of cushions on the floor, where the old man might seat himself.

The Hebrew accepted the proffered courtesy, for the strength of temporary excitement had been succeeded by exhaustion. At the same time he appreciated the full extent of the condescension, which he rightly judged was intended to conciliate him, and unseal his lips.

"Now," said Abbas, "as thou art a wise man, and not to be deceived, I will tell thee, O Moussa, how this matter stands, and what I seek of thee! and thou mayest benefit thy friends likewise, if thou art frank with me!

"My Grand Meglis has found a judgment against the estate of the Khasnadar for many thousand purses; but Zoulfikar Pasha, who hath the estate in charge, reports that, save the landed property, which is of no great value, he can find no traces of the reputed wealth which all men spoke of. Therefore Justice cannot be satisfied: nor can we discover whither the children of Askaros, who might tell us, have fled.

"Now, in this strait, as men say thou wast the trusted friend and business agent of the Khasnadar, who visited thee the very day he died, I seek to know where all that wealth is lodged, promising a rich reward, which thou mayest name, for thy revelations ! "

He ceased, fixing an anxious eye on the old man's face, which was as immovable and impenetrable as that of a stone statue.

"And if I tell thee all I know, O Effendina ! — waiving the reward, for I need no bribe — will your Highness permit me to add a word of counsel afterward ? "

"Certainly ! so thou wilt but tell me where those treasures really are ! " he added, eagerly; his dull eye lighting up with avaricious hope.

"Effendina, I will. But they are neither within my reach nor thine ! "

The countenance of Abbas fell, and he cast a sinister and malign look, from under his brows, on the placid face of the old man, who observed it, and added, hastily:

" But I can suggest a way, I think, in which some of it may be secured ! "

"In the name of the Prophet! man! then talk out plainly, and read me no more riddles ! for I am growing weary of them ! What hast thou to suggest ? "

" This, Highness ! The younger Askaros is now in Europe; at Venice when last heard from. He is the sole heir; the girl El Warda being only an adopted daughter of the Khasnadar, and not entitled to inherit. She therefore is useless in this affair. The consul-general, who, as protector of Askaros, claims now to protect what are his estates, is a stumbling-block in the way also. Is it not so, Effendina ? "

Abbas assented, by an impatient nod of his head, and a lowering brow, as though the mention of that name irritated him.

" The Elchee — whom may Sheitān seize — hath had

24

the insolence to set up some such pretext," he said;
"thou art well informed as to what passes in the secret
sessions of my Grand Meglis!"

The old man did not notice the sneer, but resumed:

"Well, then, Highness, why not offer the consul-general to mediate between thy Government and Askaros,
by proposing that he shall be rëinstated in thy good
graces, and enjoy his inheritance, on payment of an in-
demnity agreed upon, in liquidation of the Govêrnment
claim against his father's estate?   For I assure your
Highness, the money invested abroad — a very large sum
— is entirely under the control of the young man now;
and to seize upon his lands would lead to a quarrel with
the consul-general."

Abbas reflected a few moments, then replied:

"I believe thou speakest truly, O Moussa! and the
wisdom of thy counsel is worthy of thy great ancestor,
after whom thou hast been fitly named.   I will take warning of Thotmas, and not only allow thee to depart in
peace, but adopt thy counsel also, and take thee and thine
under my special protection henceforth.

"Go thou to the consul-general, and suggest this thing
to him, as though I knew not of it; for it is not fitting
the proposal should come from me.   I rely on thy discretion to protect my dignity therein; and thou must not
even hint to him that the thing will not be new to me.
Bakaloum!   Thou mayest now depart; and I thank thee
that thou hast reminded me that the Prophet hath ordered
the toleration of all faiths, though there be no salvation
except through Islam.

"*Salaam Aleikoum,* old patriarch!   Peace be with
thee!"

The old man rosé up, made his reverence, and retired

with a lighter heart than he had entered, feeling like one who has safely emerged from the den of a tiger.

As he passed through the courtyard he encountered Daoud-ben-Youssouf, who was just entering the palace gates. The recognition was mutual, as also the surprise.

" What seeks the fox in the cave of the tiger ? " thought Moussa.

"What can have brought that old dotard here?" thought Daoud.

But each only greeted the other courteously, exchanging no words, and passed on his way.

The Hebrew mounted his white donkey at the gate, and ambled slowly home — a smile on his aged face — thinking of the good tidings he had to tell El Warda, still his secret guest.

CHAPTER XXIV.

THE VICEROY PAYS THE SYRIAN.

WHEN Daoud-ben-Youssouf was ushered into the presence of the Viceroy, he found him apparently in good humor, smiling from time to time as though some pleasant thought tickled his fancy. His reception of the Syrian was bland and encouraging in the extreme — more patronizing and cordial than it had ever been before; which Daoud regarded as a good omen.

"So, thou hast come swiftly at my summons!" said Abbas, chuckling to himself; "and with a good appetite for the feast, I trust? for thou hast hunted down the fat quarry: and now cometh the banquet. Is it not so?" and he laughed again until the tears trickled down his face, as at some capital joke.

"Effendina! I know not why I was summoned. But it is my duty and my pleasure to respond promptly to my lord's call!"

"But thou hast a suspicion as to why thou wert sent for? Thou knowest that Abbas Pasha ever keeps faith, and fulfils his promises to the letter. Surely thou hast not forgotten mine to thee, when first we talked of the affairs of the late Khasnadar — now so happily concluded — in which thou hast more than exceeded thy part."

"Effendina, I remember everything!"

"Ay! Thou hast a good memory, I believe. Canst thou, now that the judgment hath been rendered, give me any clue to the hidden wealth of the Khasnadar? Thou mayest have met the Jew, Moussa in the courtyard? He pretends to know somewhat of its hiding place."

"Effendina! if any man does know, it is he. Did he reveal it?" he asked, eagerly, forgetting his caution, and the presence in which he stood, in his burning anxiety.

But Abbas did not take offence at the impertinence of the question. His good humor seemed impenetrable. He only rebuked the rash youth, as one would a forward child.

"Thou art here to answer questions, not to ask them!" he said; then added: "but I will indulge thy curiosity so far as to tell thee, that he doth give me information which is truly valuable. A wise man and a true one, indeed, is that old Yahudi! He hath improved my opinion of his people. But this concerneth not thee! Hast thou any information to impart to me? Any more useful treachery to sell? If not, our accounts might as well now be closed!"

"Effendina! I have told all I know, and have nothing more!" replied the Syrian, who did not fancy the snarling earnestness of the Viceroy's last remark, nor his manner, which seemed too soft and playful to be entirely natural.

So he thought it best not to protract the interview, but boldly said:

"Effendina intimated to his faithful servant that, now his work was done, his reward would be forthcoming. Shall I kiss his Highness's hand in token of thanks for his bounty?"

24 *

"But I promised thee the girl as well as the gold!" responded Abbas, seemingly much amused at the impatience of the Syrian to clutch the promised purses. "How can I give her to thee, when she hath disappeared like the Fairy Princess in the 'Thousand and One Nights'? Hast thou yet found any clue to her hiding-place?"

"Effendina! I have not. She has disappeared like a bubble in the air, or a circle on the water."

"Well, then, thou canst not blame me," said Abbas, still smiling, "if I pay thee but half of what is due thee!" Then turning to his chamberlain, gave him some instructions in a low voice, and dismissed the Syrian, saying:

"Go thou with Mahmoud Bey, who is an old friend of thine, and first introduced thee, who will conduct thee to my Khasnadar, who will give thee the half of thy reward — the other thou must find for thyself!"

Not quite satisfied with the ambiguous smile which accompanied these satisfactory words, Daoud followed the footsteps of Mahmoud Bey through the passage, and just as he emerged through the palace-door into the courtyard, felt himself suddenly seized — his arms pinioned to his sides by a strong cord which was flung over his head — was thrown on his face flat on the ground — his legs lifted in air, his slippers and stockings torn off in a twinkling, and the heavy blows of a palm stick fell thick and fast on the soles of his delicate feet, of which he was as careful and proud as a woman.

Utterly stunned and bewildered by the suddenness of the treachery, and writhing under the pain of the bastinado — one of the most terrible of Eastern punishments — the Syrian made no useless struggles, uttered no cry, but submitted with stoical fortitude to the pain, which was acute and agonizing, while the shame he felt at the degradation almost equalled the physical torture.

At length, blind and dizzy with the pain, his brain reeling, his feet beaten almost into a jelly, with sharp pains racking his spine and his whole frame — exhausted almost to fainting — his torturers ceased their blows, and rolled him over like a log, into a corner of the court-yard — for he found he was unable to rise or stand, upon making the attempt — and there they left him.

A mocking laugh from an upper window of the palace roused him from his dizzy swoon. He turned his blood-shot eyes in the direction of the sound, and saw Abbas Pasha standing there, above his head, looking down and apparently enjoying his wretched plight, as he had wit-nessed his punishment.

"Ho! ho!" laughed Abbas again, as he caught the eye of his victim. "Have I not kept my word? thou dog of great promises and small performances! who hast dared trifle with thy master, and sought to fill his eyes and ears with sand!

"Said I not that thou shouldst be paid half of what I promised thee? For thy two hundred purses thou hast had one hundred stripes of the bastinado — the other half I reserve the payment of, as thou shalt merit it. Go, now, and remember that, though thou art a sleek young tiger-cat, whose claws are sharp, thou shouldest not venture to play pranks with a full-grown tiger!

"Pray to thy saints soon to heal thy delicate and dainty feet, or bear thee to Cairo on their wings; else wilt thou not walk for many days to come!

"Consider thine account settled, unless thou shouldst prefer to call again for thy balance! — Ho! ho! ho! —

for after having seen thy feet, I care not ever to look upon thy face again !"

No word escaped the Syrian's lips ; no muscle of face or body moved, as he lay upon the ground, bruised, beaten and bloody, with the foam upon his pallid lips, and shame, agony, and impotent wrath gnawing at his heart.

But if looks could kill, the glances he shot from his dilating pupils at the man who mocked at his misery and laughed at his degradation, after having duped and betrayed him even worse than he had betrayed his former friends, that glance would have been as deadly as Medusa's.

He felt the hot blood surging up to his brain, as he realized the utter impotence of his wrath, and his thirst for vengeance on his smiling enemy, and, with a sound like the rushing of mighty waters booming in his ears, darkness came down over body, brain and heart, and he saw or felt no more — lying there more like the corpse than the living body of the baffled schemer, whose punishment was almost as great as his crime, coming, as it did, in the hour of his fancied triumph, and plunging him down from his highest heaven of hope into the deepest hell of despair.

The Viceroy looked coolly down on the inanimate form, then withdrew from the window, and took his way to his mother's apartments, still chuckling to himself at his own excellent practical joke.

The smile was still upon his face as he raised the curtain of the door, and passed into the hareem, where he found his mother, but not alone, for an unveiled female was sitting on the divan beside her.

Seeing this, Abbas was about to retire, when the

woman rose, disclosing the bold beauty of Nezlé Khanum ; and Abbas, coming forward, greeted her with great apparent cordiality, and took his seat beside the two women.

After the usual compliments had passed between Abbas and his kinswoman, the latter said :

"Thou hast the air of one, O Abbas ! that hath just heard pleasant tidings, or witnessed some amusing sight of late, for thou wast smiling when entering. Let us poor women, ever shut out from the sights abroad, share in thy mirth !"

"Truly it was but a small matter, O Khanum !" returned Abbas. "Yet, of a verity, fit food for mirth. I have just witnessed the paring of a wild-cat's claws ; and truly it was amusing !"

"Thou speakest in parables, my son, like a Santon at a tomb, or a Mollah in a mosque," said his mother, with the curiosity of old age, "with thy talk of wild-cats and other vermin ! What was the sight that so pleased thee ? Tell thine old mother !"

Thus solicited, Abbas, with grim humor, told the whole story of the Syrian, ending with the payment just made him ; suppressing, of course, the more material facts, which he did not desire to be known ; winding up with his parting remarks to Daoud.

Both the women seemed much amused by the recital ; but the small bright eyes of Nezlé Khanum never left the speaker's face after the name of Askaros had been mentioned in connection with the affair, and under her ready and noisy laughter might have been detected a sardonic twitching of the mouth, by a less preoccupied observer than Abbas.

When he had concluded, and they had all paid their

tribute to his good story, Nezlé, affecting to wipe from her eyes the tears which her laughter had caused, asked:

"And what became of the young wild-cat, after his claws were trimmed so adroitly?"

"Oh," said Abbas, "lying in the courtyard still, I suppose! The creature can crawl away when it has recovered sufficiently. I gave orders to my people not to interfere with it."

"Peki!" said the Khanum, "I wonder if it was the young man I saw coming in, as an old Yahudi left the courtyard, as I was looking down through your mother's window, half an hour since?"

"Most probably," responded Abbas, "my fair kinswoman, it was the same."

"He was very good-looking, then; beardless, with a smooth skin like a girl's, and the daintiest little hands and feet imaginable. Had I known what he was coming for, I should have interceded for him. Pretty boys are growing scarcer every day in this country."

"This one would have made a good Mameluke," said Abbas; "the very boy to watch one's slumbers, keep the flies off and hand the sherbet. I am sadly in want of some good ones."

"I am promised some from Stamboul soon," replied Nezlé, carelessly, "and if Effendina wants some, he may take his choice."

"Thanks," said Abbas. "We shall see, for we know thy taste to be good in all that appertains to youth and beauty — in our unworthy sex," he added, sarcastically.

But the mother of Abbas, who loved dearly the visits of the princess, who brought her all the latest gossip from the baths and hareems of Cairo, saw the rising storm on the brow of her guest, and the ominous flash in her eye at the equivocal compliment of Abbas, and hastened to divert it by turning the conversation into a less dangerous channel.

Abbas, too, whose love for the princess was by no means equal to his fear of her, seconded his mother in this hospitable intent, and apparently succeeded.

An hour later, when the Syrian revived from his death-like swoon, still weak, dizzy and faint with pain, exhaustion and excitement, he found himself to his surprise, lying in a small room attached to the hareem kitchens, with two stalwart black eunuchs taking charge of him, bathing his wounded feet with balms and unguents, and tending him with great care.

To his question as to whether they did this by the Viceroy's orders, they shook their heads, and one of them answered : —

"A high and noble lady, who hath seen thy piteous plight and compassionated thee, hath ordered us, her slaves, to bind up thy wounds and take thee safely home, which we are now ready to do, when thou art strong enough : for thy litter, since thou canst not ride, is now ready for thee without."

"Let us leave this Sheitan's den at once, then," said the Syrian, savagely, raising himself up from the divan on which they had laid him. The eunuchs glanced fearfully around, and placed their fingers on their lips, as though to warn the rash speaker that the walls might have ears ; but proceeded instantly to lift him up, since he could not stand — so swollen and useless were his bruised feet and discolored limbs — and to bear him to the outer air.

"What is the name of this kind lady who has taken pity on a bruised worm like me?" asked Daoud, as they carefully bore him forth and placed him on a litter, borne by two strong *hamals* (porters).

One of the eunuchs stooped down and whispered in his ear a name, on hearing which the Syrian's astonishment seemed to deprive him of speech, for he spoke no other word until safely deposited in his own house. Then, bestowing a liberal *backschisch* on the eunuch who had accompanied the litter on horseback, he dismissed him, with thanks to his mistress, to whom he tendered his future life-long services, in gratitude for her charity.

But when left alone, stretched on his divan in his own dreary house, he muttered savagely to himself through his clenched teeth, an Italian proverb:

"He laughs well who laughs last!"

CHAPTER XXV.

"THE OLD, OLD STORY."

SPRING had returned once more, the buds and blossoms were awaking again from their winter's sleep, and the soft winds whispered gently among the green foliage, and ruffled the smooth surface of the lagoons into mimic waves.

Venice, the ever desolate though ever lovely, was donning her summer robes again, and endowing herself with that fatal beauty, under which lurked the seeds of death for the imprudent stranger, whom her Circe-like spells beguiled to linger there.

The winter which had been passed by our friends, the Americans, in Venice, had witnessed some strange changes in that household; though the family still occupied the place they had leased for the winter months.

Sir Charles had succeeded in finding the Egyptian, the morning after their unexpected rencontre near the Bridge of Sighs, and had brought him to visit his former guests at Cairo; and the consequences of this intervention were very serious for all parties.

For the simple narrative of his misfortunes from the lips of the young Copt, and his present exile and desola.

tion, had so wrought on the excited heart, or the imagination of the young American girl, as entirely to overpower her judgment or cooler reason; and what had been a mere fancy before, soon developed itself into an ardent passion for the hero of her dreams.

She was too frank and too honest to conceal this change in her sentiments from him who had the best title to know it; and Sir Charles, though cut to the heart by her avowal that she found she could not love him well enough to be his wife, and wounded both in his pride and affection by his failure, was nevertheless too proud and too generous to urge his suit on cold or unwilling ears.

He left Venice abruptly the day after she had spoken to him; leaving a note for Mr. Van Camp, stating that his daughter would inform him why the engagement had been broken, as it had been solely on her urgent solicitation that he had abandoned a hope so dear to his heart. He further stated that he should never marry; but if at any future time he could be of service in any way to him, or his, they had only to call upon him, for he ever would cherish sentiments of the warmest friendship for Miss Van Camp and her father.

The old gentleman was both mystified and mortified on receipt of this note; and the spinster was furious. But Edith calmly and gravely assured them she had considered the matter thoroughly, and could not conscientiously wed a man she did not love.

So the old gentleman consoled himself with the thought that now he should keep his daughter; but Miss Priscilla mourned, as one not to be comforted, at the vanished dream of figuring among lords and ladies, and of presentation at foreign courts. Moreover, she saw, with eyes sharpened by disappointment, that as the figure of Sir

Charles receded from the foreground, that of the young Egyptian came forward ; and that on one pretext or the other, he was constantly either at the palace where they dwelt, or accompanying them in their excursions, and that Edith and himself conversed in so low a tone that it was impossible to hear what they were talking about.

These things disturbed the mind of the sagacious spinster, and she imparted her suspicions to her brother-in-law, who only pooh-poohed her, and resumed the after-dinner nap she had interrupted to make her confidential communication. So Miss Priscilla, though sorely disquieted, and not daring to interrogate Edith on the subject, whose temper had grown more and more uncertain, alternating bursts of fitful merriment with equally fitful periods of despondency, grimly watched and held her peace.

The *dénouement* came sooner than she had anticipated ; for one day Askaros came to visit them, with a face of unusual gravity and sadness, so that they feared he had received tidings of some new misfortune ; but it was quite the reverse, for he had received an intimation from the consul-general, who had befriended and protected him in Egypt, that the Viceroy had made a compact with him, that if Askaros would return, on payment of a stipulated number of purses to the Egyptian Government, they would quash all proceedings against his father's estate, placing him in full possession of all appertaining to him as heir, and acknowledging him as a *protégé*, and official of the foreign consulate-general, which would assure his personal safety. He was therefore urged to return immediately, to take charge of his interests. El Warda had enclosed a little note also, in which, among other matters of gossip, the fact was carelessly stated of the departure of Princess Nezlé for Constantinople, it was supposed by order of Abbas, with whom it was said she had quarrelled.

This news, which ought to have filled the young man's mind with joy, seemed to produce directly the contrary effect. He was sadder and more abstracted even than usual; and, strange to say, the fair Edith seemed to share in his despondency.

Seeing this, the young man was emboldened to speak again of his admiration — his love — for the fair American. And this time he was not repulsed, but listened to in silence he knew not how to interpret, as he wildly poured out the mingled agony and ecstacy of his soul, in the burning language of Eastern passion — until venturing to look up at the face which he worshipped, he saw something there that encouraged him to hope, and in a few moments more the "old, old story" had been wildly repeated, and as earnestly listened to as in any tale of true love: and the young Copt knew his love was returned.

It was hard to say whether the usual calm and composed father, or the eccentric aunt, was more horrified and indignant, when the young Egyptian formally repeated his proposal to them, adding that he was authorized to do so by Edith herself.

We pass by the stormy scenes that ensued — the indignant refusal by the father, the hysteric indignation of the aunt, the mute misery of Edith, whose dream was thus rudely broken, but who proved staunch to her strangely-selected lover. Mr. Van Camp broke up his establishment in Venice, and took his daughter away, forbidding her to correspond with Askaros on pain of his displeasure, or even to see him; which the half broken-hearted girl promised to obey, having never in her lifetime disobeyed her indulgent father, whose native Dutch obstinacy, once aroused, was impervious to argument or entreaty.

"If she had chosen any civilized man, however poor or obscure," he said, "I might have given my consent; but to marry an Egyptian savage — to mix the pure old Knickerbocker blood with that of an African ! — I would rather see her in her grave ! " So he hurried off the girl to Rome, to Naples, to Paris, seeking by change of scene and of society to divert her thoughts, and banish what he considered this insane freak from her mind ; but all in vain. Although the girl submitted with a patient sweetness to all his requisitions, and never complained, yet a settled sadness took possession of her. She lost color, appetite, spirits, sleep ; a hectic flush spread itself over her pale cheek, and a hacking cough, the herald of the insidious disease of which her mother had died, shook her enfeebled frame. The physicians whom he called in, gravely shook their heads, and advised a milder climate than Paris, where they then were — some recommending Nice, others Egypt — until the fond father fairly worried out, summoned his daughter to him one day, and told her that he repented of his rash declaration that he would sooner bury her than see her the wife of the Egyptian ; and, as the choice seemed to lie between the two things, he would allow her to choose the latter, if she still were of the same mind.

His only answer was the clasp of a pair of soft arms round his neck, while he was half smothered with kisses ; and wiping his eyes, in which unwonted moisture had gathered, he said :

"I know I am a fool in giving way to you; but it can't be helped."

25 *

Had the consulting physicians seen Edith the next morning, with hope once more in her eye and a fresh bloom on her cheek, which seemed to have grown round again in a night, they undoubtedly would have indefinitely postponed the voyage to Egypt they had before so strongly recommended.

Yet that was the voyage they were now preparing for ; and in two weeks' time Mr. Van Camp — with many forebodings as to the wisdom of the step he had been seduced into, sorely against his will and judgment — was sailing back, with his family, in one of the Peninsular and Oriental steamers, for the land of the Pharaohs once again.   Immediately after the peremptory rejection of his suit by the father of Edith, the young Askaros — reckless, and desperate, and careless now of what befell him — had returned to Alexandria, and there Mr. Van Camp expected to find him.

The spring by this time was well-nigh over, and the heats of summer were rapidly coming ; but at Alexandria they knew the sea-breeze tempered the rays of the sun, and that it was as cool as most European seaboard cities, and determined therefore to stop there, before proceeding to Cairo — since, through the consular agent, they could easily ascertain all they sought to know of the fortunes and fate of the young Egyptian.

CHAPTER XXVI.

THE VULTURE SCENTS HIS PREY.

AND thus it chanced, thanks to the consistent friendship of the consul-general, and the subtle skill of
the Israelite, as well as the precautions taken by his
father, that Askaros found his path smoothed for him,
on his return, and free to sit once more the master of his
own house, and the acknowledged heir of his father's
estate.

He had to pay a heavy price for this reinstatement, it
is true; but it took only a portion of the large fortune he
had inherited, and he still had enough left to make him
one of the richest among the wealthy class to which he
belonged.

El Warda refused to return to the dwelling of him
whom she and all the world knew not to be her brother,
but took up her residence with some distant kinsman.

Her unaffected happiness at his return made the young
man fonder of her even than before, and the increased
softness and tenderness of his manner toward her, caused
her heart to flutter wildly with newly-awakened hopes as
to the possibility of the formation of a newer and stronger
tie between them, now that the greatest barrier, in the
shape of the Frank woman, was removed. But the poor

girl's new waking dream of felicity was soon disturbed
and dissipated for ever, by the unexpected return of the
only woman on earth her gentle heart had at once hated
and feared.   For, with the return of the American party
to Egypt, and the renewed devotion of Askaros to the
girl of the azure eyes and sunny hair, the prophetic soul
of the loving girl warned her of the dissolution of that
dream.   Even had Askaros failed in his suit, El Warda
was not the woman to share a divided heart, or accept
the cinders of one consumed by a vain flame for another.
With the sad stoicism of the Indian widow, who mounts
the funeral pile prepared for her incremation while still
full of life and hope, El Warda, with true Oriental fatalism, meekly and heroically accepted her disappointment,
and sought, though vainly, to banish from her heart the
image that haunted it.

She became very religious — frequented the Coptic
convent much, and busied herself in works of piety and
charity, and seemed bent on seeking from heaven that
consolation, and that sweet hope in the future, which
earth seemed destined to deny her.

In the interval her more fortunate rival, under the
curative effect of hope restored and happiness secured,
again found the rose returning to her cheeks, the light to
her eye, the springiness to her step, and her gay laughter
gushed out once more, like the carolling of the bird that
swings itself on the spray, and chants from mere over-
flowing of its heart.

It was arranged that the marriage of Askaros Effendi
— for such was now his title as inheritor of the wide
lands and large fortune of his father — with the young
American girl should be solemnized at the Consulate
first, and afterward at the Coptic Church, as is the cus-

tom in all mixed marriages in Egypt. The only condition exacted by Mr. Van Camp, on consenting to the union, was the solemn promise, on the part of the Copt, that he would arrange his affairs in Egypt as speedily as possible, and make either Europe or America his permanent residence, only visiting Egypt from time to time, as his affairs demanded his presence there, on which occasions Edith was to be left in charge of her father.

Askaros, who, to secure Edith's hand, would have promised almost anything, cheerfully subscribed to these conditions, not being over anxious himself to remain in Egypt. Especially after he found the Princess Nezlé had returned, after a short visit to Constantinople, and was said to be in higher favor with Abbas than ever.

This he deemed the only cloud which lurked on his horizon — like most mortals blindly ignorant of the quarter whence the storm was to come.

There was no unnecessary delay interposed after these arrangements had been made, as Mr. Van Camp and his family were anxious to leave Egypt before the summer heats set in.

The marriage took place as agreed upon, the bride looking as lovely, and the bridegroom as self-conscious as is usual on such occasions. Among the first to congratulate her new sister was El Warda, who, while pressing a kiss on her fair brow, threw around her neck a costly string of Oriental pearls. Although looking paler and thinner than when Edith had last seen her, she had become more lovely, her face having gained in expression what it had lost in girlish gayety, and while more serious and thoughtful, was not sad — but with a sweet resignation stamped upon it, like that of a saint. At the same time she made her gift, she presented the bride also with a bouquet of choice flowers, all virgin white, and exhaling a rich perfume.

"I can bring my brother's bride no rich gifts," she said, in a low sweet voice; "but I bring her these pearls; and these flowers — white as her face, pure as her soul, sweet as her lips, but sooner to fade than her affections. Next to him I hope to hold a place in her sister's heart, if she will find a nook in it for a poor ignorant Egyptian girl, who loves both very dearly?"

Edith, moved to tears, she knew not why, by the simple pathos of the girl's speech and manner, though not suspecting the deeper tenderness that was veiled under that sisterly affection, responded warmly, and while kissing her dark cheek, urged the girl to share their home, as a sister should, both in Egypt and abroad. But El Warda gratefully, yet firmly refused.

"I thank you from my heart, O wife of my brother!" she said; "but my ways of life are not as yours, neither are my pleasures nor my tastes. I should only be an encumbrance on your household, and miserable myself, trying to live like a Frank. I shall live and die in Egypt, which is my home, and I have no desire to see strange people and strange lands. My own suit me best. It is more than probable that I shall take my place in one of the convents of my people, for I shall never marry. So trouble not yourself, nor allow my brother to be troubled about the little Copt girl; who will be very happy in her own way, although that way be very different from yours. Now, may Sitta Mariam protect you both, and guard this house from evil spirits and evil men!"

Stooping, she impressed a light kiss on the bride's forehead, and, ere she could reply, had glided from the apartment and the house, returning to her own residence.

Left alone, for her husband had gone to the door to bid farewell to his wedding guests, the young bride fell into a reverie; the strangeness of the new situation impressing her like the repetition of one of her day-dreams in Venice, when she first began to listen to the whispers of her own heart.

A sound like the whirring of wings aroused her. Something brushed her sunny curls, settled down upon her shoulder, and rubbed its soft head against her cheek, with a cooing sound. She saw it was one of the Barbary doves of Askaros, and the moment after the young man passed through the door, laughing.

"I thought I would surprise you with an unexpected visitor," he said. "Do you not recognize the bird you saved on the Ezbekieh, when chased by a hawk? He is rightly your property, since his life would have been forfeited but for the shelter of your bosom. Now he is yours by a double right, for all that is mine is yours also. From whatever point you let him go, he will come back here. Recollect this: for who knows but you may want to use him, when carried off by some one of the Genii, or some wicked prince, and imprisoned in an enchanted castle."

Edith replied in the same tone of badinage, and the conversation turned on their friends, who had embarked for Marseilles immediately after the marriage and ceremony that morning, from Alexandria.

"What are they doing now, I wonder?" said Edith, wistfully.

"Let me look into my magic mirror, and I will tell you!" said Askaros, with mock solemnity; and gravely pouring out some ink into the hollow of her hand, in imitation of the Cairene magician who mystified the travellers at the hotels, he peered earnestly into it. "I see," he said, "an elderly gentleman lying flat upon his back, and resisting the importunities of the steward to come to dinner. I see a young gentleman, smoking a strong cigar with no relish, and a very pale face, whose sea-legs are nothing to speak of, but who stoutly stumbles over the deck, getting entangled in coils of rope, and having his eyes blessed by the sailors. I see also a maiden lady, lying on what looks like a cupboard-shelf, fearfully sick — let us say, at soul — and peering anxiously at the 'old willow pattern,' in the bottom of what might be, but is not a soup-tureen! And I see also a stewardess tendering her a tumbler containing a mahogany-colored liquid, fearfully like brandy and water. All this I see, O lady fair! accompanied with much movement, and shaking up and down, and salt spray, and scalding steam; and the vision vanishes!"

It was as Askaros had humorously described it. Her relatives were all tossing on the Mediterranean, and Edith, for the first time in her life absent from them all, left to the society of her Haroun-el-Reschid, did not appear disconsolate at such desertion, unnatural as it may seem.

The days glided on, and the weeks moved noiselessly past, guided by the fleet velvet-footed hours, until there remained but one week more of their honeymoon, at the expiration of which Askaros was pledged to return to Europe, his affairs having been put in a satisfactory condition, and the settlement with the Egyptian Government completed.

Abbas had even condescended so far as to permit the consul-general to bring Askaros in his suite on a visit, and had allowed the Copt to kiss his hand, making some

gracious speech to him at the time, which the blackness
of his brow contradicted ; for Abbas never either forgot or
forgave, had a tenacious memory and much patience.

He had encountered the Viceroy on another occasion.
As he was driving out his wife one evening on the great
Shoubra road, under the grand old trees planted by
Mehemet Ali, in his American wagon presented by the
younger Van Camp, he met the cavalcade of the Viceroy,
which came thundering down the road from those wonderful gardens, now the property of the generous young
prince Halim Pasha.

Recognizing the royal cortége, Askaros drew up to one
side of the road to let it pass, as is the etiquette.

First came the mounted guards in rich uniform, then
the Viceregal carriage. Abbas was sitting in an open
calèche, the hood thrown back, with one of his ministers
sitting on the front seat.

As he passed he recognized the salutation of Askaros
by no movement or look: but a sudden gleam came into
his dull vulture-like eyes, as it fell on the fair face and
golden hair of his companion, and a dark flush reddened
his swarthy face. He stared hard at the unexpected apparition, with a bold unflinching gaze, which disconcert-
ed its object, and brought the bright color to her face,
neck, and bosom, giving a fresher glow to her beauty.
Then he leaned forward, and seemed eagerly to interrogate the official riding with him, and, turning his head,
again gazed back until the winding road hid them from
each other's view.

"Is that the Viceroy!" asked Edith, a cold chill
creeping over her, she knew not why, as memory brought
back the scene of the serpent presence visibly to her
eyes, when she had experienced a similar sensation.

26

"It is the Viceroy," answered Askaros, whose face, light and joyous the moment before, now wore a sombre and pre-occupied expression.

"What an evil face he has!" added Edith.

"Not more evil than his nature, of which it is the reflection," answered the young man.

"How he stared at me! In an European it would have been absolutely rude. But I suppose," she added, laughing, "as the Turks think women have no souls, and also that an unveiled woman has no modesty, and only uncovers her face to be looked at, his manners are Turkish, and must be pardoned."

She turned in surprise, for her husband neither echoed her laugh, nor replied to her remark, and the serious expression of his face alarmed her.

"What is the matter?" she asked, anxiously. "Are you ill? or what has happened to worry you? I hope you did not take seriously my complaint about that ugly old man's staring at me; for, sir," she added, saucily, "a great many old, and young gentlemen too, will stare at the pretty young wife of Askaros Effendi, or Monsieur Askaros, when they return to Europe; and I am sure I won't mind it very much, if you don't."

But even the raillery of Edith, for the first time, seemed to fail in awakening a corresponding cheerfulness in the heart or in the manner of Askaros. Although he made an effort to appear lively, his gayety was forced, and his laugh hollow; and the remark he made on reaching home did not tend to reassure his young wife.

"Safe at home at last!" he said. "Truly sung your American poet, whose song echoes over the world:

‘ There's no place like home!’

But I vow a silver candlestick to the shrine of Sitta Mariam, on the day that sees us safe out of this accursed country."

When pressed by Edith to disclose the reason of his disquietude, he first evaded the subject, but being urged more strenuously by those soft lips he could never resist, he accounted for his gravity, by telling her he had that day received the news that his protector, the consul-general, was to be transferred to another mission very shortly, leaving to replace him an old and timid man, as acting-consul, until his successor arrived.

"This would be a bad thing for me, were my affairs still unsettled," added Askaros; "but it matters little now, as we shall probably leave Egypt before he does."

And so the matter dropped.

CHAPTER XXVII.

THE CEREMONY OF THE DOSEH.

ANOTHER week had passed, unmarked by any event of importance, and, as the cloud had quickly passed from the brow of Askaros, and its shadow from his soul, the young wife forgot the vague apprehensions his conduct had inspired, and was as gay and happy as a bird again — carolling through the spacious old palace, and flitting over it, like a winged thing — all life and joy and hope.

For, within a few days' time she was to leave Egypt with her husband, to rejoin her father and family, and pass the summer in Germany, and autumn in Italy — not to return again to Egypt until the ensuing year.

Askaros, too, seemed rejuvenated by the prospect of speedy departure, and the two romped together like boy and girl, through the spacious apartments of the solemn old palace, to the great amazement of the staid and lazy old servants — Ferraj included — who could not comprehend how any one could take pleasure in running about, when they might enjoy *"keff"* sitting still, smoking and eating sweetmeats — the Arab idea of supreme felicity.

The large-eyed silent Copt women, who came to see the new wife of Askaros, sat and stared silently at the strange Frank woman, smoked their pipes, ate their sweet-meats, sipped their lemonade — and never came a second time.

Turkish hareems she held in horror — the visit to that of the princess having entirely satisfied her curiosity.

Nezlé Khanum sent her a message to come and see her; but Askaros made her decline it, on the plea of illness, which did not deceive that astute lady, who laughed to herself, and said :

" The boy is afraid to send his little white doll to me ! Is hè afraid I may poison her ? or does he have the vanity to think I have not forgotten his existence, long ago, though I was angry at the time, and for a long time after-ward? I really believe that young Syrian Abbas treated so shamefully, is the better-looking, after all ! But I have had enough of boys: ripe fruit is better than green. But this baby of Askaros' shall see me again, in spite of his wise precautions ! "

In pursuance of which determination, Nezlé, whose love of intrigue and trickery amounted almost to insanity, disguised herself as a *Dellab,* or saleswoman, and piloted by the Frenchwoman, actually visited the house of Aska-ros, and saw and spoke to his unconscious wife through her interpreter.

" What fools these men are ! " she said, with a roar of laughter, while the obsequious Frenchwoman was divest-ing her of her disguise, on her return to her own palace. " Why, Askaros might have taken El Warda, who was dying of love for him ; and she was worth a dozen of that faded-looking *Ingleeze,* both in looks and character. *Wallah !* what fools the men are, indeed."

And so, the princess buried her indignation against her former lover in contempt for his bad taste. Cruel and

26 * U

unscrupulous as she was, she was equally capricious: and both her fancy for, and resentment against the young Copt had now died away, having been obliterated by other intrigues, without which she could not live. In fact, the courage displayed by the young man, in effecting his escape on that memorable night, as well as the fidelity with which he had guarded the secret of his intrigue with her, no whisper of which had ever got abroad, or reached the Cairene gossips, had inspired her with a feeling of respect for him which was almost friendly. But of this he knew nothing, and looked to that quarter as the one from whence all the clouds on his horizon came.

About this time there was an unusual gathering one morning on the Ezbekieh, and Edith, who was riding on horseback, accompanied by her husband, noticed it, as also the great apparent excitement of the people, who seemed to have deserted their ordinary occupations, and streamed out in crowds toward the gate, which opened on the road leading to Boulak.

She observed also in this crowd many wild-looking figures, naked to the waist, with only a sheepskin round the loins, whose wild haggard faces, and long matted hair, hanging from unshaven heads, made them unlike any of the residents of Cairo she had seen before.

On inquiry, Askaros told her these were *Santons*, or saints — grim fanatics who dwelt in caves or the open air, and lived on alms bestowed by pious Mussulmans, chiefly women, who considered their prayers as specifics against illness, and all the troubles of life, and who were such privileged characters, that even were one of them to kill a man, the common people would not seek their punishment.

The wild-looking howling dervishes, whom she had seen performing their strange rites — not entirely unlike those of the American "Shaking Quakers" — who also wore their hair in long elf-locks, and were clad only in long loose gowns, with high conical caps, were likewise out in great force.   Edith, therefore, rightly judged it was some religious ceremony or festival that was in agitation : which opinion Askaros confirmed, informing her that the procession of pilgrims or *Hadjis*, from Mecca, was to enter that gate, headed by the *Sheik-ul-Islam*, or spiritual chief of the pilgrimage.

He further explained that the return would be signalized by the annual ceremony of the Sheik's riding over the bodies of a lane of living men, mounted on horseback, and that the *Hadjis* were supposed to obtain a remission of their sins by submitting to the test; since it was a mark of the displeasure of Allah, if during the performance of this miracle any person was killed or seriously injured.

This ceremony was called the *Doseh*, and would take place that day, over the space leading from the Ezbekieh to the gate before mentioned, a distance of about one hundred and fifty yards.

"What a terrible sight it must be!" said Edith.   "Let us hasten home to avoid it.   I would not look upon such a sight for worlds.   And the looks of those wild people terrify me so.   Come, let us go back."   And giving her horse the rein, they turned back from the Ezbekieh, and rode rapidly home again.   "And they call this religion!" said Edith, shuddering, "and think such cruel sacrifices can be acceptable to a God of mercy, whom we know to be a God of love.   Well may we echo the cry of Madame Roland in the French revolution, 'O Liberty, what crimes are committed in thy name!' and apply it to religion — if we can call a terrible superstition like this by so holy a name."

Askaros fully shared in her indignation and disgust at such a profanation, the native Christians in the East retaining much of the old Scriptural belief in the active agency of devils and other evil spirits in human affairs, which European faith has discarded. But he informed her also, that it was his unpleasant duty to accompany the consul-general on his official visit to that ceremony after mid-day, it being his policy, for the moment, to identify himself with the Consulate as much as possible. He told her the sight would be a novel one to him also, as he had carefully avoided seeing it hitherto, and would not now, were it not compulsory upon him; having ever regarded it as a kind of devil-worship, or shadow of the old heathen practice of human sacrifice, to propitiate their cruel divinities.

At the appointed hour, however, he accompanied the consular cortége, and found himself, with them, provided with a place in a large window in a house overlooking the scene, at which the Sheik was to dismount after his fearful ride. Glancing his eye over the places reserved for the high officials, he observed that the Viceroy was not present, although represented by several of his Ministers. This he considered strange, for the cruel nature of Abbas delighted in such exhibitions, and he had revived, under his reign, the rigor of these rites, discouraged by his more humane grand-father and his more civilized kinsmen.

This was the strange scene they saw, to which earth can offer no parallel, save in the procession of the car of Juggernaut, in the remoter East — a kindred superstition, yet more bloody and cruel than the Doseh, because involving a greater loss of life.

In the open space below was packed a dense crowd of people, of all classes and conditions, from the Bey or Pasha, on splendid Arab charger, with crimson velvet saddle and housings, and jewelled head-stall, to the respectable merchant, decently clad ; thence lower down to the half-naked *Fellah* in blue shirt, or totally naked *Santon* or *Fakeer*, half-crazed with fanatical frenzy or self-imposed privation.

Under the trees of the Ezbekieh might be seen the adroit Eastern jugglers plying their trade, and exhibiting wonderful feats in the open air. Dancing-girls and singing-girls also were posturing and screaming to excited audiences ; for all police rules are relaxed, and all is license on the day of the Doseh.

Snake-charmers were also there, who not only played with huge cobras, in the midst of a circle ranged at respectful distance around, but bit and tore with their teeth pieces out of the writhing reptiles, which they seemed to swallow, almost maddening under the effects of their poisonous meal.

Other jugglers there were: swordsmen who not only went through the sword-exercise and mimic gladiatorial conflicts, but thrust knives and swords through different parts of their own naked bodies and cheeks, until they were skewered with them ; but no drop of blood flowed, yet the illusion of the trick was perfect.

Over all this crowd rose the confused hum of the sound of many voices ; the deep gutturals of the Arab men blending with the shrill shrieks of the women, and the hoarse cries of the jugglers and Santons, mingled with the discordant sounds of the rude Egyptian music, accompanying the singers and the dancing-girls.

It was as confused a bedlam of sounds as of sights: but suddenly silence fell on the noisy wrangling crowd, a stillness so sudden and so deep that any single voice could have been distinctly heard, and all eyes were strained toward the open gate, through which was now borne on the breeze the dull muffled sound of the *darabuka*, or fish-skin drum, announcing the approach of the returning pilgrims.

They had not long to wait; for soon there passed under the arch of the gate the sacred camel, white as snow, and richly caparisoned, with a kind of turret on his back, in which were the holy carpet and the sacred palm-branches — the *mahmal*.

Then followed a long succession of camels and horses, with men mounted upon them, and on foot the *Hadjis*, or pilgrims, made holy by their visit to the sacred city of Mecca, purified by prayer, and absolved from earthly sins by that pilgrimage.

Then came riding on a strong white horse a large heavy man with a stolid face, richly dressed, on whom all eyes centred, for he was the Sheik who was to ride that horse over a lane of living bodies, from the gate even to the house wherein sat Askaros among the officials.

There was a movement in the crowd, and a lane was quickly formed, as if by magic, in the very midst of that mass of humanity, apparently so compactly jammed and wedged together but a moment before, that it had seemed impossible to make space for a child to pass between them. A living wall was promptly formed on each side of this new lane, composed of the dusky bodies of the spectators who stood back, leaving space enough for a man to lie at length across the road. Very soon that strange living pavement was laid down by men who took the bodies and ranged them, like logs, side by side on the path thus made, the head of one alternating with the feet of the other, and the bodies packed down and levelled so as to present the smoothest possible surface, no leg or arm being allowed to display itself. The men came forward voluntarily, many from the surrounding crowd, others from the Hadjis, or pilgrims. Askaros observed that most of the men looked as though drunk with excitement, or drugged with opium, foam hanging from the lips of many, and the eyes of most of them dull and bloodshot.

Still this strange work went on. Still the only sound which broke the silence was the dull monotonous beat of the drum. Still the Sheik sat motionless on his white horse, a man on either side supporting him on his saddle, in which he swayed heavily from side to side, like one half drunk or half asleep.

The preparations seemed now complete, and there was a dead pause : then the drum beat faster, and the attendants of the Sheik urged the reluctant horse to take his first step on the slippery footing of human bodies, over which his path lay.

The horse, more humane than his rider, recoiled and refused, snorting with terror ; but the attendants and the crowd forced him on, and led by one man dragging at his bridle-reins, scourged by another from behind, while two men ran alongside over the bodies, supporting the swaying Sheik in his saddle, the heavy horse, shod with iron, bearing the heavy man, commenced his terrible journey, passing slowly over the bodies which packed the path to the house, a distance of full one hundred and fifty yards.

Every forward step the horse took he appeared to recoil, throwing back the whole weight on his haunches; but, forced onward by the attendants, would put down first one forefoot, then the other, cautiously, like one treading upon ice. Whether his recoil crushed the unfortunate human beings on whom his full weight thus was thrown, and on whom his hind feet rested, was impossible to be discerned; for the crowd closed in so fast behind the feet of the charger, and bore the half lifeless forms so swiftly away, that Askaros, from his elevated position, could not tell whether any injury were done to life or limb by this terrible test. The pride and vanity of relatives and friends, too, came thus in aid of this priestly juggle; for naturally no one liked it to be said or known that the displeasure of Allah had fallen or been visited on one of his kindred or friends; so if the men were hurt, their injuries were concealed, not revealed. Askaros thought he could detect blood mingled with the froth which streaked the lips of some of these poor deluded wretches, but whether from excitement or internal injuries he could not judge. Others he saw leap up briskly, and pass into a circle of congratulating friends, who seemed to have made their venture in perfect possession of their faculties; but the great majority seemed to have been drugged so heavily, as to be incapable of any active exertion of mind or body.

Such, he soon saw, was the case with the Grand Sheik himself, who, on dismounting in the courtyard of the house after his dreadful ride, had to be lifted rather than assisted from his horse; and, as he stood erect that the faithful might kiss the hem of his sacred robe, or the fat hand that hung down heavily and nervelessly by his side, he rocked and reeled like a drunken man, and his eye presented that dead, dull appearance, peculiar to the opium or haschish-eater, when the vision of external objects is entirely lost, and both brain and body are in the somnambulist condition.

So looked the Sheik after his ride ; and Askaros felt more respect for our common humanity, when he saw that even such fierce fanaticism could not war against Nature in this great outrage upon her laws, without the artificial aid of drugs, to stifle the voice of conscience, and nerve him to his repulsive task, which doubtless he deemed a duty and religious obligation.

But the crowd manifested the greatest reverence for the chief actor in this cruel scene, which, to them, was a sacred one.

27

CHAPTER XXVIII.

THE ·SEARCH THROUGH THE NIGHT.

THE Doseh was over; the crowd dispersed, and the officials departed. Askaros, after accompanying the *cortége* back to the consular residence, impatiently turned his steps toward his own house, to sun himself in the smiles of his young wife, and seek an antidote, in her society, for the disgust and depression the scenes he had just witnessed had inspired in his breast.

It was about sunset when he reached his house, and great was his disappointment at not finding Edith there to welcome him, which was the more singular since she had never before ventured out without his protection. No one could tell whither she had gone; but his anxiety was dispelled when he learned she had been accompanied, not only by an old and confidential servant, who was a kind of house-keeper, but by Ferraj and another man-servant also. He was told they had only left the house half an hour before his reaching it.

A little annoyed, and inspired by a vague uneasiness, which he condemned himself for as childish, Askaros restlessly paced up and down the long apartment, unable to sit, smoke, or read, vexed at himself for the nervous feeling he could not conquer, and almost irritated against

314

his young wife, for the first time, for the disquiet she was occasioning him.

Vainly did he reason with himself against the presentiment of evil, and the cloud of some coming sorrow, which rested like a black shadow over his soul, and which he imputed to the morbid frame of mind induced by the spectacle he had seen that day. But his reason and judgment were not strong enough to dissipate this shadow; and as the evening wore on, and his wife did not return, nor her attendants come back to notify him of the cause of her detention, his uneasiness rose to keen anxiety, and his nervousness increased to such an extent that he found himself utterly unable longer to endure it, and he felt he must go forth to seek her, and gain relief from his own suspense by active search for her.

The vague presentiment of evil, which had in the beginning been as formless and shapeless as that phantom thing of unutterable horror shadowed forth by the greatest genius of modern romance, in his "Dweller on the Threshold," now began, like that loathsome thing, to assume shape and form, and his busy fancy, under the inspiration of fear, conjured up terrible images of woe and horror. Almost every description of accident or outrage which could be visited upon a frail, timid woman, and an infidel, by the hands of the crazy fanatics let loose on the city on this day of unbridled license, ran riot in his imagination; and he shuddered as he recalled to his memory many of the repulsive and frenzied faces of those fanatics which he had seen in the crowd that day, any one of whom would deem he did Allah a service by slaying or maltreating an infidel woman and a Frank.

True, Ferraj was with her, and would protect her. Yet he was only one man, and powerless against numbers. A thrill of fierce anger against Ferraj and the female servant alternated with the grief at his heart. Why had they not warned Edith of the danger of going out that day? They well knew it! and he cursed the blind obedience of Eastern slaves, which made them renounce almost the right and the exercise of independent thought in such cases as this.

But had anything really happened, one of the servants would have come back to tell the tale. He was 'disquieting himself idly. Edith had only gone to visit El Warda, feeling lonely in his absence, and not knowing how soon he would return. What a fool he was to torture himself needlessly! He would go to the house of El Warda forthwith, where he was sure to find Edith, and they would have a good laugh over his imaginary terrors, of which he began to feel ashamed; yet there was a sinking sensation at his heart which belied these hopeful thoughts. Having formed his determination, he proceeded hastily to carry it out, and, leaving a message for Edith, in case she should return in his absence, strode away in the direction of the house where El Warda resided, which was not far distant.

With hope and fear fluttering wildly at his heart, he reached the house, and to his eager inquiries the Boab responded that the Sitta Edith had not been there that day, he was quite sure, and that the Sitta El Warda herself had not been home since mid-day.

"They are together, then, somewhere," said Askaros to himself, catching at that hope, after the first cold thrill of disappointment had passed; "perhaps at the Coptic convent. I will see."

Arrived at the convent, he was told, in answer to his inquiry, that El Warda was there, but not his wife, whom they had not seen. He asked to see El Warda, and learned from her, to his surprise, that she had neither seen nor heard from Edith that day; but suggested she was in the habit of visiting the American missionaries' wives very often, and might have gone there.

Askaros caught at the idea, and rushed off immediately to the Syrian quarter, where dwelt the missionaries, to reach which he had to cross the Ezbekieh, as it was on the opposite side of the city.

To his inquiries there, at each house successively, the same response, "She had not been there!"

Turning his footsteps homeward, he consoled himself with the thought that while he was racing over Cairo after his wife, she, doubtless, had returned home, and was impatiently awaiting his return also. At the thought, he quickened his pace, and almost gayly ran through the garden on reaching his house, framing some tender reproach for her as he went.

But a bolt of ice seemed to penetrate his heart when the Boab, in response to his eager question, answered:

"*Sitta barra — Moosh foak!*" (The lady is out — not come home).

He staggered against the door, and gasped for breath, like one who has received a deadly blow. A horrible thought crept into his brain, and curdled his blood.

"Could the vengeance of the Princess Nezlé have taken this direction, and stricken him in the point she knew the most vulnerable? Were his pleasant vices, by a dreadful retribution, thus to be made the whips to scourge him?"

His hair bristled on his head at the thought of Edith's being in the power of the wicked woman, whom, in the

27 *

revulsion of his sentiments from fondness to loathing, he
believed fully capable of the commission of any crime.

Had she not warned him that her hate was as strong as
her love, and her vengeance sure against all who offended
her! By a refinement of cruelty, might she not have
seized his heart, his soul, and keep it in her hands to
torture? Nay, was not her purpose already effected, and
the commencement of her triumph insured by the torture
he was then undergoing? Might not she, adept as she
was in cruelty, protract the agonies of that suspense until
they became unendurable — until his brain gave way under
the intolerable pressure which weighed upon it, and her
work ended, as with her own father, in the madness of
the victim? Was he not on the eve of going mad now?
for he felt the hot blood surging up into his head, and
bounding madly through his arteries, while his eyeballs
were injected with blood, and his brain grew incapable
of connected thought — one idea, like the echo of a
cuckoo-clock, alone ringing through his mind:

"Go and find her at Nezlé's palace! Save her from
the tigress!"

All that has taken so long to describe, passed with
electric rapidity through the mind of Askaros as he leaned
against the door of his own dwelling, after receiving the
Boab's answer.

Raising himself suddenly from that support, the astonished Boab saw him rush wildly back through the
garden-path by which he had come, heard the gate close
heavily behind him, as, with despair in his heart, and
desperate resolve on his face strained almost to insanity,
and with wild bloodshot eyes, which seemed not to see
the objects before them, but to be strained on vacancy,
the half maddened husband staggered forth like an in-

toxicated man into the starless night, bent on carrying out his desperate resolve of rushing again into the den of the tigress, from which he had before so narrowly escaped.

The night was an unusual one for Cairo, for it was a stormy and a black one. Neither moon nor star was visible in the black rack of clouds which obscured the sky, and hung, like a pall, over the still city, as though the angry heavens frowned on the place and people who had offended them by the spectacle of that day. From the side on which lay the desert came a low moaning sound, with a puff of hot air — the breath of the distant Khamseen then howling over the desert; and blood-red gleams on the black sky, in the same direction, followed by fitful flashes of forked lightning, showed there was a tempest brewing in the elements, as well as raging in the soul of the solitary man, who swept along on his mad errand, heedless of all the presages of earth, air, and sky, regardless of the coming storm, and as fully possessed by devils which rent and tore heart, body, and brain, as was ever demoniac in Holy Writ.

On through the deserted city, he rushed out upon the road to Boulak. The hot wind from the desert, bearing its fiery sand with it, swept wildly over the open country, and with it, for the first time in seven years, rushed down a deluge of rain, which excited mothers, crouching in the half-opened doors of their mud-huts, were showing their astonished younger children, who had never seen such a sight before as water falling from heaven !

The forked lightning following the crashing thunder, which pealed like artillery, played around the distant dome and minarets of the Citadel, and lit up with a lurid glare the rushing river, the sharp cones of the Pyramids,

and the solemn stone face of the Sphinx, looming out
more weird-like and ghastly under this spectral light.

But all these sights and sounds of terror were unheeded
by the solitary living creature to be seen on that deserted
road — every dumb animal, as well as man, having
sought shelter — who rushed on regardless of howling
Khamseen wind, burning into his brain — of rain that
drenched him through his thin garments — or lightning-
flash that played around his head, striking sometimes a
palm-tree close at hand, whose shivered boughs and scattered dates would strike him.

Onward ! ever onward he rushed, on as wild a race
and in almost as spectral a shape as the horseman of
Bürger's ballad, who sought also his bride — but to bear
her from this to another world — until the fire in his
brain could sustain his failing limbs no longer against
fatigue and exposure to the elements, while the fever riot-
ing in his blood was fed by the poisonous Khamseen wind,
scorching brain and marrow.   But still he staggered forward — until, as he reached the central market of Boulak,
yet pressing on toward that fatal palace, the earth reeled
under his feet as in an earthquake, and he fell, stretched
on the ground, without sense or motion, just as the Muezzin's cry proclaimed the midnight hour.

At early dawn a party of Fellahs bringing their produce to the market, found lying there the body of a man,
not dead, for the breath came gaspingly from the laboring chest, but sore stricken with fever, and when they
sought to question him, raving wildly, in their own and
strange tongues, of secret foes and deadly perils to be
met and conquered.   Among his ravings their quick ears
caught the name of Nezlé Khanum — on which they

shook their heads, and imitated to each other the sipping of a cup of coffee — in suggestion of poison.

Finding him richly dressed, with a precious ring on his finger, they summoned the Sheik of the quarter, who caused him to be placed upon a litter, and conveyed to Cairo, where he was placed in the mosque called the *Mauristan*, the madhouse of that city, where he would be kept until his friends should claim him — nothing found on his person indicating who he was, or whence he came.

And there for the present we must leave him, resuming his interrupted search for the lost wife — so nearly now a widow.

V

CHAPTER XXIX.

DAOUD-BEN-YOUSSOUF.

ALARMED, she knew not why, by the sudden apparition of Askaros at the convent, and his sudden departure, as well as by the evident excitement of his face and manner, El Warda, whom the storm had kept a close prisoner at the convent all night, early next morning repaired to the house of her brother, to reassure herself, half ashamed of her own apprehensions.

For, with the suddenness common in these climes, the storm of the past night had sobbed itself to rest, far away in the great desert of Sahara, and the only traces left of its visit on the preceding night were the scattered boughs of the trees, and unusual dampness of the earth in the garden which surrounded the house of Askaros.

Above, the sky was as blue and clear, and the golden sunshine as bright, as though the storm had only been a bad dream; and the young girl's spirits rose in harmony with the freshness and gladness of earth and sky.

Blessed privilege and faculty of youth! to bathe itself in the influences of external nature: to which it draws more near than in later years, when hope and joy revisit not so readily the barren fields of the wearied heart,

322

strewn with the ashes of many of their flowerets, which once bloomed and blossomed there; and memory haunts the shrines her younger and brighter sisters were wont to occupy, and send forth their oracles in vague thoughts and wishes, all the more enchanting because of their indistinctness.

So the young El Warda, her calm countenance reflecting the serenity of her soul, soothed by the fresh beauty of the morning, half smiled to herself at the disquietude her brother's visit had given her the previous night, as she walked slowly up the garden-path. But the smile faded from her face when the Boab told her that neither the Effendi nor the Sitta had returned home the previous night, adding, in a mysterious whisper, "but Fatima (the female servant) came back this morning at dawn, and has strange things to tell."

With an ominous sensation of having to hear of some dreadful thing, El Warda pushed past the Boab, and ran up into the house to the apartment of Fatima, whom she found sitting on the floor, rocking herself to and fro in an agony of grief, and wailing at times, as though following a funeral.

At the presence of her young mistress, of whom she was very fond, the old woman ceased her moan, rose to her feet, and seizing the hand of the young girl, pressed and kissed it fervently; then resumed her seat, and her wailing once more, like one who mourns, not to be comforted.

Alarmed, more than words can tell, by this conduct on the part of one usually so stoical as the old Copt woman, El Warda first sought to tranquillize her, and then, in broken fragments, extracted from her the strange story she had to tell.

It seemed that on the previous evening, about an hour before sunset, while Edith was sitting in her own room, with Fatima in attendance, playing with her Barbary dove, which had been made a great pet by her, she received a letter that seemed to give her great pleasure, which she told the woman was from her friends in Europe, who were then daily expecting her to join them. She had taken a small gold pencil which hung to a chain suspended round her neck with other trinkets — a gift from Askaros — and was sketching on the blank page of the letter a rude outline of the steamer she expected to sail in, to give Fatima an idea of it, she never having seen any boat larger than a *dahabieh*, when a messenger was announced, who would deliver his message only to Edith herself.

The man being ordered to come in, presented himself and said he was, as he seemed to be, one of the native *Dragomen*, who swarm about the hotels, to act as guides to travellers. He spoke a little French, and explained in that language that he had been sent by the landlord of the Hotel d'Orient to say to the wife of Askaros Effendi that an accident had happened to her husband — how, he did not precisely know — and that he was then lying there under charge of a physician. The landlord had further bid him say that as the wife might wish to come immediately to her husband, who could not be removed, he had sent a carriage for her, that she might do so, and that Askaros, though severely, was not dangerously hurt.

The man added this was all he knew, and that the carriage awaited her at the end of the street opening on the *Mooskie.*

Edith, immediately rising up in great agitation, declared her intention of going at once, gave the man a liberal *backschisch*, and, accompanied by Fatima as well as by Ferraj, who insisted on taking another man with them, followed the Dragoman through the garden and up the narrow streets leading to the *Mooskie*.

They had gone about half the distance, and were in one of the narrowest streets, which was perfectly deserted, when their conductor gave a low whistle, a door suddenly opened from what seemed a hareem wall, and six black eunuchs, well armed, rushed out, and threw cloaks over the head of her mistress and herself, and bore them rapidly away to a carriage at the end of the street, in which they were conveyed, bound and gagged for what seemed to her a great distance, though in what direction, in her confusion, was impossible to tell. When they stopped, she as well as her mistress was lifted out, and where they took the latter she had no means of knowing, as she had never seen her since.

She had heard the clash of arms when first seized, and supposed that Ferraj and the other slave had made some resistance, and been overpowered. She herself had been left lying all night on the floor of a room. She was given food, but her eyes had been kept blindfold, and had been taken up again a few hours before, placed on a donkey before a man, who held her, and dropped in the street near the garden of Askaros, still bound, where she had been found by some passers-by and released, after which she had come home, to find her master gone also, whither no one knew.

Neither Ferraj nor the other slave had returned, and though she had gone to the spot, or as near it as she could recollect, the rain had washed away all traces of blood, if any had been shed, and she could not be quite certain

as to the exact place where the thing happened, there
were so many doors in the wall leading to so many different hareems. This was all she knew or could tell.

"Oh, the unhappy house!" she moaned, wringing her
hands, and rocking her body to and fro. "Never has
there been any luck in it since my old master died, and
you left it. Even the Barbary dove, the Sitta Edith loved
so much, has left it too, for I have tried vainly to find it
among the others. I would have known it, since it has
a blue ribbon round its neck the Sitta's own hands had
tied there."

A ray of hope shot through the heart of El Warda as
the old woman wailed thus, doubtless the dove, with
which she had been playing, had been forgotten by Edith
in her agitation, and nestling in her bosom, as was its
wont, must have been borne away with her. Its com-
panionship would be a consolation to the poor girl in her
captivity, and it possibly might bring a message from her,
did her captors not discover it. To so slight a spar of
hope will a loving heart cling when all looks desperate,
that El Warda felt a glow of pleasure at this discovery.

But where was her brother, whose counsel and courage
were so essential to unravel this mystery and punish this
villany? No one in the house could give her the slightest clue, except the Boab, who told the little he knew.

Was it possible then that the tale was partly true, and
he was lying at the Hotel d'Orient, possibly wounded by
the same treacherous villains who had set the snare for
his wife? Anything was better than suspense — she would
go and see. So taking Fatima and a man-slave with her,
the girl bent her steps to the hotel.

She was courteously and kindly received by the landlord — who knew the Askaros family well — who assured

her he had never sent the message, nor seen Askaros, and that the whole story was a pure fabrication.

In utter bewilderment and despair the half-distracted girl, forgetting her maidenly scruples, and all except the necessity of some friendly aid and counsel, repaired, for the second time in her life, to the house of Daoud-ben-Youssouf, near by the hotel, in the hope that he, with his craft and sagacity, both of which she rated very high, might be able to penetrate this mystery, which had so suddenly enveloped the two beings nearest and dearest to her of any on earth — the one for his own sake, the other because so dear to him.

A second time then, accompanied by Fatima, unannounced, she passed up the steep narrow steps, and into the sitting-room where their previous interview had taken place, and again found the master of the house alone.

But she started back with surprise and a feeling of pity, when she saw the change which a few weeks had wrought in the Syrian's face and mien since she last had seen him. Daoud was sitting moodily on his divan, his neglected chibouque fallen from his hand, upon the floor, no books or papers near him as usual, his head sunk on his chest, his shoulders stooping like those of an old man. He was plunged in a reverie which, from the expression of his face, was painful, and so deep that he did not observe her entrance until, gliding up to him, she touched him on the arm to attract his attention — Fatima guarding the doorway as before.

Startled by the touch, Daoud looked up, and her heart smote her as she saw how wan and wasted looked now that once smooth face, on which deep lines of care or pain had been suddenly and prematurely traced, as though by the burning plowshare of passion; while the sunken bloodshot eye, formerly a still deep well of dark light, with a wolfish glare looked out from two deep hollows surrounded by livid rings, like the baleful eyes of a ghoul glaring out of the face of a corpse. The Copt turban had been pushed away from his head, as though to cool the fever which consumed it, and streaks of gray were visible among the thick curls of his dark hair, while his whole air and attitude indicated the extreme of physical and moral depression — almost despair — strange to witness on a face she recollected well so youthful, smooth and smiling a few short moons before.

Shocked and astonished too much to speak or act, with a sick feeling of remorse at her heart at a change which she attributed to a hopeless passion for herself, the young girl stood spell-bound and motionless; but that feeling was changed to terror, as the Syrian sprang up, a gleam of madness in his eye, and clutched at something in his breast with his right hand, waving her off from him with his left, with a gesture full of wild fury not unmingled with fear.

"Avaunt, devil!" he hissed, in a low strained whisper. "Dost thou hear the wicked whisper of my heart, and come to tempt me in the shape of the only angel this foul earth holds, reeking as it is with treachery, crime, and sin? Lost as I am, and reft of earthly hope, not yet am I ready to sell my soul, even at the price of the delusion and the snare thou hast so cunningly set for me! *Apage, Sathanas! Vade retro!*" and he made the sign of the cross in the air. " If the monks and priests lie not, that spell should disperse thee into foul vapor, and drive thee back to Gehenna again!"

And with wild straining eyes, and heaving chest, the

Syrian stood still, as though to witness the effect of his incantation.

"Poor Daoud! to whom I promised to be as a sister," stole in on the madman's ear the soft, sweet tones of the voice he loved best to hear: "What frenzy possesses thee to rave thus, and to look so wildly? Art thou ill? Hath too much labor of body or mind so shaken thy nerves, that thou mistakest thy sister El Warda for an evil spirit to be banished by incantations? What sorrow or pain hath wrought this fearful change in thee, making thee prematurely old? Confide it to thy sister: and though she is sadly in need of consolation, coming hither for counsel in her deep distress, she yet will strive to share thy sorrow, and soothe thy pain; for strange woe and trouble have fallen again on the home of her childhood and thine, O Daoud, my brother!"

The effect of the harp of David over the moody madness of Saul, was not greater than the magical change which passed over the Syrian's face and mood, as the music of that beloved voice fell upon his ear, and stole softly, like the dew from heaven on arid soil, into his parched and thirsty soul. His rigid countenance relaxed, the deep lines disappeared, his face resuming its look of youth once more, as cloud after cloud seemed to roll away from brain and heart, which they had kept so long in dark eclipse.

The light of intelligence shone again in his eye, replacing the wild glare of the moment before; his collapsed and shrunken form appeared to dilate with the rapid heaving of his heart: and El Warda saw again before her the Daoud she knew, not the spectral distortion of him she had looked upon the moment before.

Slowly, like one awakening from a dream, the Syrian
28*

passed his hand wearily over his brow, as though to
collect his scattered thoughts, a deep sigh broke from his
overburdened heart, his right hand stole away from the
object it clutched at in his breast, and fell to his side,
the other played nervously with the sash around his waist,
while his large eyes filled slowly with tears, which glistened but fell not.

To her surprise he made no step forward to take the
maiden's hand, but standing as if carved out of marble,
let the slow utterances fall from his trembling lips, like
one talking in a trance.

"And it is not indeed an apparition sent from Gehenna,
in answer to the prayers of my mad and desperate heart,
to tempt me to perdition, but the angel of light herself, in
bodily presence, that comes to look upon the lost man
that was once Daoud-ben-Youssouf?

"Thy hand I dare not touch! for my presence alone
is pollution to one so pure and saint-like as thou! oh,
bright star of the morning of my youthful hope, now
shining so purely down on the dim depths of the night
of my despair!

"I hear the music of thy voice, but my weary senses
have caught not the meaning of thy words.   Comest thou
to me, oh, pure of heart and spirit! from the companion- .
ship of the white-robed Coptish nuns — those saints on
earth — to bid me, the lost sheep from their flock, take
the counsel as given by the wife of 'the man of Uz' in
the Holy Book, 'Curse God, and die'?"

"Art thou then mad indeed, O Daoud?" said the
maiden shuddering, more terrified by the sad impiety of
this blasphemous speech, made without passion and excitement, than by the frenzied fierceness of his previous
manner.   "Art thou then mad indeed, that thou speak-

est such strange wild things, which make me shudder?
Is this meet greeting for a friend who cometh to thee as
a sister, and expecting sympathy, meets only insult? I
have remained here too long already then! Farewell,
unhappy Daoud. May God forgive thee for thy sins!
my forgiveness thou hast already — if that matters anything! I shall pray morning and evening to Sitta Mariam
for the renewal of thy health of body and mind, for
surely both are strangely sick at present. Farewell!''

As she turned to go, her words and movements seemed to
break the spell which bound the Syrian. A more human
expression came into his face, and his dilating eyes, still
moist with unshed tears, looked wistfully into hers, as he
stretched forth both his arms with a pleading gesture, as
though to detain her.

''Stay, for the love of God! for the love of thine own
patron saint! for the love of Sitta Mariam! Is it possible
thou hast not heard!'' ——

''Heard what?'' asked the girl, in astonishment at the
eagerness of his face and gesture, like those of a man
whose very life hung on the answer to his question.

''Of me?'' gasped Daoud. ''Did not the Hebrew
tell thee?—for I know now where thou wast hidden, but
knew it too late!''

''He never breathed thy name,'' answered El Warda;
''and since my brother's return he hath been away on
business, in Jerusalem, among his people. Now I see
why thou wert hurt and angered, thinking Moussa had
told me of thine illness, for I see thou hast been very ill,
O Daoud! and I fear me art still so; and having had no
word from me, thought it unkind. But believe me,'' she
added, tears rising into her soft dark eyes, ''I did not

know it, but thought thee well and happy, else thou shouldst have heard from thine old playfellow.''

As she spoke, with sweet, serious earnestness, incredulity gave place on the face of Daoud to conviction, and a wild hope shone in his eye and stole into his soul.

She did not know then of his treachery? Moussa either had not known, or had not told her. Possibly Abbas, for reasons of his own, had kept his secret! and it was safe now and forever, for the same reasons would always restrain the politic tyrant from divulging it. But one other knew it too, and that a woman! a bold, bad, unscrupulous woman! But between her and .El Warda was a difference as of light and darkness, and it was not probable the pure child would ever willingly see that wanton woman again, whose very name was a hissing and scorn in every coffee-house and bath at Cairo — more so of late than ever. He was safe then, where alone he dreaded detection, contrary to his worst fears, which had scourged him like scorpions.

As these thoughts swept like lightning-flashes across his subtle intellect, he felt a thrill of fierce joy pulsating in his heart, and a secret hope re-awakening in his soul. With the renewal of that hope came swiftly back the craft and the courage which could defy man and God, and the dogged resolve, to win the woman before him — or die.

Those thoughts and that resolve passed through his brain, even while El Warda was speaking, and when she ceased, his answer was prompt and ready.

'' Pardon me, sweet angel! '' he said, pleadingly, ''if I did you injustice. But I have been very ill, and am still far from perfect recovery, as thou canst see — sick, too, at heart as well as in body, when it seemed to me the whole world had deserted me.

"The frenzy of my fever was upon me but now, and I know not what wild things I may have said and done! Something outrageous I fear me, else thou never wouldst have taken offense at the poor half-crazed sick man. But thy voice and presence and gentle pity have chased the fever from my blood, and I feel the spring-tide of returning health flowing in as the sickness ebbs. But thou wilt forgive me?—and already in my selfishness I have talked too much of one so insignificant as myself. Thou hast something to tell and to ask of me? Whatever Daoud can do, El Warda has but to command, and it shall be done."

Greatly relieved by the change in Daoud's manner, and his restoration to a healthier frame of mind and body, El Warda proceeded to relate to the astonished Syrian the mysterious disappearance of Askaros, and the abduction of Edith.

The Syrian listened in silence, only occasionally putting a brief question, and when she had finished all she had to say, mused a few moments. Then raising his head, and fixing upon the blushing girl an eye full of respectful admiration and deep devotion, took her hand, laid it gently on his heart, and said:

"While this heart beats, the wish of El Warda is its law! Within two days, if thy brother and sister be alive, thou shalt know where! If human skill and courage can extricate either or both from any peril that may menace them, thou mayst rely upon their safety. Should I need aid from any quarter thou canst influence, I will advise thee. It is not well that I should be seen at thy dwelling, nor seemly that thou shouldst come to mine; therefore send Fatima to me, when thou hast aught to communicate.

"Thou little knowest how much good thou mayst have done, how much evil have spared a soul pining in pain, by this visit. Sheitan hath lost, and Sitta Mariam gained a servant through thee this night."

Then, as she rose to go, he stooped and reverently kissed the hem of her garment, muttering to himself: "*Thou* art my patron saint! thus I devote myself, body and soul, to thy service!"

The girl, not hearing the words, but interpreting the look and gesture, blushed again, raised her finger as though in warning, smiled upon him, and glided away, leaving him alone in the chamber so dim and desolate before, but now brightened and sanctified by her late presence in it.

"Ha! ha!" he laughed softly to himself; "the omen was false after all! Though the hawk's wings have been sadly shorn of late, he may catch the dove yet! But now to unravel the thread of this double mystery! I think I can find the clue, and if not, why, the woman can find it for me. But I will not try that resort until all others fail. It is hard to play with fire without getting scorched, if not consumed. Is *her* hand in this? We shall see! we shall see!"

Revolving many thoughts and many plans in his subtle intellect, now roused into activity once more by his renewed hopes and vanished fears, the scheming Syrian spent that night in pacing up and down his room, receiving the reports of various emissaries, whom he sent abroad to make inquiries in different quarters.

Then, as the first gray dawn broke forth in the east, he threw on his cloak and sallied forth, muttering to himself:

"I have found one! Now to find the other!"

CHAPTER XXX.

THE DOVE IN THE VULTURE'S NEST.

W HEN Edith recovered from the surprise and stupor into which the sudden assault of her captors had thrown her, she found herself being hurried rapidly along in a carriage, the blinds of which appeared to be closed.

No one seemed to be in the carriage with her except Fatima ; but as both were fast bound, gagged and blindfold, it was impossible to know positively, or to communicate with each other.

After making several frantic but useless efforts to liberate her hands, or uncover her eyes, Edith desisted in despair, and resigned herself to her fate without further struggle. Thus she proceeded on her strange journey, for what appeared to her many hours, in a silence broken only by the stifled sobs of her fellow-captive.

She was so utterly bewildered by the whole occurrence, that she found it impossible to think ; her brain whirled, and her thoughts came so crowded and confused as to have no sequence or connection. The whole thing was such a mystery, she could not begin to fathom the meaning or the purpose of her abduction ; for she was conscious of having no enemy, and the thought of any baser motive never entered the pure mind of the American girl, whose knowledge of evil was limited to the confession made every Sunday in the church service, but which had never conveyed any practical idea to her mind.

Her education had been of that careful kind which instructs a woman in ancient and modern history, and keeps her utterly ignorant of the living and breathing world around her, and which considers purity and virtue to consist in the utter ignorance of evil, not in its knowledge and resistance. All sights and sounds, as well as books, that could offend maidenly delicacy had been carefully kept from her by her instructors first, and her fond father afterward; so that she had attained the age of womanhood, and had become a wife, with the innocence and the heart of a child.

Romances she had not been allowed to read, except those of the Puritan type approved of by Miss Primmins; and her imagination, therefore, was not so excitable, nor filled with the same images as those of her schoolmates, who had surfeited on the sweets of "Lady Audley's Secret," "Strathmore," and other sensational novels of the day.

She therefore had not the terrors of a prurient imagination or a morbid fancy to increase the pain of her actual situation; and, although naturally terrified at her strange position, the fear of something worse than danger or death, which can haunt a woman under such circumstances, did not find a place in her pure mind.

And, even in the midst of her own peril — whatever that might be, of which she had a very misty idea — one thought brought sweet consolation to her. The woman

and the wife felt a joy in the conviction that the story of
her husband's accident was false, and that, happen what
might to her, he was in no danger, nor had suffered any
injury; and, womanlike, in that thought she found alle-
viation for her own pain.

None of these thoughts consoled the Arab woman who
lay groaning by her side, and who appreciated better
than her mistress the real nature of the peril which
threatened, and the purpose of the abduction; for her
training and knowledge of life were of the kind to make
her comprehend both, and no doubt entered her mind
on the subject, except as to the person who had planned
it; and here she was as utterly in the dark as her
mistress.

At length the carriage stopped, and by a great effort
Edith raised herself up from the seat on which she had
been thrown. As she did so, she felt something fluttering in her bosom, and immediately recollected that her
dove had nestled there, as was its wont, just before she
sallied out to go to her husband, and had been forgotten
in her excitement. The consciousness of the presence
of even that helpless thing she loved, near her in this
hour of unknown danger, sent a thrill of pleasure through
her breast. It seemed to her an indication that she was
not quite deserted, while she felt this friend nestling near
her heart; and this little incident did more to reassure
the sensitive girl than a more material fact might have
done. So she bent her head down with difficulty, to
keep the bird in his position, fearing it might be taken
from her, did her captors see it; and the dove, as though
it comprehended her design, nestled quietly down again,
and was still once more.

As the dove moved, he had pushed some hard substance next him against her breast so as to give her pain, and Edith remembered that, before leaving home that morning, Askaros had playfully armed her with a small jewelled dagger, scarcely more than a toy, telling her, with mock solemnity, that every Turkish Odalisque wore one of those, and that she ought to adopt the customs of the country in which she lived. She had never thought a second time of the dagger, as she did of the dove, for it never occurred to her that in any emergency she might have occasion, or could nerve herself to use it.

When the carriage stopped, she was carefully lifted out by two persons, and borne up what seemed to be a long flight of steps, and deposited on what felt like a soft divan — her eyes and limbs still bound — and then left alone.

She could hear the stealthy footsteps of her conductors stealing from the room, and a door close behind them; then she was again left to silence, solitude, and her own reflections. The excitement of her mind, and the critical nature of her situation, prevented sleep, worn and weary as she was, and the predominating feeling in her mind was that of wonder, not unmixed with curiosity, as to what all this meant. Lying there undisturbed for some time, she began to believe she was the sport of some practical joke, which, had it not been so cruel, she would have attributed to her husband; and the vague fears which had at first assailed her, from the strangeness of the situation, began to wear away, and to be succeeded by an impatience to know what it all meant, and rejoin her husband.

But she was not destined to remain much longer in this suspense. Again, in her darkness, she heard the rustling of the curtain over the door, as some one put it aside, followed by shuffling steps and the sweeping sound of a woman's dress passing over the floor. The moment after, a hand was busy with the mufflers which covered her head and bound her arms, and she was at once restored to sight, and the free use of her limbs once more. Her eyes, half blinded by their sudden exposure to a blaze of light, fell first on the face and form of a Circassian woman, both of which must once have been beautiful, from the traces still left, but the expression of whose countenance was not prepossessing now — hard, leering, cunning and cruel. She was very richly dressed, in Turkish style, and on her fingers, neck and hair glittered gems of great cost and size. She peered insolently and inquisitively into the uncovered face of Edith, ran her eye rapidly over the slight girlish form, and burst into a roar of derisive laughter, as though equally amused and disgusted at the survey, and with some ideas it excited.

Repulsion, terror, and indignation struggled successively for mastery in the bosom of the gentle girl, who recoiled instinctively from the hag, though without the slightest suspicion as to who or what she was, or clearly understanding whence the repugnance rose.

She turned her head away to avoid looking at the woman, and in the act of doing so her eyes fell for the first time on the objects surrounding her, and rested upon the details with wonder and admiration. Never in her life had she seen, never had her imagination pictured the possibility of such luxury and lavish expenditure as were displayed in the apartment in which she now found herself. It was not a large room, and had but one window, large, and latticed in Eastern fashion, so that the occupant could see what was passing outside, being herself invisible. The roof was vaulted and very lofty, with small perforations, like lattices, on the side of the wall opposite the window, but which did not seem intended to give light, since there was no way of opening them from the inside of the room. The walls and ceiling were of the most elaborate wood-work, carved in fantastic patterns, the floor of tessellated marble, inlaid with squares of pearl and ivory. The furniture was a *mélange* of the Oriental and European, all of the richest and most costly kind, with large mirrors set into the walls on all four sides, and divans covered with embroidered damask serving for seats. Small oval mirrors set in frames of pearl, combs, brushes and other necessaries of the female toilet were strewn over *Koorsees* inlaid with pearl, in corners of the room — which was evidently one of a suite in the hareem of some very wealthy man.

Adjoining this room a half-opened door discovered a most luxuriously fitted-up bath-room of the Turkish kind.

While the astonished eyes of Edith were surveying the apartment, and all it contained, the bold, bright eyes of the Circassian woman were fixed on the fair fresh beauty and girlish figure of the young American, with a stare which certainly did not indicate admiration, but the reverse. So that when Edith turned her head again from her examination of the room, she again encountered those leering evil eyes — more like those of the lower animals than a woman's in expression — and could not suppress a shudder.

The woman saw the expression, and understood it, and her face darkened, but she only raised her hand, and pointing to the adjoining room. "*Hammam!*" (bath), she said, as though intimating the propriety of Edith availing herself of that luxury.

Edith shook her head in refusal.

Then the woman commenced talking rapidly to her in some language which she had never heard before, and which she supposed to be Turkish; and afterward in another, some words of which she recognized to be Arabic.

But Edith, who understood neither language, could not comprehend the purport of her words, and could only shake her head in reply to the torrent of words, accompanied by animated gesticulation, so volubly poured out by her companion. Failing utterly to make the American woman understand her meaning, either by word or gesture, the Circassian seemed to lose temper. She rose up from the divan, where she had squatted down beside Edith, and, with a gesture of impatient anger, muttering the words *"Homar Fransowee!"* (ass of a Frank) hobbled out of the apartment, not only dropping the curtain behind her, but closing also a mahogany door, which Edith heard her lock behind her.

Believing herself alone and unseen, the poor girl, whose pride had sustained her in a show of courage and coolness she did not feel in the presence of that odious woman, whose character was stamped upon her face so plainly that even her innocence could not mistake it, the full terror of her situation dawned upon her, and covering her face with her hands she burst into tears of mingled fear and shame.

For the first time the suspicion flashed upon her why she had been entrapped, and the horror of the thought was almost more than she could endure. The hideous reality of that woman's presence, her look and manner, as well as the appearance of the place, spoke as plainly as words could have done the character of its occupants. She was a prisoner then in an Egyptian hareem! but

29*

whose? That question she asked herself in vain, for neither her memory nor her imagination could give her the slightest clue to that mystery.

How was she to escape? This was the next thought which entered into the mind of the American girl, under whose soft exterior there lay concealed a strong will and a resolute soul, though neither had as yet been tested in her smooth summer voyage, thus far, over the sea of life. Now that the clouds darkened and the storm disturbed those smooth waves, she felt her energy rising with the emergency, dried her tears, and rising, walked to the window to see what the outlook might be.

She started back with a cry of surprise at the scene which met her view. Immediately below the window was a large open space, surrounded by a high stone wall; beyond that again a long low range of barracks, in which she saw Egyptian soldiers. Above the roofs of the barracks, far as the eye could range, on every side there stretched the bare bald desert, dotted here and there in the distance with slow moving lines of horses, camels and men. All else what the Scriptures so strongly term, "the abomination of desolation."

With a sigh she turned from the window, more mystified than ever, for the dreariness of the view added to the oppression which weighed down her spirit. Throwing herself again down on the divan, she gave way for a few moments to the wildest hysterical grief; then rising up, threw herself on her knees, and with clasped hands and upturned eyes, prayed long and fervently that God in His mercy might sustain and strengthen, if He would not deliver her from those strange perils, coming so unexpectedly in the hour of her greatest hope and happiness. Having completed her prayer, which rose on high like incense from the altar of a pure but sore-stricken heart, to the Great Creator and Judge of all things on this small dust-heap we call a world — doubtless a small speck only in the eye of Omnipotence — the exhausted girl sunk down and fell into the heavy slumber of over-wrought brain and body, forgetting for a time in that blessed oblivion her past pangs and present apprehensions.

Little did she imagine that when she deemed the All-Seeing Eye alone beheld her in that chamber, apparently so secure from outward intrusion, that a human eye — a dull, greedy, sensual, vulture-like eye — was gloating over her charms, and feasting on the beauties of her person — from the wealth of her dishevelled golden hair, streaming loose on her ivory shoulders, having broken free from restraints of comb or other fastening during her ride; over the dainty symmetry of her delicate form, just ripening into perfect womanhood from immature girlhood, down to the small feet peeping out from beneath the long Frank dress, suggesting the symmetry of the limbs it so decorously concealed. This novelty piqued and excited the imagination of the jaded voluptuary, wearied and sated with the undisguised beauties of his own hareem, and the immodest exposures of persons by which they sought to stimulate his failing appetites. So to him the fresh pure womanhood of this young American, was as provocative as a new dish to the palled palate of the epicure.

For the vulture eye which glared down through that lattice which Edith had thought a window — but which allowed the occupant of a small *entresol* chamber to look down into her apartment unseen — was that of none other than Abbas Pasha himself.

While he was gloating down on his unconscious captive, the door of his hiding-place opened, and the Circassian woman we have seen below, making a profound salutation, stood behind him in the narrow space, speaking no word, but evidently awaiting his pleasure.

Abbas turned round at her entrance with an impatient sigh, and reluctantly averted his eyes from the fascinating vision below to the bold, bad face of "the Mother of the Hareem," for such the woman was who had Edith in charge, and who now came for further orders from her master, formerly her lover and her slave — a fact which she had not forgotten, although Abbas had. Abbas spoke first.

"How find you the Ingleeze woman, O *Zuleika*, mother of houris?" he said. "Is she not truly a pearl of price? a very white lily of the valley, such as the great King Solomon sang of, and would have joyed to possess in his palace built by the genii? Is she not, indeed, a rose?" And he glanced down again into the chamber, unwillingly reverting his eyes to the painted face of the Circassian, who, forgetting her faded charms, still retained the desperate hope of reclaiming her lord's allegiance.

"A white rose then," responded Zuleika, sneeringly, "for her face is as white as a Santon's tomb, and she has neither *kohl* on her eyes nor *henna* on her hair or fingers, and her figure is as thin as a half-starved camel's after the pilgrimage to Mecca."

But, witnessing the gathering cloud of wrath on Abbas's brow at her sarcasms, which seemed to anger him, the Circassian hastened to correct her blunder, adding:

"Yet my great lord is right. Under all this, which to ordinary eyes would look like ugliness, his eagle glance has detected the rare beauties which lurk beneath.

For, when properly bathed and anointed, her eyes and eyebrows darkened with *kohl,* her hair and finger-tips tinged with *henna,* and in a costume which will display, not hide her figure, she will indeed be a rose, pleasant to look upon, and sweet of perfume ! And these things my lord's most faithful servant, Zuleika, charges herself to attend to — if it so pleases my lord, the king ! that the foreign woman may be made worthy to come into his sight, and fill the place in his hareem which he has condescended to assign her.''

Abbas impatiently nodded his head, as though wishing her to be gone ; but the woman lingered, as though wishing, yet fearing to say more.

" What is it? Speak !'' said the Viceroy. "I see thou hast something to say. It is permitted.''

'' May it please my great lord ! the Frank woman speaks neither Turkish nor Arabic — nothing but Ingleeze, which no one in the hareem understands. My lord had commanded his faithful mother of the hareem to prepare the mind of the Frank woman for the honor which is destined for her, before he visited her. But how can this be done, since we are all as dumb women to her?''

The suggestion seemed to strike Abbas, who mused over it in silence for a few minutes, and then replied :

'' There is good sense in what thou sayest, and it is necessary the Frank woman should be made to see the honor and the advantages of what is destined for her. Neither can I myself speak to her without an interpreter, since, the Prophet be praised, I speak no language of the Infidel ! Hearken unto me ! Canst thou not find in Cairo some woman, known to thee, that can be trusted, to whom we may confide this duty?''

" Highness ! to hear is to obey ! Just such a woman

I do know; and she shall be brought hither, if my lord commands."

"Frank or native?" asked Abbas.

"A Frank by birth, who hath lived here so long that she is one of us; as I know, thoroughly trustworthy, and with small love for the women of her own race, among whom she is an outlaw."

"*Peki!*" said Abbas; "thy face is white in my presence! It is well thought of! Let the Frank woman repose herself; and do thou send to Cairo, and procure the woman thou speakest of. When she arrives, let me see and speak with her, before she sees or knows of our new bird. This is a serious matter; and I must judge if she can be trusted. I have spoken."

The Circassian took the hint, and withdrew; and Abbas, after another long, lingering look, turned away, descended the steps which led to his spying-place, and passed on to his own apartments, in the other wing of the palace.

An hour later, the poor girl awoke from her heavy slumber, and found herself still alone. At first, she could scarcely believe all that had passed to be more than a feverish dream; but the painful reality soon forced itself upon her mind, as her eye fell on the unfamiliar objects surrounding her.

She rose up and passed to the door. It was locked. She passed into the bath-room. There was no egress thence. She searched for some other door of communication, but could find none. She then went to the window, and looked out. The height from the ground was full forty feet, and below it was a space enclosed by a high wall.

As she stood gazing out upon it, she felt the dove flutter

in her bosom, and suddenly what Askaros had suggested to her, as to its uses and training, flashed upon her memory, and inspired her with hope.

The dove should be her messenger to her husband! Hastily she took from her pocket her aunt's letter — on which she had traced the steamboat for Fatima — and with the gold pencil, which hung suspended from her neck, she traced on the blank page these words:

"I am a prisoner in a palace, the window of which overlooks the desert. Safe and well otherwise. Come and rescue your Edith."

Addressing this small square note to "Askaros Effendi, Cairo," she took out the dove, which caressed her with its soft bill, carefully tied the note under its wing, attaching it to the blue ribbon about its neck, and kissing it over and over again, while her tears rained down on its soft wings, launched it out into the air.

The bird seemed unwilling to leave her, for it circled outside of the window, and returned to perch on her shoulder again.

Twice she essayed the experiment, with the same result. The third time, she repulsed it, on its return, and threw it roughly out again; and the bird did not come back, but instead of darting off in a straight line, circled up into the air to a great height, before proceeding on its way. She soon had reason to admire the instinct which had prompted this act, and its previous conduct — for she soon saw that a hawk had espied the dove, which was high up in the air above him, and was striving to rise to its level, to give it chase.

A few minutes of intense anxiety for Edith ensued, as the hawk strove to rise higher than the smaller bird; but ere he could effect this, the dove darted away with the swiftness of an arrow, leaving the baffled pursuer far out of range.

"He will take my message safely!" said the glad girl, whose spirits rose with this success; "and Askaros will be sure to find and rescue me! If he does not—and there is need"—she whispered to herself, while a settled resolve shone on her fair young face—"although I have sent away one of my friends, the other still is left!" And she touched the jewelled hilt of the dagger at her bosom—then knelt down to pray again.

CHAPTER XXXI.

THE MAD-HOUSE OF THE MAURISTAN.

WHILE these events were transpiring at the Abas-sieh, equally important ones were happening at Cairo. When Daoud-ben-Youssouf sallied forth at early morning, he bent his steps to the Turkish quarter, and walked rapidly along until he reached one of the largest and handsomest mosques in Cairo. Both in its architecture and its exterior it was one of the finest specimens of the old Moorish architecture to be found in the city.

This was the *Mauristan*, which, long disused as a mosque, had been converted into a mad-house, whither were sent those unfortunates who, from any cause, had lost their reason.

In the East the victim of insanity is looked upon with a reverential feeling unknown in other countries.

The madman is regarded not as one laboring under a physical disease, but as resting under the direct visitation, as well as under the special protection of God.

A peculiar sanctity attaches to the object of this visitation ; and no Eastern man, even to protect himself from bodily injury, would harm a lunatic, believing he would thereby incur the direct displeasure of Allah.

Nations which boast of more culture and a higher

:ivilization may scoff at this superstition, and regard the madman as they do any other human being, the normal exercise of whose functions has been disturbed ; yet there is something very striking and very touching in it, nevertheless. Moreover, it cannot be denied that in the three great attributes of Hope, Faith, and Charity, the uncultivated Oriental immeasurably excels his Western brother ; although the first may often darken into fatalism, and the second into fanaticism, yet the third, in practice as in precept, is the faith of Islam. In respect for old age, and for all who have been afflicted in mind or body by Providence, the West can learn most profitable lessons from the East.

Hence, although no state provision, such as the public hospitals common in other countries, exists in the East — private charity supplying their place — there was a place assigned at Cairo for the care of idiots, madmen, and all others deprived of reason, who were taken charge of and attended to at public expense.

This place, as before stated, was the *Mauristan*, which Daoud now entered, the interior of which was supported by a range of strong pillars, to which were chained down many human beings, howling like wild beasts. Others, whose insanity was of a less violent type, were moping over the wide space, or gathered in groups, amusing themselves as they best might, under the superintendence of keepers armed with heavy clubs. For although these unhappy creatures were regarded with a peculiar kind of reverence, as suffering from more than a mere physical malady, yet, by a strange inconsistency, their treatment was most cruel — as we would consider brutal. This arose not from intention, but through ignorance of the proper sanitary measures. As there are no professional *Hakeems*, (doctors,) among the Mussulmans, who believe the prayers offered up at some Sheik or Santon's tomb to be more efficacious than medicine, maniacs were treated in the rudest and simplest manner. The violent ones were chained to pillars, pinioned in such a way as to prevent their doing any injury to themselves; the milder cases left to the curative power of nature alone.

Daoud, whose nerves had been sorely shaken of late by illness of body and mind, shuddered as he entered this horrible place, with its sights and sounds of woe and pain, as vivid an image of the dwellings of the lost as ever was conceived by the gloomy imagination of the great Florentine who had "been in hell;" or pictured forth by the weird genius of Doré, which has given shape and form to those ghastly fancies with his painful pencil.

Wolfish eyes, gleaming with a baleful fire which seemed not of this world, glared upon the Syrian from the bundles of misery huddled together at the base of each stone pillar, curdling his blood with the demoniac malignity of their expression, more like the eyes of lost souls in pain than those of living men.

The shrieks and yells of the more furious alternated with the gibbering laughter of the imbeciles: echoes from deserted seats of reason, untenanted now by thought.

No women were among them. All were men; or, rather, creatures whose outward semblance was that of men, but in whom the noblest part of humanity was utterly lost, or in sad eclipse; bodies in which brutal instincts had survived and dethroned reason — that breath of God which elevates the human clay above all the other works of the Omnipotent Hand.

As the Syrian, inspired by a loathing repulsion, which rose almost to horror, cautiously picked his way through this mass of diseased humanity, he compelled himself to peer carefully at the faces and forms of the poor wretches he passed, one by one, as though seeking some person he knew might be found among them.

At length he stopped, breathed a deep sigh of mingled relief and pain, like one whose quest was over, and stooped down over a form which lay huddled together, as though in the death-like exhaustion succeeding a vio- lent paroxysm. The form was now relaxed and nerve- less — the extreme of lassitude and weakness indicated by the position of the limbs and features of the face, which was that of a young and handsome man, and which, though haggard and death-like, did not wear the strained intensity of insanity.

He seemed to slumber; for the long-drawn, laboring breath came with the regular inhalations of sleep, while his chest rose and fell regularly, though slowly.

"It is he," said Daoud, "and the crisis is past. That is not the fitful and broken sleep of a disturbed brain. The prayers of his guardian angel and mine have saved him not only from death, but from worse than death — the demoniacal possession men call madness, and priests the visitation of God. He must have had a violent paroxysm of fever, and these fools mistook his ravings for insanity, and chained him here, like a wild beast!" And he glanced down with loathing at the ropes which bound the sleeper's limbs, and attached him to the strong pillar. "I am no *hakeem*," he resumed, "but I am sure that is never the face of a madman. When he knows all, perchance he may wish he had lost his reason; for those tidings, to his soft nature, will be almost equal to the death-pang. I begin to repent my wrath against him, and my plots, which, though they brought woe to him and his, brought greater pain and shame to myself. Is it too late to repair the wrong I have done him, or at least to expiate it? No, no! Have not our priests told me that Daoud, the great king, whose name I bear, sinned more grievously than I in many ways, and yet became the chosen servant of the Lord after his repentance?"

As he muttered thus, looking down pityingly on the still form beneath him, the sleeper stirred uneasily and muttered eagerly a few broken words, as though calling on one he wished to see, with an impatience half chiding, half fond.

The Syrian's brow darkened and his small hand clinched until the nails were driven into the delicate flesh, while a look of painful suspicion crept into his eyes, the pupils of which contracted and dilated like those of a bird of prey. He stooped down over the sleeping man and placed his ear close to the lips, which continued to repeat the impatient call, in sounds scarcely as audible as a whisper. But what the listener heard reassured him, and his face lighted up as though a heavy burden had been lifted from his brain and heart, while an expression of joy, blended with contempt, stole over his delicate features.

"Ephraim is joined unto his idols; let him alone!" he muttered, with that familiar everyday use of Scriptural phrases so common to the Eastern Christians, who, like the New England Puritans, distort the text of Holy Writ to meanings far different to those for which they were designed.

"The poor fool calls on the name of his wax-doll! not on that which I permit no lips to invoke, no heart to enshrine but mine — unfit shrine as that heart may be for such a saint! It is well for him and well for me that it was so, for Sheitan was busy with me again for that interval of suspense.

"*Apage Sathanas, vade retro!*" and he crossed himself. "I spit at and defy thee and thy works. But now to business!"

Gliding away with the noiseless swiftness that characterized all his movements, Daoud left the sleeping man, happily unconscious of the great peril he had so narrowly escaped in the rambling utterances of his disturbed slumber. For had that other name, which the mad jealousy of Daoud suspected, been uttered by those fever-parched lips, the pitiless Syrian would surely have abandoned him to his fate, which a protracted residence in that place would have made death or madness, ere aid from other quarters could have reached him.

As it was, the Syrian sought the head keeper of the Mauristan, to whom the young Copt was well known by name and reputation, explained to him the object of his visit and the success of his search, and obtained from him a ready permission at once to remove him to his own home. This was speedily effected, and shortly after sunrise, Daoud, in charge of his rescued rival — as he once had deemed him — knew not whether to feel most pleased or pained on receiving the tearful thanks of the glad girl, on his delivery to her at his own house, and saw, at the same time, the look of passionate grief and devotion she threw upon the wreck of the man, so brave, brilliant, and strong but yesterday — now lying collapsed and almost lifeless before her.

He had, however, no excuse to linger longer in the paradise of her presence, and was reluctantly about to withdraw, after having protracted the interview by art-

fully prolonging his detail of the search and discovery
of Askaros, when, to his surprise, the girl requested him
to remain, and accompanied the body of her brother —
as she called him — from the room.

Impatiently the Syrian awaited her return, with mixed
emotions of hope and fear agitating his breast, as to her
reason for detaining him, which even his ready wit could
not supply. His suspense was short, for El Warda soon
returned and put into his hands the note she had just received through the dove, but a short time before his arrival. He read the note carefully over several times,
then turning to the anxious girl, who watched his face
and hung upon his first words with breathless interest,
said :

" I begin to see through this mystery, I think ! The
desert view from the window confirms my first suspicions.
Send back the dove with this answer '' — and he suggested
the words which the dove bore back — "and I will labor
to find your sister, even as I have found your brother.
Even should he be better when he awakes, disturb him
not with these matters, for he will still be too weak in
mind and body to be of use, and it will only harm him.
Should he inquire for his wife, tell him she has gone to
Alexandria to the consul-general, to enlist his aid to find
him, and will soon be home. Now I go to discover
further traces of this villany. Fear not ! doubt not !
hope ever ! and trust to one who will keep his pledge ! ''

Trusting himself to say no more, the Syrian left the
house with a lighter heart than he had worn in his breast
since the fatal morning he had passed into the Viceroy's
palace exultant, and been borne out bruised and broken
in body and hope.

One little incident had escaped even his vigilant eye

which might have given him uneasiness; and it was this: as the exhausted form of Askaros was borne away from the Mauristan, a man glided out also, and followed at a distance, until the garden gate closed on his conductors, then hurried away like one whose work was done.

Daoud spent that day, so trying to poor Edith in her captivity, in fruitlessly seeking a clue to her disappearance, in which he was not so fortunate as he had been in the case of her husband. The facts relating to the latter's having been found at Boulak, and carried to the Mauristan, had been easily gathered from the gossips of the Cairene coffee-houses, which afford a substitute for the evening newspapers, and telegraphic despatches of civilized communities, and probably retail as accurate information. Of course the incident only was stated, as Askaros had not been recognized, but the quick apprehension of the Syrian supplied that omission.

But how to trace the missing wife? Here the gossips could give him no clue, for the whole matter was still shrouded in secrecy and mystery outside of the household of Askaros. True, his suspicion fell upon Abbas; but how could he verify them? how proceed? The window overlooking the desert made him suppose the Abassieh her place of confinement; yet not a certainty. His thoughts fell on Nezlé Khanum, as the sole human being that could unravel the mystery, and give him aid were such the case. For the consul-general would be powerless here, even were there more than vague suspicion to proceed upon! The sanctity of the harcem, inviolate from step of man, or even the arm of law, shielded from detection or punishment many criminal acts, as well as afforded a sanctuary for all encompassed within its walls. No man can enter there. True! but a woman might.

What woman could he find who would dare the vengeance of Abbas? even for all his hoard — the savings of his laborious and frugal life — which he would devote to bribe her. He racked his brain in vain to think of one, with the craft and courage necessary to venture into the Abassieh, and ascertain whether the captive were really there?

Suddenly the thought of the Frenchwoman flashed upon his mind. She would do it, for the darker motive of avarice, which he could tempt, and for the purer one of love for El Warda. He would go and find her! for he suspected, though he did not know, the darker and more disreputable employments which she occupied herself with, in connection with the hareems, to which she had free entry.

It was now night, and he hurried to her house, to learn, to his chagrin, that she had gone off at mid-day, no one knew where, not to be back possibly for many days. This was a very great disappointment; so the Syrian unconsciously wandered in the direction of the house where his heart was, and carefully examined if any traces of any kind had been left in the narrow street where the violence had been committed, but could find none.

He then went into the house, and made old Fatima repeat her story over and over again, in the hope of getting some clue; but the garrulous old woman could give him none, always repeating the same story he had heard her tell before, with wearisome iteration. Neither Ferraj nor the other slave had ever returned, nor any trace of them been found.

Wearied out and almost hopeless, he returned to his own squalid home — now seeming to him, from contrast with his dreams, more dismal than ever — and throwing himself on his divan, fell into the heavy slumber of utter exhaustion, having had no sleep for many nights previous, when almost mad with misery.

He did not awaken until the sun was shining into the apartment the following morning, and rubbed his eyes after unclosing them, to convince himself he was really awake, for there stood before his divan, gravely regarding him, a tall black eunuch, the richness of whose dress indicated he was attached to the hareem of some distinguished personage.

Though in face and figure he presented the same peculiarities which give a family likeness to the members of this unfortunate class, there was something in his countenance which recalled to Daoud the recollection of having seen him before under peculiar circumstances, when or where he could not at the moment bring to mind. But it flashed back on his memory with the first words his visitor spoke, in that strange squeaking voice peculiar to his class.

As Daoud rose up from his divan and saluted him, the eunuch gravely returned the salutation, and said :

"The noble lady, my mistress, whom you vowed to repay for a service rendered you in a sore strait, has sent me to say she now claims the fulfilment of that promise, and would see you, to explain her wishes. If the waters of oblivion have not washed away your memory, follow me, and I will conduct you to her."

"What seeks she of me?" answered Daoud, whose astonishment was only equalled by his reluctance to obey such a summons; and over whose memory there flashed the many strange stories told of the bad, bold woman who commanded, rather than invited his presence..

"The great lady is not in the habit of confiding aught

but her will to her servants, far less of having her orders
questioned where she honors such as you with a message!" said the eunuch, haughtily; adding, after a moment's pause: "The noble lady bade me remind you,
if you showed any reluctance to come, that only half of
your promised reward had been paid, and a reminder to
your debtor would insure the balance. Have you already
then forgotten whose mercy and pity saved you from
open shame, and from being the gibe and scorn of every
coffee-house in Cairo, O most ungrateful and thankless
of infidels?"

"There is truth in your words and in hers, though
they are not over-courteous," replied the Syrian, who
had now recovered his constitutional coolness and courage, and felt the force of the eunuch's statement, sting-
ing as it was; and who knew, furthermore, he could not
afford to convert so powerful a friend into an enemy, as
his refusal to obey her summons might.

"Fear cannot move me, but gratitude can! For life
or death, I am at the disposal of the noble lady who suc-
cored me in my sore need! Lead on, I follow," and
he pointed to the door.

The eunuch grinned a ghastly smile, which exhibited
his black teeth through his skinny and livid lips, while
his dull eye, deep sunken in its orbit, and surrounded by
a livid ring, glanced over the spare form of the Syrian
and his beardless face, as though in wonder at this last
fantasy of his mistress. He shrugged his shoulders,
made no reply, but turned, and silently led the way
down-stairs, followed by Daoud.

At the door stood another eunuch, holding two horses,
richly caparisoned, one of which his conductor immediately bestrode, signing Daoud to mount the other,

which he had no sooner done than both took the road leading to Boulak at a headlong gallop, as though their lives depended on their haste.

No words were exchanged between them as they swept along, the early travellers on the road making way for them, as, like two spectral horsemen, the black and his pale companion rushed into sight and passed out of it, under a cloud of dust, almost as rapidly as they had appeared.

The palm-trees and acacias swept past them in their swift race, to the eyes of Daoud, until they reached the wall of the palace of the Princess Nezlé, when, suddenly curbing his panting steed, just at the secret gate through which Askaros had formerly entered, the sable guide dismounted, and tapped three times on the wall. The gate swung open, and two slaves appeared, one of whom respectfully assisted the eunuch to dismount, the other taking the bridle of Daoud's horse, and motioning him to do the same.

He saw, to his horror, that these slaves were mutes, and began to comprehend why the princess's secrets were so well kept, surrounded as she was by these ever-silent attendants.

His conductors motioned him to follow, and he passed through many winding avenues to a small postern door, up a narrow flight of steps, and found himself in the same chamber already described, from the window of which Askaros had leaped into the Nile. On the divan sat a veiled lady, whom he at once guessed to be the terrible princess herself. The eunuch prostrated himself with lowly reverence, rose, and withdrew at a gesture from the lady, without uttering a word, and Daoud was left alone with her he dreaded, yet longed to see.

The princess broke the silence with a slight laugh : "So!" she said, "gratitude yet dwells on earth, and thou hast remembered past favors. Or is it fear brings thee here? I fain would know the metal of which thou art made. Bad as I may be, I am not so cruel as men call me in the idle babble of the bath and coffee-house! If dread of my displeasure alone hath brought thee here, and thy heart fails thee, depart in peace; for the work to be done requires courage, of all things, and thou lookest, as Abbas said, more like a girl than a boy. I need a man, and a resolute one, for the thing for which I summoned thee."

"Great lady," said the Syrian, "mistrust me not because I hide not the heart of a lamb under the shaggy hide of a lion; and my looks are girlish, as thou sayest. The deadliest cobra may conceal its venom under the softest skin. Neither do me the injustice of believing that fear instead of gratitude brought me here. Well do I know that, once within these walls, my liberty and life are thine; that I might disappear forever, like a bubble that bursts on yonder river, and no man know my fate. But so long as I chose to remain outside, even thy hand could not reach me, and Abbas, in his capricious tyranny, would never waste a thought on one like me. Speak, then, freely, O lady, and I, a free man, say to thee, in the language of thy slaves, 'To hear is to obey!'"

He paused, and, stepping forward, knelt down gracefully, and kissed the hem of her robe with a reverential gratitude; then, rising up, folded his arms across his chest, and awaited her pleasure.

The boldness of his speech did not seem to displease the princess, but, on the contrary, to gratify her.

"Thou art a saucy boy, indeed!" she said, "and

31

somewhat lacking in reverence to speak so boldly; but I forgive thee, and in token thereof, as thou art scarcely yet a man, will let thee see the face of the monster, men have told thee such terrible tales about." And, laughing aloud, she threw off the heavy veil, as though it encumbered her, and disclosed to the eager gaze of the Syrian the small regular features and eagle eyes of the Princess Nezlé.

The evident surprise and admiration of the young man pleased the princess, whose womanly vanity craved the tribute now more than in her earlier years.

"So you see Sheitan is not so black as they paint her, nor am I a ghoul or a jinn, but only a woman after all. Thou art a pretty boy! and there was a time when I should have had softer talk for thine ear than what I have to tell thee now. Though thou art Youssouf, I am not the wife of Thotmes, of whom the old story is told. If I speak to thee of love, it is of thine for another, young like thyself, and how thou mayest win her yet — of her whom Abbas promised thee! Ha! that start, that change of color! Thou seest I read thy heart, and know all!" And as she spoke, as though enjoying his confusion, she fixed her penetrating eyes, not without a scornful pity lurking in their dark orbs, full on the face of the astonished and discomfited Syrian.

"Furthermore I tell thee," she resumed, "that El Warda" — smiling as she saw him start at the mention of that name — "was here with me at early dawn. She told me she had but one counsellor and friend in Cairo, in the matters of life and death on which she prayed my aid, and strange to say of so modest a maiden, thou art that man!" And again those searching eyes seemed to read his very soul.

"Great Khanum!" said the Syrian, to whom her last words seemed to have given new life and energy, "if the matter for which I have been summoned here be that on which she came to thee, and which I know, brain and body, life and soul, thou mayest command of Daoud-ben-Youssouf!"

As he spoke his slight form seemed to dilate, his nostrils expanded, and in the steady light of his eye shone desperate resolve.

The Khanum looked on him admiringly; her unflinching spirit responded to his; she felt the attraction which draws one strong nature to another, and it echoed in her voice as again she spoke.

"Rightly did Abbas call thee a tiger-cat, but wofully did he err when he boasted he had pared thy claws! I take thee at thy word. But before pledging thyself I warn thee it is no slight service, no child's play I may have to ask of thee; but to do and dare things, the very mention of which may cause thy flesh to creep, and thy blood to curdle! For thou art very young," she added, musingly, as though to herself, rather than to her companion.

"Great Khanum! I see thou dost still distrust; but hear me, I beseech thee. There is nothing, however desperate, I am not willing and ready to do or dare, if it lead to *her*, or even if it be in her service. Ay, even though it lead me to the pit of Eblis; or lower still, back into the palace and presence of the man from whom thou didst rescue me."

"Is it indeed so?" said the princess slowly, her eyes kindling with a glow which seemed the reflection of his own. "Thy vaunt shall be tested. It is even there I would send thee! Danger will dog thine every step, and detection be certain death, under slow tortures, to which the tender mercies dealt thee before will be but as thistle-down in comparison. Wilt thou indeed dare this, and for the reason thou hast given?"

"Great Khanum! yes. Try me!"

"I will. Return to Cairo. Go to the bath. There cause thy head to be shaven, and the beard to be removed from thine upper lip. Take this vial, and with the liquid it contains tinge thy skin, that thou mayest come forth looking less like a fair Georgian, and more like a brown Circassian than at present. Should I need thee, at sunset I will send for thee. If not to-day, perhaps to-morrow. But leave not thy house in the interval. Possibly this trial may even yet be spared both thee and me. *Inshallah.* But we shall see. Now go."

Clapping her hands as she resumed her veil, the eunuch reappeared, and at a sign from the Khanum took away the young man, to whom she vouchsafed no further look or parting greeting.

Let alone, her brows knitted together, and her small white teeth were clinched together, while her dilating eye glared, as though some deadly passion, hate or fear, or both commingled, wrought in her stormy soul.

The spasm seemed but momentary. She shook it off as though her strong will had met and mastered the difficulty or the danger, whichever it might be, that menaced her; and, with that sudden change of mood habitual to her wayward temper, her mind suddenly reverted to the late interview, and she laughed sardonically.

"I thought Askaros was a fool about his doll!" she said; "but surely this Syrian boy is a greater one with his; which he not only has not possession of, but most probably will never get at all! Ho! ho! what fools all these men are, bearded or beardless, young or old, and, oh ! how weary I am of all of them ! But I believe this boy will keep his pledge. *Bakaloum !* And now to prepare for my interview with Abbas."

Rising up from her divan, the princess betook herself to her haschisch, to drown her hopes or fears in the sooth- ing influence of that pleasing poison, ere she made her perilous and decisive visit to her royal kinsman.

Critical that visit was evidently intended to be, for as she passed into her inner apartment she muttered to her- self through her set teeth :

"The crisis must have come, and the danger be press- ing, when she sends that seal to me ! I fear me the prophecy of the stars must speedily be fulfilled, for this moon hath almost waned."

31 *

CHAPTER XXXII.

A STRANGE FRIEND IN A STRANGE PLACE.

THE first day of her imprisonment in her gilded cage
had almost passed, and the shades of evening were
fast falling, blurring the outlines of the desert view, as
Edith stood at the casement, and, gazing eagerly out in
the direction her winged messenger had gone, speculated
on the incidents of his reception by her husband.

She was so busily weaving such fancies that she did not
hear the key turn in her door, nor the shuffling sound of
slipshod feet approaching, until they were close beside
her. Then she turned hastily, and saw the Circassian
woman standing with another female close beside her.

Several times during the day, black female slaves had
noiselessly entered the room, depositing silver salvers,
containing food, fruits, confectionery, iced sherbets and
colored drinks of various kinds, then vanished as noiselessly as they came. She had partaken sparingly of the
fruits only, fearing to try cooked dishes, and had drank
water alone. Save these blacks she had had no other
visitors.

Now, when the Circassian woman returned, accompanied by another, Edith nerved herself for some new

trial, but she was disappointed, for, motioning with her hand to the stranger, as though in introduction of her to Edith, the mother of the hareem turned again, and shuffled out of the apartment. This stranger, who remained, was also in the Turkish costume. She raised the veil which she wore, and disclosed to Edith features strangely familiar to her, though she could not remember where she had seen her, and gazed at her with an expression in which recognition struggled with doubt. Seeing this, the woman addressed her in the French language, as though it were her native tongue.

"The wife of Askaros does not know me," she said, "but well do I remember her, and much it grieves me to see her here. Has she forgotten the day when, with El Warda, she visited the hareem of the Princess Nezlé, near Boulak? Has she forgotten her who was their interpreter on that day?"

Like a gleam of light in the dark flashed back upon Edith the recollection of the woman at these words. She rushed up to the astonished Frenchwoman, ere she had finished speaking, kissed her fervently, and clung to her neck, much to her alarm lest any one should spy upon them. The other hastily pushed her back with the hurried whisper:

"On thy life and mine! treat me as a stranger," and resumed her former attitude.

But tears were in those hard eyes, which had not known moisture for years before, and the sardonic mouth twitched and worked in the convulsive effort to suppress a sob, at the trusting confidence of the young girl, who recognized her as a friend under such suspicious circumstances. The human heart, which still beat — indurated as it was with long suffering, and stained with sin — in that withered breast, leaped up to meet the affection of this pure young soul, with a mother's yearning. And Edith's impulse had secured her, in a moment, a friend for life or death.

When the woman next spoke it was in the cold, measured tone of a servant addressing a mistress, but she did not repeat her lesson as given her by her employer, though a listener who did not understand the language in which she spoke would have deemed, from her manner, that she was doing so.

"Friend of El Warda, my adopted daughter, what evil star, what foul treachery has brought you here?" she said, "and how long have you rested within these polluted walls? Where was your husband when you were stolen away? for I see that you are a prisoner here, not a willing guest."

"Where am I? What palace is this? Can you tell me?" asked Edith, eagerly. "Who are these hateful people to whom it belongs, especially that woman who seems its mistress? And what does she want with me?".

"And you have seen no one but her?" asked the woman in return, not replying to her question. "You do not know into whose power you have fallen? Thank God! There is yet time — it is not too late to save you yet!"

"No — no!" cried Edith impatiently. "Tell me, for mercy's sake — for all this mystery is maddening!"

"Then listen," replied the Frenchwoman, still standing as motionless as ever; "and make no start when I answer, which might betray us both, for there are eyes behind yonder lattice, which you see not, watching us — eyes hard to deceive, and a hand swift to punish what he would consider treachery in me. Are you able to stand the test? For what I will tell, will demand all your fortitude, to stand without blenching."

"Say on! I will not falter, nor betray you," answered Edith, faintly. "But what you tell me makes my heart stand still. You can trust me, as I trust you."

The woman gazed at her steadily a moment, then she replied:

"Then I will speak, for it is necessary you should know. You are in the palace and in the power of Abbas Pasha! And I am sent to prepare you for the honor he intends — of making you the head of his hareem. Keep all your courage. Remember two lives, and more than life to you, may depend upon it."

In spite of every effort she could make to nerve herself against the shock of this dreadful news, the face of Edith grew as colorless, and the features as rigid, as those of the dead. She gasped for breath, and a suffocating sensation seemed to stifle her. Though her dry lips moved, no sound came from them. She stretched forth her arms wildly, as though imploring protection, reeled forward, and would have fallen to the floor, had not the strong arms of the Frenchwoman supported her fainting form.

"A bad beginning!" muttered the other, impatiently. "I hope he is not watching us up there, or I shall have to explain this — he is so suspicious. I will go and see. Better meet danger half-way!"

And depositing her lifeless burden on the divan, she passed up the narrow stairway, which seemed familiar to her, and peered eagerly into the small hiding-place. It was empty, and she breathed more freely as she ran down again to resume her place by the side of Edith, who still lay motionless, her heavy breathing alone denoting her a living woman — not a livid and pallid corpse.

Y

Gradually she revived, and a mother could not have exhibited a more tender care than did the habitually callous old woman. The tender spot in her heart seemed to have been stricken, as miraculously as was the rock, from which the living waters gushed, when stricken by the rod of Moses.

Edith turned her grateful eyes upon her, and pressed her hand in thanks, as she assisted her to rise; then besought her pardon for such weakness, promising that now the first shock was past, she should see no repetition of it. Then she resumed her seat upon the divan, the woman again assuming the respectful demeanor of a servant, at the proper distance, and any one watching them during the conversation that ensued would have suspected nothing.

She obtained from Edith all she knew concerning her abduction, and a complete narration of everything that had occurred since her entering the palace. Among other things, she learned the despatch of the carrier-dove, which she assured Edith would be certain to wing its way direct to the house of Askaros; and she did not discourage the hope of the fond wife, that he would discover her prison, and rescue her, by the aid of the consul-general.

But the woman knew at that time how vain was that hope; for the mysterious disappearance of Askaros had been the talk of the Cairene gossips all that day, having been spread over the coffee-shops by such idlers as had learned it from the keeper of the Hotel d'Orient.

But she also knew — which Edith did not — that El Warda had again taken up her residence at the house of her brother, to strive and penetrate the mystery of his disappearance; though the Frenchwoman had not seen her, having only just received a message from her, when the imperative mandate of the Viceroy hurried her off to the Abassieh.

"He wants to see you this evening," the old woman wound up. "But he shall not, my poor child, if I can prevent it ; and I think I can. ° Time is everything ; for if help does not come by to-morrow, we can then see what is to be done, to get you out of this vile place. You may trust me. I swear to you by the soul of my dead daughter !—dead many years ago, before her mother had become the miserable wretch she now is ! And you looked so like her when you lay there—just as she looked before they hid her from my sight forever !— and I went mad first and desperately wicked afterward. Trust me, my child ; and when this cunning brain and these wicked strong hands have freed you, call me *'mother'* once more, as you did just now, and kiss me once again ! Then I will ask again, what I vainly asked the day she died : 'Lord, let thou thy servant depart in peace !' *His* servant ! What profanity in me to use that word ! I who have been the devil's bond-slave for so many wicked and weary years !

"But I must not now think of these things. I must keep my brain clear, to cope with that incarnate devil who now has you in his keeping. But fear not, my child, and trust me. Now I will go report to my gracious lord," she added, with a bitter emphasis on the words, "that the Frank woman is too ill in body and mind for him to see her ; and that I will prepare her to listen favorably to him by mid-day to-morrow. Then, if absolutely necessary, I can make you really ill with some herbs, powerful yet not poisonous."

"Stay, mother !" said Edith, humoring the strange fancy of her new-found friend and ally. "I have not yet shown you my protection in a last resort;" and she showed the hilt of the dagger, on which the diamonds glittered as she displayed it.

"Conceal that carefully. It may be useful in extremity, though not for the use you meditate," the woman answered; and a strange gleam came into her eyes that was not pleasant to see. "Abbas is a rank coward, and quails before any danger to himself in person, even if menaced by a woman. And stay! I can anoint its point with a poison so potent that the slightest scratch from it were certain death! Give it me, and you shall have it back ere the man visits you. Better use it on him than on thyself, and rid the world of a monster all men hate and all women fear. But his days will not be long in the land," she mumbled on, rather to herself than to her listener, "if the stars have not lied to me. I cast his horoscope and made my divination two nights since, by request of Nezlé Khanum, who loves him not over-much. Danger and sudden death lurk in his house. He was born under the malignant planet Saturn, and is doomed to die by violence ere this moon wanes! Who knows?—who knows?" she rambled on; while Edith, not knowing how strong a hold superstition, and the practice of illicit arts, can take on a strong, but ill-regulated mind like that of the woman before her, listened to her wild utterances, and deemed her utterly mad.

She stubbornly refused, however, to give up the dagger for the purpose so coolly proclaimed; smoothing over her rejection of the offer with words of grateful acknowledgment for the feeling that prompted it.

The Frenchwoman did not press the matter; but telling Edith to remain tranquil until her return, left the room, locking the door behind her. A suspicion that she had acted indiscreetly in reposing such implicit confidence in such a woman, whose character and life she now saw had been far blacker than the Cairene gossips or the simple-hearted El Warda had dreamed, came to disturb the mind of Edith, as soon as the door had closed. But she reassured herself by the reflection, that neither the woman nor Abbas himself could outstrip the flight of the dove; and after all, therein lay her sole hope of rescue from without.

And the woman had seemed honest. The very wild way in which she had talked was proof of sincerity. Such were not the weapons of a practised deceiver; she could not but put faith in her. Yes, she *would* trust her; for she saw that, next to the dove, the only hope of escape from the perils that surrounded her lay in her alone.

The evening darkened into night; the stars came forth, one by one, each in its appointed place in the heavens. Up rose the round bright moon, shining softly and sadly upon the desert — wasting its silvery light upon the bare brown earth, without shrub or tree, or blade of grass, to rejoice in its beams. The howl of the jackal and the hoot of the owl — the only living things that seemed to inhabit its sandy wastes — alone broke the stillness and silence of the night, which seemed to sympathize with the aching void in the heart of the lone woman — a prisoner in that palace — far away from her kindred, in a strange, savage land, with but one arm to lean on, one heart to trust — a prey to all the wild fancies which the time and place and situation inspired.

The night rolled on, and still the Frenchwoman returned not.

Silent and obsequious slaves had glided into the cham-

32

ber, deposited bread and drink, and noiselessly retired, uttering no word, like the goblin attendants in some enchanted castle. The Circassian woman had not come again, since placing her in charge of her substitute.

Edith looked restlessly at her watch. She was very weary, but her excitement was too great for even the thought of sleep. She rose and looked out listlessly into the night. As she gazed out over the desert, a dark object, coming rapidly toward her, obscured the moonlight; and she saw it was some winged night-wanderer, probably a bat or an owl. The next moment her own messenger-dove had nestled down upon her shoulder.

Her heart bounded high with hope; then stood still. She snatched eagerly at the ribbon which bound its neck, and saw under its wing either her own note or its answer. She tore it eagerly away, opened it, and saw by the light of the moon — as brilliant as that of day — the writing was neither her own nor her husband's; but a few lines traced in a small, cramped hand, unknown to her. Dizzy and sick with a vague dread, and the pang of hope deferred, at not seeing her husband's writing, as she had expected, she ran her eyes rapidly over the scroll. It was in French, and contained only these words: —

"The clue given is sufficient. We strongly suspect where you are. My brother is from home, so I answer you. Send another message the same way, with all you can discover to aid our search. Trust in God and Sitta Mariam. Your friends will save you. Your own
"WARDA."

Her brother not at home!

"Searching for me, poor fellow!" mused Edith. "I can give them certain information now; but I will wait until the return of my new friend first. But she is a fearful woman! I will determine whether to trust her or not, about my dove's return, after I have talked with her again."

And mindful of the warning that eyes were on her when she knew it not, she hastily kissed her faithful messenger, and hid him again in her bosom, which throbbed less wildly now she knew her friends and her husband had heard from her, and were hopeful of rescuing her.

After some time longer the Frenchwoman glided into the room; and the first glance at her face convinced Edith that she was ill at ease. But there was a red spot on her cheek, and a gleam in her eye, that indicated anger as well as apprehension.

"The brute beast!" she said; "how he tried my patience! I could not come to you before, for I had to watch him, and find what new devil's dish he was cooking with Mahmoud Bey and the Kislar Aga. But I did discover it by hiding behind his old mother's divan, which is in front of the curtains. The old woman is ill; and he sat there while he conferred with the Kislar Aga, who is his head demon! I could not get away, for the beast fell asleep, and I dared not stir. Had he waked and seen me, it would have been all over with me, and with you, too. But I know all now. More plots — more villany! Oh, that I could send a message into Cairo! Your dove, were he here now, could save more lives than one; for I cannot leave you, and there is no one in this accursed place I dare trust. Oh! for the dove!"

"Is this a stratagem to find if my messenger has returned?" thought Edith.

She looked hard into the woman's face, on which

strong anxiety, and, she thought, sincerity were depicted. Her resolve was taken.

"Swear to me by your daughter's soul," she said, "that you are sincere, and I may aid you."

The woman looked up eagerly.

"By that most sacred of all oaths to me," she answered, "I swear it. And may these eyes of mine, or my disembodied soul, never look upon my lost darling, if in life and unto death I be not true to you!"

"Enough," answered Edith. "I believe you. Behold the dove, as also the message he brought back to me."

The Frenchwoman clutched at the letter, and read it eagerly through.

"I see! I see!" she cried. "I understand El Warda, and the more need for prompt action. Have you another piece of paper, and a pen?"

Edith showed the fragment of her letter and the pencil.

"That will do," said the other. "Write this: 'At the Abassieh. Lose no time. *Gonsul Kibbeer* (Great Consul). Askaros, too, in peril. Send this seal to Sitta Khanum — quick. She will understand.'"

As she finished, the Frenchwoman took a piece of black ink from her pocket, stamped it with her signet-ring — which she wore, like a man, on the forefinger of her right hand — enclosed it in the slip of paper, and tied it under the dove's wing. Then, taking from her pocket a small box, she gave the bird a small lump of some black substance, which he pecked at eagerly and devoured. The effect seemed almost magical. Wearied as he had appeared the moment before, with dull eye and drooping wing, he had scarcely swallowed the food given him, when strength and spirit seemed thoroughly restored.

Then the woman leant from the casement, launched the dove into the air, and away he flew into the night, the bright moonbeams gleaming on his white wings, until he dwindled into a speck in the distance.

"Now!" she cried, fiercely; adding in a hoarse whisper of exultation: "Eblis guard thine own! for I have summoned by my spell a far worse devil than any of thy favorite's guardian demons! I will counteract and turn aside the evil he meditates — if not — perhaps — will consummate the fate, decreed two nights since by the stars which lie not. Who knows? Who knows?"

"What mean you?" anxiously asked Edith, whose faith in the woman's sanity was shaken by what seemed her wild raving. "You seem to have forgotten my peril, and your promise to save me from the doom worse than death, while you plot and plan with that terrible woman, of whom I have never heard aught but evil."

The rigid lines of the woman's face relaxed, and a gentler expression came into her sad, solemn eyes.

"Trust me still, O child — living image of my dead darling!" she said. "No hair of thy head shall be harmed. Obey me, and thou shalt be safe. But there are many things that thou hadst best not know. Trust me; and now sleep while I watch by thee; and if any creeping reptile crawl near thee, it will come but to its death! Ay, though it be Abbas Pasha himself." And she exhibited to Edith a long, keen dagger, which she wore concealed in her bosom.

"But *he* will not trouble thee, for the cup of coffee his mother made, and I handed him in the hareem, an hour since, will cause him to sleep till late to-morrow. Hum! A cautious man is Abbas," she muttered on; "but what his precautions are worth against a woman's wit he may

32*

soon learn to his cost.   But sleep now, my child, for to-morrow you will need all your strength of body and of mind !''   And again she muttered, as if to herself: ''Let me but tide over until to-morrow's sunset, and all is safe ! If not, Sheitan only can tell what may happen.   But sleep now, and thy mother will watch over thee, my child.   Sleep.''

She passed her hands several times quickly over the brow of Edith, who felt a sharp pain dart through her brain, and sparks glitter before her eyes as she sunk into a sound, mesmeric slumber.

CHAPTER XXXIII.

THE LOST MESSENGER.

THE Frenchwoman kept her word, and Edith, thanks to her, received no visit from Abbas during the day succeeding the second mission of the dove. She was told to feign illness, which she did, lying on the divan so that the Viceroy, from his spying-place, might see her when brought by the Frenchwoman, who, by cosmetics and other means, had given a deadly pallor to her cheeks, and every appearance of desperate illness. So Abbas, though he growled at the delay to which he was subjected in having his interview with the captive, had to admit its necessity.

It was with delight Edith heard later that he had gone out to drive ; for it left her perfectly free from espionage, and she stood at the window, watching for her dove's return with mingled impatience and hope. She saw the carriage and *cortége* of the Viceroy disappear on the dusty road, which she knew, by the direction of her dove's flight, led to Cairo. Along the same road she also saw come riding on their fleet dromedaries, two Bedouins of the desert, their long guns slung over their shoulders, and their white bournous fluttering in the wind, as their gaunt, ungainly animals jerked along with the swift but peculiar motion produced by the movement of both legs on the same side in advance at once.

When the Bedouins approached the palace they relaxed their speed, and finally stopped for a short rest, to eat and smoke, before resuming their journey. So near were they, and so still was the air, that Edith could distinctly hear the guttural sound of their voices. She was watching their movements with the interest of an unoccupied person with nothing to amuse her, when her attention was attracted by seeing them both rise suddenly, unsling their long guns, and point to something that their keen eyes distinguished afar off, but which her unpractised vision could not see. Straining her eyes in the same direction, however, she soon saw what appeared first a speck, then a dark object, gradually growing into shape and distinctness, as a bird swiftly winged its way straight toward the palace. She felt it was her dove, and flying so low as to be in easy range of the unerring marksmen, who had seen and awaited its coming. A sick feeling crept into her heart at what seemed almost a fatality against her, mingled with affection for the faithful messenger that had nestled in her bosom, and was now her sole connecting link with the world beyond her prison.

Nearer came the bird; and watching still, with their bronze faces turned in that direction, their long guns ready, the flint hammers cocked, stood the expectant Bedouins.

Nearer still came the dove, as if to certain death; watching, as it seemed, the sky above it, not the earth beneath, for danger. The long-range guns of the Bedouins were already raised, when one of them, signing courteously to the other, resumed his seat and laid down his gun, as though leaving so small a game to his companion.

Edith breathed freer — there was one chance less against her bird — one was more apt to miss than two ; so she watched and waited. The Bedouin had already raised his gun to his shoulder, his eye glancing along the barrel, when suddenly the bird wheeled back instead of darting forward ; and, with a grunt of surprise, he lowered his weapon. Both he and Edith soon saw the reason. A desert-hawk suddenly sailed from one of the pinnacles of the palace, where he had been watching for prey, and now pursued the bird he had sought to intercept.

Up into the air again, in wide circles, narrowing as they rose, mounted pursuer and pursued, until their flight brought them again just over the heads of the children of the desert, who watched the struggle with the same intentness, if not the same interest, as Edith.

The dove shot downward at last ; and, as he did so, the hawk, from high in air, swooped straight down upon it. As he did this, Edith saw the Bedouin, who was still standing, raise his gun suddenly to his shoulder. Down came the hawk toward the dove, swift and straight as an arrow ; but the gun flashed, his torn plumes floated on the air, and Edith saw with joy that *he* was the mark at which the man had aimed with skill too deadly to err !

But she saw, too, with a sharp pang, that the intervention had come too late to save the thing she loved, and which bore beneath its wing tidings of life or death to her, which now she would never see. For though sorely wounded, the rapacious instinct of the bird of prey, coupled with the impulsion of his downward flight, drove him headlong against his cowering quarry. With a shudder she saw the cruel beak and talons strike her favorite — saw victor and victim dash heavily upon the sand together !

The Bedouin rushed to the spot where the birds had fallen, and stooped over them. She saw him pick up the hawk ; and then, to her amazement, the dove feebly fluttered from the ground, and with wavering flight and unsteady wing, slowly struggled upward. Neither of the Bedouins made any motion to arrest its flight, but left it to its fate, as though it had earned a reprieve from them, by its recent escape.

Edith watched the unsteady flight of her pet with beating heart and bated breath. She feared it could never rise to the height of her window ; and, leaning far out, caught it as it came, and smothered it with kisses, as though it had been a human friend. The dove, whose back and breast were dabbled with blood, and whose dim eye and laboring breath indicated failing strength, feebly pecked at the loved hand which caressed it ; then a shudder shook its delicate frame, the eyes closed, the limbs stiffened, and Edith held in her hand a dead, instead of a living, friend. Faithful until the last, the bird had exerted the last flagging energies of life to fulfil its mission — had done that — and died !

As Edith, forgetting for a moment, in her grief for this faithful friend, to secure the letter it bore, bent over it, she heard a step behind her. Turning her tearful eyes, she saw the Frenchwoman, who, without ceremony, snatched at the ribbon, which she tore from the dead bird's neck, and handing a note to Edith, said, impatiently :

"This is no time for weeping over dead doves ! Death or deliverance may be in that answer !"

Recalled to herself by the harsh truth of these words, Edith read the answer, which she could not comprehend; but it seemed to satisfy her companion, who smiled grimly and said aloud, but as though to herself:

"I thought that would bring her! We must decide when she comes — for I do not see the way clearly."

Then she sunk into· musing, and Edith was made too happy at hearing from her husband to heed her much. At length the old woman said:

"Listen! we have gained a day, and your messenger's loss matters little now. She I sent for comes, and we can get no other help outside. If she will, she can save you, and I think she will. Now let me put away the body of that bird, lest its presence here cause suspicion."

Although unwilling to part with the body of her favorite, Edith saw the force of these suggestions, and with a sad heart and many tears, kissing again and again the dead beak of the unconscious thing, she surrendered it to the woman's keeping.

A few hours later, while again gazing from the window, she saw the cortége of the Viceroy returning up the dusty road, then heard the noise of his arrival in the court below, and felt that her trials — suspended for a few brief hours — were now again actively to recommence. Soon after the Frenchwoman returned in an excited manner.

"What devil's news can he have heard in Cairo?" she said, more to herself than to Edith; "for he is in high good humor. She must find out when she comes. It means mischief!"

Another hour passed, and Edith, gazing listlessly toward the Cairene road, saw clouds of dust arising from it, as if a carriage were driven along at a furious pace. A moment after the vehicle emerged from it, and she knew it must contain a woman, for it was accompanied by a guard of black eunuchs, as well as a troop of cavalry — the guard of some royal personage. On it sped toward the palace, which it entered at the same headlong rate that it had come.

The Frenchwoman, peering over her shoulder, chuckled joyously.

"It is she! It is she! I must go to the mother's hareem to watch my chance to speak to her. Rest tranquil, my child. *He* dare not disturb you while *she* is here!"

"But who is *she?*" asked Edith, curiously.

"My mistress, and your safety!" was the sole response; and the woman left the room, locking the door behind her, and left Edith alone, a prey to her own sad thoughts.

And there we, too, must leave her for the time.

CHAPTER XXXIV.

"A LITTLE MORE THAN KIN AND LESS THAN KIND."

AS the Frenchwoman reported, Abbas had returned from Cairo in high good humor, and very much exhilarated by something he had seen or heard during his visit.

He was sitting in his mother's apartment taking his mid-day repast — prepared as usual by her hand — and chatting to her gayly, when the Princess Nezlé was announced. The smile left the lips of the Viceroy, and his gayety seemed suddenly dissipated at the mere mention of that name, which seemed to jar upon his nerves.

The next moment the princess swept into the room, and Abbas, as best he might, endeavored to smooth his clouded brow, and resume his interrupted flow of speech and spirits. The princess seemed to be in the most exuberant good humor, laughing, chatting and making herself so agreeable to the mother and son, whom she entertained by racy recountals of Cairene and Stamboul scandals, that the moody brow of Abbas relaxed, and his good humor unconsciously returned. As Nezlé declared her intention of dining there, the elder lady pled fatigue at last, and asked to be allowed her usual siesta. This, of course, was granted, Nezlé declaring she would

take hers also, after having had five minutes' more talk
with her kinsman, whom she had not seen for so long a
time ; and the mother, fondly kissing the son's brow, retired to her repose.

No sooner had she left the room than a change came
over the countenances of both Abbas and Nezlé, each of
them seeming like a wary athlete, who nerved himself for
a struggle with a worthy antagonist. Abbas spoke first.

"To what do I owe the honor of this visit, Khanum?"
he said. "For well I know thou hast not come here to
talk gossip only, or to enjoy my mother's society, or
mine, agreeable as that may be. Speak frankly, then,
for between friends, such as we are, it saves time and
misapprehension."

"Thy sagacity is not at fault, Highness," Nezlé answered, calmly. "I have much to say, which it befits
thee to listen to with an attentive ear. Truth seldom
reaches crowned heads. Few can, and fewer dare tell it
when unpalatable."

"Then thine is disagreeable?" said Abbas. "Speak
on ; I thank thee for the warning, and promise to be
patient, for thou hast ever been a good friend to me.
To thee I owe my throne, and through thy influence at
Stamboul I hope to secure the succession of my son, El
Hami. We cannot quarrel."

"Firstly, then, as to what concerns thyself," said
Nezlé. "The affair of Askaros is a bad one from beginning to end, and may do thee harm both in Egypt and at
Stamboul, as well as injure the succession of thy son.
The consul-general should be conciliated, not made an
enemy by this new breach of faith I learned just before
reaching Cairo."

"Thou hast heard, then, that I have again put him in

safe-keeping," said Abbas, surprised. " Well, it is true. But thou dost not know that his protector has gone, and been replaced by that old dotard, his deputy, who is as a nose of wax between my fingers. So fear not on that account. I shall have no trouble, for Askaros hath only *disappeared;* no one can track him this time, for the accursed Nubian, who proved the abduction before, has been also imprisoned for some time in the citadel. He was hurt some time since in an affray."

"Yes, I know," answered Nezlé, carelessly. " In the affray in which the wife was carried off. Come, Highness, let us be frank ! Thou mayest deceive others, but not Nezlé Khanum."

"I believe Sheitan himself could not !" growled Abbas ; but he responded with a smile : " I believe you do know most things ; but this is a guess, and a bad one too. I know nothing of that matter ; however the tongues of Cairene gossips may malign their lord and master."

"Then, Highness," answered Nezlé, with almost mocking quiet, "I must ask the immediate punishment of one of thy people, who hath not only had the audacity to abduct her, but to secrete her in this very palace ! Nay," she added, stopping him by a gesture, "this I can prove to your Highness."

Abbas stared at her in blank amazement, and only said, shortly : " Produce the proof."

" Certainly. Behold it in her own handwriting, sent me by a carrier-dove she had with her when stolen away. The poor child knows me, and in her distress flattered me so far as to believe that I was still human, and might help her."

And so saying, narrowly watching the changing countenance of Abbas as she did so, Nezlé handed Abbas the slip of paper bearing the words, "*I am a prisoner at the Abassieh.*" The rest was torn away.

"Where is the rest of the note thou hast torn away?" growled Abbas, as his brow grew black; "and how canst thou, or I, know that this is written by the wife of the dog Askaros!"

"Highness, thou must ask the dove for the rest of the paper since that is all he brought me. The note is hers, I know; for the dove and the handwriting both are well known to me. So thou seest it must be one of thy high officials, who hath committed this outrage upon her and upon thee."

"A truce to idle babble!" cried Abbas, fiercely. "Thou hast my secret; for Sheitan keeps none from thee, it seems! What is the woman to thee? that thou shouldst quarrel with thy best and almost thine only friend, about her, or her miserable husband! Ask any other grace in the power of Abbas Pasha to bestow, and it shall be fully granted thee. Even to my mother I would not grant this! I need both the man and the woman, and both will I keep! Ay, even though El Hami should never sit upon my throne, and though Sheitan himself should claim me the moment my love and my revenge were both gratified together!

"Urge me no more!" he added, savagely, as he saw the princess was about to speak; and his brow grew black as night, and his face purple with passion. "If thou hast removed one Viceroy from the throne of Egypt, in the person of that drivelling old dotard men called 'the great'—thy father!—know that Abbas knows thee too well to take any draught from thy hand, or to trust himself in the power of one — woman in form, but *afreet* in soul!"

As Abbas spoke these words in the frenzy of a fury which made him forget his habitual fear of the woman before him, in the hate raised by her attempt to thwart his avarice and his lust — the two ruling passions of his nature — his face was as the face of a fiend.

But the blood of Mehemet Ali — which flowed more purely through the veins of the woman than of the man — was insensible to fear. The wild-beast rage of Abbas excited only the withering contempt of Nezlé, though her cheek grew lividly pale, and her eye flashed, at the insulting reference to her father, and to her own imputed, though involuntary crime. She raised her head loftily, and fixed on the savage beast before her a gaze, in which shone that steadfast light of human intelligence and courage, which can subdue the most bloodthirsty of the lower animals, when its fascination arrests their bloodshot eyes. The paleness of her cheek, the slight twitching of the corners of her mouth, and the dilatation of her nostril, like that of a war-horse snuffing the battle, alone showed the smothered wrath glowing in her breast, at the insolence of Abbas.

He now walked the room like a tiger in its cage, chafing under the eye of its keeper — and striving to lash himself into the fresh rage. When the woman spoke again, her voice was clear, calm and cold, devoid of passion or irritation, but too measured in the accents to be quite natural.

"Abbas Pasha!" she said, "are you mad? And has your frenzy for revenge on a wretched Copt man — your lust for his Ingleeze wife — led you so far from common reason, as to cause you to insult *me?* — me, whose hate

33 *

you well know is as strong as my friendship!—me, to
whom you owe so much! You well know there was
never any love lost between you and me. We were
necessary to each other—we are so still! But I brook
not such treatment from living man; and unless you
make ample apology for your words of insult, I shake
the dust of your house from my feet forever, and you
have made one enemy more—dangerous as all the
others!

"For the stars, that cannot lie, have revealed to me
that *thy* destiny is in *my* hands. Our houses are linked
together, since we both were born under the planet Saturn; but my place in his house controls thine! I have
spoken!"

When the princess commenced speaking, Abbas—as
though heedless of her words—continued pacing up and
down the chamber. Gradually he checked his steps as
she went on, finally stopped, and, as she closed with that
appeal to his superstition, the color fled from his face,
and terror succeeded wrath. His eye quailed under the
calm contemptuous gaze of the princess; but with as
much dignity as he could summon to his aid, he said:

"Let there be peace, I pray, between me and thee, O
Khanum! Pardon and forget the hasty words which
should have been addressed to no woman; and least of
all to thee, to whom I am indebted for so many past
favors, and to whom I look forward for aid and counsel
now! Ask any one thing but that thou hast demanded
of me, and it is granted before it is named. And even
that request I will seriously reflect upon also, and in it
will do all I can to meet thy wishes. Art thou content,
O heart and brain of man, under most winning guise of

woman? And shall we be friends again for life and death?"

"Ay!" answered Nezlé, with a winning smile, that showed all her sharp white teeth. And taking the hand he held out in amity, her small fingers closed on it like a vice. "Ay, Abbas, my kinsman, for life and death!"

"Why dost thou echo my words?" asked the Viceroy, anxiously, not half satisfied with the peculiar emphasis she laid upon them. "Can I make further atonement to thee for my folly?"

"Oh, no, no! I am quite satisfied with thee now," answered the Khanum, carelessly. "But we cannot quarrel again for many months to come. For in truth the chief purpose of my visit to-day was to make my adieux, as I go to pass several months at Stamboul — perhaps to remain there permanently. I am tired of Egypt; and the gossips of the coffee-houses have made me unpopular here with their slanders and vile stories."

The tidings seemed to give the Viceroy real pleasure, though he strove to repress its manifestation, and politely expressed his regret at the loss he should sustain, and his hopes of her speedy return. The reconciliation between the pair seemed complete; and when, in the evening, at parting, Abbas placed upon her finger a costly ring of brilliants and rubies, the Khanum's manner showed she considered friendly relations as perfectly re-established.

As they parted at the door of the hareem, the princess said, carelessly:

"Oh! as I had forgotten to say before, as I am going to Stamboul, I can let you have two charming young Mamelukes. They were lately sent me as a present from the Sultana, and would just suit you. Some time since-you said you were in need of handsome boys, and you know you can depend upon my taste."

Abbas, who was again in high good humor, thanked her warmly for the gift, declaring he was much in want of two Mamelukes near his person, such as she described. Promising to send them to him by her head eunuch — and mentioning one was a Georgian and the other a Circassian — Nezlé left her kinsman with mutual smiles, and their quarrel was apparently forgotten.

A crowd of officious female slaves accompanied her to the carriage-door, and assisted her in. As the door closed, she beckoned to one of them, whose veil was down, and whose whole appearance indicated great age, so bent, and bowed, and feeble, looked she, as she shuffled along.

Into this woman's ear the Khanum whispered these words:

"Thou hast done well to summon me. Watch and guard her still. This evening I send two auxiliaries; and when my signet-ring is shown thee, prepare the draught! The rest leave to me. The stars have not lied — the horoscope will be fulfilled, and the new moon comes after to-morrow!"

The old crone nodded her head in response, but said no word; and, as the carriage drove off, she tottered into the hareem-door, and up the stairs that led to the apartments of the mother of Abbas. Arrived there, she threw off her cloak, and disclosed the features of the old Frenchwoman.

"What does she meditate?" she muttered. "She is a fearful woman! I think I know — but how will she do it? I would have done it for her, had she commanded. And so I told her when I revealed the plot against her life. Lucky I was to be hidden behind Abbas' divan, and overheard the plot against her life, as against that of Askaros. But she only laughed, and said, 'that was not woman's work; and that she could always find fit tools to do her work, so long as men were such fools.' Then she laughed again; but it was not a pleasant laugh to hear, and it boded ill to somebody And then her parting words about the horoscope, and the waning moon! She means mischief! I doubt me she means mischief!''

And still muttering in this strain, the old Frenchwoman threw off the rest of the disguise, and sought the presence of Edith.

CHAPTER XXXV.

THE SWOOP OF THE VULTURE.

A S Abbas Pasha, ill at ease with himself, in spite of
the reconciliation he had effected with his dangerous kinswoman, and chafing under the consciousness
of having put himself more thoroughly than ever into her
power, wended his way back to his mother's apartments,
the idea occurred to him of feasting his eyes upon his
fair captive once again. Quietly stealing up the narrow
stairs to his hiding-place, he looked down upon the two
women, who, deeming themselves secure from observation, were not on their guard. To his surprise he saw
Edith — no longer lying ill and languid on her divan,
but apparently restored to her usual vigor, though still
pale — now standing near the window, and conversing in
eager tones with the old Frenchwoman. And the latter's
manner struck him as less deferential and more confidential than he liked.

His suspicious nature was roused by this sight; so,
returning as noiselessly as he had come, he passed back
to his own private chamber, took from a cabinet a red
velvet case of oblong shape, and opening the door of
Edith's prison, passed quietly through. So noiseless
were his movements, the first intimation the startled

394

women had of his approach was the sight of him standing within a few steps of them, intently regarding them both, and listening to the conversation he could not comprehend, as though to learn its purport from the looks and gestures of the speakers.

The Frenchwoman was the first to recover her composure ; blank terror and dismay were stamped upon the features of Edith. Making a lowly obeisance to the visitor, the former stood like a statue, her head bent down, waiting his sovereign pleasure. Edith, whose trembling limbs could scarce support her quivering frame, leaned against the window for support, her dilating eyes fixed upon the intruder, whom she recognized at once, with a mixture of dread and abhorrence; yet by the fascination of terror unable to withdraw them from his repulsive countenance, now rendered still more odious to her, by the look of stolid satisfaction the features wore.

Abbas enjoyed their confusion in silence for some time ; but when he spoke, it was with a grave courtesy, not without dignity.

"Say to my fair guest," he said to the interpreter, "that it rejoices me to see that her health is again restored. Say that I have visited her thus unannounced, to tell her this palace and all it contains are at her disposal, including its master, who now stands before her."

The woman, instead of giving word for word the Viceroy's speech, slowly and like one rendering a full translation, simply said :

"He offers you the house and all it contains. Answer him, and say you are sensible of the honor he does you, but do not know why you were brought here."

Edith did as suggested, and the interpreter gravely

turned the words into Turkish for the Viceroy, who turned sharply upon her.

"Have you not explained this to her, and prepared her for my visit?" he growled.

"Highness, I have done my best," she answered, calmly; "but the Ingleze are very stupid and very stubborn — not like the women you have known."

"Tell her, then," answered Abbas, "that I could not live without her, and resorted to stratagem to secure her, out of my great love for her; that I intended her to be the head of my hareem, and Queen of Egypt. In proof of this, I have brought her a trifle as a present, which I beg her to accept." And opening the velvet case, he took thence a splendid parure of diamonds and pearls arranged as a coronet, and a necklace and bracelets of fabulous value. These he proffered to the shrinking girl, who made no motion to accept them, but only stared at him and his gift with wide, open eyes full of terror.

"Tell him that your acquaintance is yet too brief for you to accept his presents, and determine if you can return his love," prompted the Frenchwoman. "Say something, for God's sake! and don't stand staring there, and I will tell him what is best. I fear to anger him; so rouse yourself, and look less like a bird under the eye of a serpent. Your fear will encourage him, and then may follow violence, which I cannot resist. Gain time! it is everything. For your *husband's* sake, if not your own, be a woman and not a child!"

Thus adjured, Edith nerved herself to the repulsive task; and just in time: for the patience of Abbas was well-nigh exhausted, and the evil gleam began to shine in his dull eye. He roughly questioned the old woman

as to what she was saying to the Ingleez — which she explained in her own way — and as he saw Edith assume a
more friendly manner, credited the explanation.   He
laid the sparkling parure upon the window-ledge and
drew nearer the girl's side — though not offering to take
her hand, nor to touch her — and, through the interpreter, talked to her in that strain an Eastern man thinks
most likely to please a woman.

He paid her florid compliments, full of hyperbole ;
compared her complexion, eyes and figure with all animate and inanimate objects, proffering unbounded affection and untold wealth and luxury, if she would but smile
upon him and return his passion.

To all these the Frenchwoman answered for Edith in
vague terms ; not actually repulsing him, but urging the
necessity of longer time and more intimate acquaintance.
This plan, adroitly as it was managed, seemed only to
have encouraged the brutal nature and gross instincts of
the Viceroy ; and the Frenchwoman saw with terror she
had finessed too much, when after an hour of this weary
talk, Abbas rose from the seat he had taken, and, instead
of offering to go, motioned her to withdraw, and leave
him alone with his captive.

For a second the woman seemed to hesitate ; but reflecting on the impossibility of resistance, she withdrew,
casting on Edith a look full of meaning, and touching
significantly the handle of the dagger hidden in her
bosom.   The gesture was unseen by Abbas, who looked
not at her, but gloated upon the charms of his destined
victim.

The momentary hope inspired in the breast of Edith
by this gesture, and the wild idea that the old woman
might slay Abbas where he stood — suggested by her des-

34

peration —died away when the woman passed out, closing the door noisily, and dropping the curtain before it
inside.　But neither Edith nor Abbas observed that she
softly reopened it, and stooped down behind the curtain,
peering eagerly through into the room, fierce resolve
written on every line of her haggard face, and a long,
keen dagger bare in her hand — a crouching tigress ready
for the spring!

"If it comes to the worst," the woman muttered,
"this shall cut it short!　Who can tell but the stars have
assigned this expiation to me?"

And so, wan, worn, terrible, with glittering eyes, like
a wild beast at bay, she watched and waited there; more
dangerous than any beast of prey — than any desperate
man — in the recklessness of roused feminine ferocity!

Abbas — undreaming of danger and possible death
lurking so close behind him — uttered a grunt of satisfaction as she left the room, and approached the terrified girl, who seemed to shrink within herself, as his
loathed form drew near her, as she still leant against the
window.

Unable to converse with her, he took up the case of
jewels, and selecting thence the coronet of pearls, essayed
to place it on her brow.　Half stupefied with terror, the
girl made no resistance to this overture, but shrinkingly
submitted to it, her pallid face and wild, agonized eyes
offering a fearful contrast to the sparkling gems that
blazed and scintillated on her brow.

Emboldened by his success — or mistaking the terrified
submission of his captive for pleased acquiescence—Abbas
next placed the necklace around her neck.　In doing so,
whether by intention or by chance she could not tell, his
clammy hand touched her bosom.

But that touch roused to indignation and horror the terror that hitherto had paralyzed the faculties of the insulted wife. The hot blood surged through her veins; her courage rose to desperation, and raising her arm, she repulsed the officious and revolting admirer with such force, that he reeled several steps away, and would have fallen, had he not staggered against a divan. Here he supported himself, gasping for breath through mingled astonishment, rage, and baser passions still.

But the violence done him seemed to have roused the wild beast within him, sometimes dormant but ever ready to awaken; for with a hoarse cry, and with an unmistakable expression on his sensual face, he sprang forward to seize the helpless form of the frail woman in his strong arms.

And then the seconds of Abbas Pasha's life were well-nigh numbered! For, at that cry and movement, there glared from behind the curtain a face, more fiendish and more fell, than ever woman's was before — a face like those that Greek and Roman painters feigned for the Furies—full of eager hate, and hot thirst for blood.

In the long, lean, sinewy right hand this terrible shape, like avenging Fate, held — not the fabled snaky scourge of Tisiphone — but a keen, gleaming dagger. And, as Abbas rushed forward, it rose to its feet, ready to bound upon him!

The next moment, it sunk back and slunk away into concealment; for Abbas recoiled more suddenly than he had advanced, and — with craven terror in every feature of his vile countenance — cast a hurried backward glance at the door-way, as though meditating flight.

Gathering courage from despair, and with womanly modesty exasperated into recklessness, the American girl had drawn up her figure to its full height, her bright blue eye flashing the fire of outraged womanhood, and had thrust her hand into her bosom.   Then, as Abbas rushed to seize her, as the vulture swoops upon its prey, in the uplifted right hand of the maiden he saw gleaming a dagger, apparently menacing his own precious life.

Dastard as he was sensual — craven as he was cruel, the seducer fell back, not knowing — from the wild cry with which she accompanied her act — that in utter desolation, preferring death to dishonor, the blow she meditated was for herself — not him.

"God be merciful to me, a sinner!" was that cry. "Better this than worse, O Askaros! my husband! for whom is my latest prayer — my last thought — my parting breath!"

But she arrested her upraised hand, as she saw the baffled ravisher recoil, and stand irresolute in the attitude of a beaten hound, shame and cowardice struggling on his face — no resolve left on his brow — no courage in his eye — but, like all the meaner animals in peril, meditating flight.

The fierce eyes that watched him from behind the curtain saw this too; and as a grim smile convulsed the firmly set lips, slowly stole back the dagger to its sheath, and the wild figure crept outside the door, as though all peril were past, and, like the hunting-tiger of India, the human beast within, baffled in his first spring, would try no second.   Nor was she wrong; for scarcely had she closed the door, and concealed herself, than it was flung violently open, and Abbas pushed noisily through.   With the deadly sin of Tarquin adding another stain to his ulcerated soul, which knew shame and fear, but not remorse, the baffled tyrant crept away from the presence of his victim that might have been, his prisoner still — all unknowing of the deadly peril he had just escaped — of other dangers lurking in his path — and only plotting to carry out by force, or fraud, his vile infraction of the laws of God and man.

But the small cloud no bigger than a man's hand, which neither he, nor the woman, saw or knew of, was still rolling down toward him, charged with his doom.

The Frenchwoman crept back into the room, and there found Edith, still standing like a pythoness, with dilating eye and expanded nostril, the dagger still uplifted in her hand — gazing with strained intensity on the door through which her insulter had slunk away. She did not seem to see the woman, when she entered and came up to her; and it was only when she spoke, that Edith, with a start, recovered her consciousness, and, kissing it first, hastily replaced the dagger in her bosom.

"Well done! my daughter," the old woman said; "I saw it all; and strange to tell, you saved the life of yonder dastard by menacing your own! He thought the menace was for him. Cowardly and cruel, the two go together. My dagger would have made a new Viceroy for Egypt, in one second more, had he gone forward instead of back! I thought it was his Kismet to die by my hand, ere this moon wanes; but it seems not. Yet the stars cannot lie! But lie thou still, here," she added, as Edith, in reaction from her late excitement, fell upon her neck, and burst into a flood of hysteric weeping. "Lie thou still, my daughter. The tiger will crouch awhile before he ventures another spring. He will consult me first, and employ me to drug thee — I know him well! So, he is easily baffled, thou seest. Rest tranquil; for

34 *   2 A

the Khanum has promised, who ever keeps her word. She told me, 'This evening I send two auxiliaries. The stars have not lied! The prophecy will be fulfilled — the new moon comes after to-morrow!' Knowest thou what that means, my child? It signifies deliverance for thee — ay! and for Egypt, too! — for the stars and the Khanum lie not!"

CHAPTER XXXVI.

ORZMUD AND AHRIMAN.

A T noon on the same day which witnessed the great peril and escape of Edith at the Abassieh, El Warda sat watching by the couch of Askaros, in the sad and lonely house, in which had lately been enacted so many scenes of joy and of woe — succeeding each other with the rapidity and shifting changes of color in the kaleidoscope. The sick man, now restored to his right mind, but wan and worn from the ravages of the fever that had shorn him of his strength, lay exhausted on his couch, sunk in a fitful and disturbed slumber.

So weakened was he in mind and body, that it had been an easy task for the girl — no adept in deceit, and truthful always — to make him accept the preconcerted story that accounted for his wife's absence; but he was impatient for her return, and every time he wakened, would repeat the same question as to when she might be expected.

It is one of the alleviations of illness, that a merciful Providence sends, that the doubts and fears which would most keenly afflict us in health, trouble us but little in that shadowy realm that separates illness from death; and a kind of childish confidence in the statements of

403

friends who surround us, and minister to our wants, re-
places the exercise of individual judgment.   Therefore
the story, which in health would not have satisfied Askaros, nor quieted his apprehensions, was now perfectly
reassuring to the sick man.

El Warda watched over him with a sister's care, and
had only left him when the message brought by the dove
proved the necessity of promptitude, and induced her to
pay that visit to the princess, of which the results have
already been related.   As she sat and watched the sick
man, she fell into a reverie, in which the strange and
exciting scenes which had so suddenly broken the monotony of a life, until now so uneventful, passed in re-
view before her.

She recalled the hopes she had cherished — not fully
understood by herself until they were blasted ; and she
lingered over their memory with a fond regret.   Then
her thoughts passed on to the strange conduct of Daoud,
at the second visit she had paid him ; and to the mysterious allusions he had made, which she could not comprehend.   Her mind dwelt on him with a pertinacity
and an interest which displeased herself.   She knew she
did not love him as she had loved another ; yet she felt
a deeper interest, and certainly a warmer sentiment for
the young Syrian than mere friendship would warrant.

As the girl sat thus, with her eyes fixed on the sleeping invalid, weaving these thoughts and fancies in her
busy brain, so deep was her self-absorption that she did
not hear the sound of stealthy footsteps creeping near,
nor observe that the curtain of the door had been raised,
and several forms had glided into the obscurity of the
darkened chamber.   The first intimation she had of their
presence, was feeling something thrown over her head,

and enveloping her arms, while strong hands seized and bound her.

She could not resist, nor shriek out for help, because half stifled by the pressure of the covering upon her face; and she was gently deposited on a divan, and left there. Then she could hear the sound of persons moving softly about the room, and finally a noise as of removing a heavy piece of furniture. But what struck her as strange was that the noise did not awaken Askaros; for she heard neither the sound of his, nor of any other voice. All was carried on in silence. No one spoke, nor even whispered, that she could hear. At length even these slight sounds ceased, and all was quiet again in the chamber — so quiet, indeed, that the girl could hear the rustling of leaves in the garden, but no call from Askaros — no sound of human voice, or evidence of human presence in her vicinity.

Strange as the situation was, the suddenness of the whole thing had been so great, and she had been so gently treated, that she was but little terrified, though she could form no idea of the meaning of the strange proceeding, since it was plain no violence had been intended. But as time glided away, and no one came to liberate her, the silence of the chamber became oppressive. By a strong effort she released her right arm from its bonds, lifted a little the stifling pressure of the band over her face, and called on her brother's name, to at least awaken him, and hear the sound of a human voice. Besides, she knew he had a small silver bell near him, and could summon the slaves to release her.

But her surprise changed into alarm when, after calling, first gently, then more loudly, no answer came but the echo of her own voice. A new alarm took possession of her, and with the strength of desperation she tore away the coverings from her face, wrenched herself round on the divan, so as to command a view of the sick man's couch, and peered eagerly into it.

The couch was empty !

Then, all at once, flashed into her mind the horrid purpose of this strange visit, and the meaning of the noises she had heard. They had come to steal Askaros away, and had succeeded in their attempt. The last drop had fallen. The poor girl's cup was full ! With a wild shriek she fell back again upon the divan; and when the slaves, summoned by the sound, ran to the apartment, they discovered their master was gone, and El Warda lying senseless in her bonds.

Slowly she recovered her consciousness, and with it a keen sense of the new danger which threatened that fated house. Askaros, during the tedious hours she had sat by his bed of illness, and told her the strange tale of his previous abduction ; and she therefore doubted not an instant the quarter from which this new stroke came.

One thought alone suggested itself to her in this emergency. She must go and consult Daoud, her only counsellor, since she had learned but the day before that Moussa-ben-Israel, the only other she could trust, was still absent at Jerusalem. Her resolve was no sooner made than acted upon. She summoned Fatima and a man slave, and for the third time bent her steps toward the house of Daoud.

Let us pass before her into the house of the Syrian, and find out the condition of mind in which she was to meet him. For, at the moment of her arrival, he was carrying on a fierce conflict in his own soul, and striving to arrive at a decision, on which his whole future destiny would hang.

The Persians believe that over the birth of every male child there preside two divinities, Orzmud, the Spirit of Good, and Ahriman, the Spirit of Evil; and that the life of that man represents the conflicts of these warring angels. Sometimes the one, again the other, gets control of all his actions; and the strife ends only with his death, when the angels appear as witnesses for and against him, before the great Judgment-seat.

In the life, and conflicting influences of the Syrian, was afforded an apt illustration of this Eastern superstition; for his soul, during many months, had been a battlefield for these warring powers; and Ahriman, the Spirit of Evil, had almost gained the mastery, until the treachery of Abbas, and the gentle influence of his love for the pure young girl, had once more given Orzmud a place in his troubled soul — a battlefield strewn with the wrecks of past conflict.

When El Warda, like a ministering angel, had visited him before — wretched, miserable, despairing, and trembling on the verge of madness, and with her pure influence had caused hope to dawn again on his darkened spirit — Orzmud had gained the vantage-ground. Daoud vowed to dedicate the rest of his life to better and brighter things, and to make himself worthy of her he loved. Hence he had labored diligently and indefatigably to undo his own evil work, and to expiate it by services to the man whom he had formerly destined as his victim.

The force of circumstances, however, or as he in his Eastern fatalism termed it, his Kismet, had drawn him once more into the vortex of troubled waters, from which he had hoped to escape: and the instincts of hate and

vengeance had been revived in his soul, by renewed conflict with the wiles of Abbas, and by that interview with
the Khanum, whose skilful touch had set bleeding afresh
the wounds of pride and revenge, festering and unhealed
within his soul.

These evil impulses had almost banished the good influence, that had fallen like dew upon his heart, in the
interview with the woman he loved with all the wild
idolatry of his passionate Eastern nature. And Ahriman,
not Orzmud, was whispering to him, as he sat awaiting
the eunuch who was again to lead him into the presence
of the Khanum.

But, mingling with the tempting suggestions of the
fiend, appealing to his fiercer passions, came the chill
whispers of doubt and dread. The mission on which
the princess sought to send him he more than suspected,
for his subtle intellect did not require such broad hints
as she had given, to fathom her fell purpose. It was a
mission of life or death for him or for another, and the
odds were fearfully in favor of his enemy, whom he now
knew to be hers also. She incurred no risk — that was
all his. If he failed, on his head alone would fall the
penalty. Perhaps it was a trick, after all, and she was
acting as the instrument of that enemy to lure him to his
destruction. But his subtle spirit soon dismissed the last
suspicion. The woman was in earnest. There could be
no doubt of that; but she had saved him before, only
with the view to use him, as she was now doing. Turn
it as he would, he was her tool after all, when he flattered himself he was avenging his own wrongs.

That thought was galling to his proud spirit. Was he
doomed ever to be the catspaw and convenience of

others? he, who felt in his soul the power of originating and commanding!

Then, too, there came another suggestion. He was playing a fearful game, the price of which was his own life, which might be wrested from him, as the Khanum had told him, under slow tortures, to which his previous punishment had been as thistle-down, when weighed against them. Like many men of the greatest moral courage, and utterly contemptuous of danger, however great if only sudden, the delicate nervous organization of the Syrian rendered him morbidly susceptible to physical pain, as much so as a woman. Therefore, he shuddered at the thought of those slow tortures the princess had hinted of, and which rose to his imagination in the shape of impalement, and other Eastern punishments.

But more than all—after incurring the terrible risk of all these dangers — was he sure of getting his reward? even if successful. He had no promise, no pledge from El Warda that she would pay him the only price he coveted, and be the guardian angel of his life when he came back triumphant, when he had fulfilled his pledge to her to save those two, one of whom, he half feared, she still loved with a consuming though pure and hopeless passion.

These thoughts had recurred to him while returning from the bath, after making the changes in his appearance suggested by the Khanum; for those very precautions proved how dangerous needs must be the mission requiring such disguise. He half resolved to temporize, and, under plea of illness, to refuse to go when the princess sent for him, that he might have more time to think over an affair so momentous. For there was a desperate hope in his heart, that he might yet win El Warda with-

35

out so terrible an ordeal, without once more staining his soul and his hands with fresh sin.

He was sent for no child's play; that he knew. To gain such an angel, must he, like the old Greek he had read of, descend into hell? unlike him, not to find her there, but to drag her down from her pure sphere, to consort with one, the accomplice and tool of a she-devil?

No, he would not go! at least not yet. He would try first if more legitimate and less wicked means could not accomplish the ends he sought; means of which he could frankly speak, and she could approve. For the other black secret would hang over their future confidence, and cloud his happiness like a funeral pall. No, he would not go!

As these thoughts passed through his mind he looked out of the window over the trees of the Ezbekieh, and gazed up in the air, with a sudden remembrance of the omen he had seen there so many weary, weary days ago, when the shadows of the coming evil were just beginning to darken his soul.

High up in air, just over the Ezbekieh trees, sailed a vulture-hawk, slowly circling down, as if intending to alight.

"I see the vulture now, but not the dove," the Syrian muttered. "Like me, he is weary of the chase, and longs for rest, not evil."

Even as he spoke, an Arnaout ruffian, who was lounging, half drunk with arrackee, in front of the coffee-house, suddenly sprang up, levelled at the vulture his long Albanian rifle with twisted stock, and just as the bird was about settling to its rest, brought it heavily to the earth, fluttering in its death-agony.

"Is that an omen too?" hissed Daoud, fiercely. "Is

the foul fiend permitted ever to mock me thus, when a good aspiration rises to my soul? Oh, that I could see my guardian angel now, to confirm my good resolves!"

The almost unspoken words had scarcely passed his lips when she whom he had invoked glided into the room; and when he turned, he saw her standing at his side, gazing upon him with a half wondering look of doubt and recognition.

CHAPTER XXXVII.

EL WARDA'S SACRIFICE.

WHEN El Warda entered the silent and deserted house of the Syrian, she saw no one below, and, passing up the stairs, she entered again for the third time, the sitting-room looking out upon the Ezbekieh.

But she started back in disappointment, and in shame, at seeing another than Daoud there. The slight figure standing by the window, with the back toward her, seemed his, but when it turned toward her, in response to her light touch upon the arm, she recoiled in amazement.

Though the features were similar to Daoud's, instead of the colorless complexion of the Syrian, with the thick short hair clustering around the temples, the face she saw was swarthy as that of a Circassian; the ample turban covered a shaven head, while the beardless upper lip lacked the silken moustache Daoud always wore. The man seemed equally embarrassed, though he did not show the same surprise as herself, for he seemed to recognize her in spite of the thick veil, which she had not raised. When he spoke she was reassured, for the voice and the smile she at once knew as those of the man she

412

sought; though she still marvelled much at the strange metamorphosis.

"Welcome, thrice welcome to my poor house! whose master is ever at thy service, gentle lady," he said. "Sit down, and tell the most devoted of thy servants to what cause he owes the honor of this visit; for well he knows it is not made without grave reason. Now, as ever, thou hast only to command him."

El Warda took the proffered seat in silence, much marvelling at the masquerade that had so changed her companion, that even she did not at first know him. Lost in thought, she did not speak for some minutes, and Daoud also preserved a respectful silence, as though awaiting her pleasure.

At length she spoke, and, making no allusion to his appearance, related to him circumstantially the incidents already described; beseeching his aid a second time to save her brother, as he had done the first.

When the girl had finished her tale, a revival of the fierce conflict he had first gone through, took place in his troubled soul. He saw the dangers of the new complication, caused by the renewed treachery of Abbas, and the necessity for prompt action, if he would save both husband and wife. But his distracted brain could find no other hope of aid, than the dread woman he had sought to repudiate.

He felt the supreme crisis of their fate — of his own and of the gentle girl before him, so trusting and so dependent on him — had come. He felt his decision must be immediate, as it would be final; that the fate of all four, and of another besides, their deadliest foe, hung trembling in the balance, which a breath from his lips would incline. And at that thought, his pride and his

35 *

courage, from temporary éclipse rose into full effulgence, and his voice and mien were composed, almost commanding, when he spoke again.

"El Warda! sister, and more than sister! light of my life! pulse of my heart, and inspiration of my soul!" he cried: "the liberty of Askaros Kassis and the honor of his wife, the life of Daoud-ben-Youssouf, and of their common foe, all —strange as it may seem to thee —all now hang upon the slender thread of one word from those lips of thine! Utter it, and I go to danger, perhaps to death, to rescue those thou lovest even more than thine own dear self. Utter it not, and I fold my arms, and lift not my hand and peril not my life, for those who care not for me, and whom I regard as less than any single hair that falls from thy beloved head! With thee, and thee alone, rests the decision — and on that decision hangs the destiny of all!"

"And that word!" cried El Warda. "What is it? and how can one word from the lips of a weak girl do such great things? Oh! Daoud, dost thou too mock at my misery by such words at such a time?" and dropping her face in her hands, the hot tears trickled through them, each drop blistering the Syrian's soul! while the shudder that ran through her frame attested the violence of her grief, at the loss of her last hope — his sympathy and succor.

A spasm of pain contracted the Syrian's brow at the sight of her suffering ; but, the sublime and pitiless egotism of the passion he called love, conquered. He stood still, watching her, while every nerve and fibre of his frame quivered with suppressed pain — like that of a wretch upon the rack —at witnessing her suffering. Gradually the hysterical paroxysm passed ; the girl's sobs grew infrequent, then ceased : and she raised her eyes, still wet with tears, to the arbiter of so many destinies besides his own, in a mute appeal that he felt he must answer.

Callous as he had grown — invulnerable as Achilles to the ordinary casualties of the warfare we call life — like the Grecian, he too had his one point, through which he too might, at an unguarded moment, meet his fate. No Indian at the stake ever endured with more stoical composure the tortures that agonized body and soul, than he had outwardly witnessed the sufferings of the girl before him, crushed by the loss of her last hope. And the cynical coldness with which he had spoken, made her resign herself to the grief of utter despair.

But that look was more than the man could bear; and the suppressed passion, the grief, the love, the agony that possessed him — all found vent at last in a rush of words that almost choked his utterance.

He told her now, in words that burned with the heat of his own long stifled passions, all his love, all his misery, all his sin! He concealed nothing — extenuated nothing. Had he been standing before the great Judgment-seat in the presence of his offended Creator, he could not have spoken more fully. With the frankness of a death confession, he explained to her everything that had hitherto seemed dark and mysterious; and he opened to the astonished vision of the pure girl the black depths of sin and sorrow, unsuspected before by her guileless heart, to which evil had been a horrible, but shapeless thing.

He told his own story, concealing nothing; he revealed the iniquities of Abbas, and the crimes of the princess; he showed the actual situation as it was, with all its terrors and all its perils.

When he ceased, the excitement that had sustained him

thus far, seemed to give place to deep humility and despondency. His head sunk upon his breast, his frame seemed to collapse, he crossed his hands over his chest, and stood like a criminal awaiting the sentence of his judge — all the pride, all the passion which had animated him in the beginning, sunk into self-abasement and dread of the verdict he had challenged.

Over the expressive face of the girl, while he continued speaking, there passed many changes; from disapproval to condemnation; from pity to almost loathing; from righteous indignation to qualified approval; from repulsion to sympathy. But as the penitent went on in his confession, the change from severity to softness grew more perceptible; and ere he finished, the expression of that candid earnest face grew more pitying, more sympathetic, almost affectionate; as though the first harsh judgment had been revoked.

When he had ceased, and stood like the criminal awaiting sentence, there stole upon his ear, like the music of seraphs from above, the soft, low tones of the voice he loved so well to hear, bringing soothing words full of hope and promise to his struggling soul.

"I have heard thy strange tale, O Daoud! my brother," she said, "with mingled feelings of despair, of terror, but finally of hope and joy for thee! For the latter part redeemeth the first: for does not the Holy Book say, 'There is more joy over the sinner that repenteth, than over ninety and nine just persons made perfect?' And hast thou not repented in the agony of a self-imposed humiliation, to thee — as I know thee — more bitter far than death? And shall not thy repentance be accepted by God and man; and the joy in heaven, as it is on earth, be proportionately great therefor?"

As she raised her eyes above in the ecstacy of devotional rapture, she seemed to the gaze of her worshipper more divine than human. But his soul could never soar to those heights where hers habitually reposed ; and the impression produced upon his mind by this unselfish rapture was but transitory.

Ahriman — his lower nature — dragged him back to earth again, and tempted him to drag his idol down with him. So, in answer to the enthusiastic girl, he said:

"I thank thee for the hope and comfort thou hast given one sorely in need of both. We have spoken enough of the past ; let us now consider the present and the future. What thou hast come here to tell me, proves the necessity of immediate action. Even now I am awaiting the arrival of a messenger to summon me to the Princess Nezlé ; and I hesitate to go, for danger — perhaps death — lurks in the path over which she would send me !"

"And is there no way to avoid it ?" asked El Warda, anxiously. "Cannot the consul-general aid us ? Better far trust him, than that wicked woman."

"The consul-general has gone," Daoud answered. "Else had Abbas never dared to seize thy brother. His successor is a man of feeble mind and body, who will take no steps to aid us."

"Then you think this evil woman is our last hope ?" asked the girl, tremblingly.

"I do !" responded Daoud ; "and I will go — upon one condition only. Promise me, that if I come back successful — if I save both Askaros and his wife — that thou wilt be mine thenceforth for ever, to guide my earthly labors, and fit my soul for eternity. Wilt thou give me this promise ?"

2 B

" cannot! I cannot!" cried El Warda, wringing her hands in despair. "It is unkind, it is cruel of you, Daoud, to ask it at such a time! to make my love the price of your action! If you would keep my esteem, do not drive a bargain with me; but depend on my gratitude afterward."

"Then will I stir no step!" answered the Syrian, sullenly; "for I believe I go to rescue my rival and my enemy: since thou wilt not give the promise. It is useless to urge me further. I will not go! All that a man may reasonably do for his sister, will I do for thee; but I will not risk my life for less than this hope I have named — which looks more shadowy now than ever."

"And is this resolve final?" asked El Warda, suddenly, drying her tears as she spoke.

"As final as destiny!" was the cold answer.

"Then hear me!" she rejoined, drawing up her form, assuming an expression of determination Daoud had never seen upon her face before. "Then hear me. If there be no other means left to save them, but at the price of myself, I will pay that! But mark me, Daoud-ben-Youssouf, man selfish to the core! Even now I cannot lie to thee, and say that with my hand I will then give thee my heart: nay, nor even so much of it as I could have accorded thee a few seconds back, ere thou didst seek to bargain with the sister for the brother's blood! May Sitta Mariam pardon me for the sin, into which my desperation and thy cruelty drive me!"

The sullen gloom passed from the Syrian's brow as she spoke; and the scorn of her last words fell unheeded on his ear, which drank in greedily her promise; and he clutched at it, as a drowning man does at a plank which is to float him to shore.

"And thou promisest!" he cried. "Swear it by Sitta Mariam, and I go to the princess, to bring back those whom thou lovest better, I fear, than thou dost poor Daoud, whom thou mayest yet learn to love as he loves thee! — either to bring them back or never to return!"

"I take no oaths!" El Warda said. "They are sinful. But I say to thee on my word, which thou knowest is sacred, that when thou shalt return, having done the things thou hast promised, I will place my hand in thine, and say unto thee as Ruth said unto Naomi: 'Whither thou goest, there will I go; thy country shall be my country, and thy God my God. And may God do so unto me and more, if aught but death part thee and me.'"

"Enough! enough!" cried the Syrian, wild with joy. "I need no other pledge from lips on which truth ever sits enthroned. Mine thou art, or shalt be; and the powers of earth and hell shall not prevail against me!"

"Beware, rash man!" answered the girl; "and offend not Heaven by such impious profanity, as to weigh the decrees of Providence in the balance of thy passion and pride! Beware a judgment! for is it not written, 'After death cometh judgment'? And thou art not prepared to die. Farewell! I linger no longer here; for thou hast raised up a barrier between us. Hereafter I either shall never look upon thy face again, or — submitting to the doom I have taken on my own head — will keep my promise!"

Then waving back the Syrian, who sought to take her hand, and dropping her veil, after casting a look of reproachful pity on her companion, she rapidly left the

room, with a sign to Daoud not to follow her; passed
down the steps and out of his house; and her slight
figure was soon lost to his straining eyes as she passed
into the Ezbekieh.

"I have won her at last!" he cried, in fierce exultation. "Mine she shall be, in spite of Sheitan and his
servant Abbas! She will learn to love me soon enough,
when she sees the depth of my devotion. The clouds
of my life are over! now comes the sunshine. And
how will I bask in its beams — all the brighter for past
eclipse!"

As he raved thus, in the first intoxication of his success, a shadow fell upon him, as a dark body passed between him and the window, through which the sunlight
streamed. He looked up, and saw the eunuch of the
Khanum, who spoke no word, but saluted in silence,
and pointed to the door.

"I am ready!" cried the Syrian, responding to the
mute appeal. "Lead on, I follow."

The black turned, and passed down the steps. Suddenly he stopped as he reached the door, and turning
to the young man, with a softened and more human expression lighting up his face than Daoud had seen on it
before, said:

"Life is sweet to the young. The Khanum values not
the lives of men. Thy mission I can see means danger —
perhaps death. Be warned in time, and go not! Small
cause have I to pity men; but thou art a boy, and I do
pity thee. Once in the Khanum's hands, thy term of
being will be as brief as the ripened fruit on yonder date-
tree lasts. Whether she sends for thee in love or hate;
to make a favorite or a tool of thee, it will be the same.

Let me then return alone, and Allah will find one good record made for me in the Book of Life!"

Surprise kept the Syrian mute a second: but even this unexpected interposition did not shake his resolve, which, was now as adamant.

"I thank thee from my heart for thy warning," he said. "But go I must; I have no choice — lead on!"

The eunuch shook his head, but said no more. Both mounted fleet horses ready for them, and within a few minutes Daoud-ben-Youssouf stood a second time in the presence of the Princess Nezlé Khanum.

"The hour is come, and awaits only the man!" she said. "Art thou still willing to obey my orders, though they lead to what I said when last I saw thee?"

"Great Khanum, I am!" the Syrian answered, calmly.

"*Peki!* behold thy companion."

She clapped her hands, and a young-looking but powerful Georgian, with fair complexion. and blue eyes, magnificently attired in the gorgeous costume of a Mameluke, entered the room and prostrated himself before the princess.

"Ali, this is thy companion!" she said to him in Turkish. "Him thou art to obey in all things, even of life and death. Dost thou comprehend? For if thou failest, my ire will consume thee!"

"*Be chesum!*" (On my eyes be it!) was the response, with another reverence.

"Come thou with me," she said to the Syrian; "I will give thee thine instructions. On thine own courage must depend the rest."

Half an hour later, Daoud-ben-Youssouf, clad in a rich costume, similar to that worn by the Georgian, and so thoroughly disguised, his most intimate friend would

36

not have known him, was mounted on a dromedary, and accompanying the eunuch and the Georgian Mameluke, Ali, toward the Bab-el-Nazr, whence they all passed out upon the desert.

But as she dismissed him, Nezlé had held up her finger warningly to the Syrian, and said:

"Recollect all my instructions, and fulfil them to the letter! And remember," she added, with an ugly look of meaning in her eyes; "remember that thou returnest to me — *alone !*"

CHAPTER XXXVIII.

THE HAWK STRIKES THE VULTURE.

AT the Abassieh once more. The terrified girl, now almost hopeless of succor from without, and doubting the promises of the wild woman whom she considered half insane, watched and waited, in an agony of apprehension, the renewed importunities of Abbas.

No conversation passed between her and the Frenchwoman, who seemed plunged in gloomy reverie, and watching from the window, gazed out into the desert view. At length she uttered an exclamation, and Edith, looking up suddenly, saw three dromedaries, upon which were mounted one eunuch and two richly-clad Mamelukes, rapidly approaching the palace.

The woman made no remark, but passed from the room and glided to the hareem gate, at which she met the eunuch dismounting. Not a word was exchanged between them; he only pointed to the smaller and darker of his two companions, who showed her a ring he wore upon his finger, and said briefly: "At nine to-night, the draught."

The woman nodded her head intelligently, and returned as silently and as stealthily as she had come; and the eunuch, with his two companions, passed through the courtyard to the grand entrance of the palace.

The evening darkened into night, and Edith was not again disturbed by Abbas, who had summoned the Frenchwoman, and had a long conversation with her, ending by placing in her hand a heavy purse of gold. The final word of the woman was "Bukara!" (to-morrow!) and the satisfied leer on the face of the Vice-roy told that the promise, whatever it might be, was agreeable to him.

Nevertheless, his good-humor did not last long, and he seemed to be in a peculiarly fitful and excited mood that evening; and as it wore on he became more irritable. The unhappy attendants on his person fared badly; for not only did he lavish upon them all the terms of opprobrium of which he was such a master, but he spared not also blows, kicks, and other tangible proofs of his displeasure. Suddenly a thought seemed to strike him. He summoned Mahmoud Bey, and inquired if he had been rightly informed that the Princess Nezlé had sent the Mamelukes she had promised, and on his reply being affirmative, ordered them into his presence.

The Mamelukes entered, and Abbas looked at them both with an approving eye, especially at the fair Georgian, who, in his face, was more like a beautiful girl than a man, though heavy and clumsy of figure. The Circassian did not seem to please him so much, though the ample folds of the dress concealed the spare figure, and gave it that roundness so pleasing to the Oriental, who, in man or woman, hates leanness. Moreover, the face of the darker boy, into which he stared hard, seemed to suggest some memory, unpleasant though

puzzling, which he could not recall. He turned to
Mahmoud Bey and asked:

"Did the eunuch tell thee they were both from Constantinople lately, and were both Mamelukes?"

"Effendina, he did."

"Something strikes me as familiar in that face, or as
though I had seen it before; but I suppose it must be
fancy. I like the looks of both these boys. They will
attend me more pleasantly than these pigs and apes, that
have been trying my temper by their awkwardness and
stupidity all the evening. Send away all the others, and
let these two stay. I will take a cup of coffee, and then
repose, for I am weary; and charge my people, on no
pretext, even though Cairo should be on fire, to waken
me before I call. Now go, all of you."

His orders were obeyed.

Glancing his eye over the faces and the forms of the
Mamelukes, who stood in humble attitude before him,
again the puzzled expression came over his countenance,
and he sharply gave the command, in Arabic, to move
the pillows of his divan.

Both looked up and started forward, but neither
obeyed, the countenances of both expressing inquiry, as
though they had heard the words but did not comprehend the language in which he spoke. The test seemed
to satisfy the suspicious tyrant, who muttered to himself:

"I think I must be fanciful this evening; though it is
not my wont; I seldom have felt so strongly the presentiment of danger, or evil. I suppose my double bad
luck has made me so. To quarrel first with Nezlé, and
then with that little fiend of an Ingleez! Um! as for
Nezle, she little dreams she will soon follow that father
of hers she is so fond of! The Kislar-Aga charges him-

36 *

self with that, through some of his people! and for the
Ingleez, we shall settle that to-morrow.   Call you this
coffee, dog!'' and he dashed two-thirds of the fluid into
face of the trembling slave who had brought it from the
hareem door.   "Thy vile breath hath poisoned it, for it
is bitter as gall; and I took only one mouthful!"

Even as he spoke these last words, a quick inscrutable
expression — like a flash of lightning across the dark
storm-cloud — flashed over the dusky face of the smaller
Mameluke.   Then it instantly grew still and expressionless again.

Abbas hurled the cup and heavy chased *fingan* at the
head of the slave, and throwing himself back on the
divan, called, in Turkish, to the Mamelukes:

"Keep off the flies and watch my slumbers."

Then he settled himself to sleep.

As he had commanded, the silence and stillness of
death reigned throughout the palace; and in the chamber
no sound disturbed the hush, save the droning of the
flies, the sighing of the Desert wind without, and the
heavy breathing of the sleeper.   Abbas was a gross, fleshy
man, and his slumbers were sound, as the heavy, stertor-
ous breathing indicated.

The obsequious slaves stood at his head and feet waving
palm branches to keep off the intrusive flies, which, less
obedient than man, respected the Viceroy as little as the
common Fellah, and rudely broke in upon his slumbers.

The Circassian glided to the side of the Georgian,
where he stood at the head of the divan, showed him a
signet-ring, and whispered in his ear.   The face of the
Georgian showed repugnance — even horror, at the communication made him by his companion, who marked it,
and whispered again even more eagerly than before.

At the second whisper, doubt and hesitation seemed to pass away from the Georgian's fair face, which settled into a kind of dogged resolve. He nodded his head thrice in assent; and from that moment stood watching his companion's every movement and gesture, as though ready to imitate it.

Utterly unconscious of this by-play — which would have excited his waking suspicions to the extent of bowstringing both Mamelukes — the Viceroy slept on. But he slept not tranquilly, for his rest seemed broken and fitful, and he started often and muttered in his sleep — like one whose brain is busy weaving those strange incongruous medlies of fact and fancy — of fragments of the real past blended with wild impossibilities — which come through the Gate of Horn to wander through the avenues of the human brain, restlessly traversing them, while memory and will seem both to have deserted the body, as though in a partial death.

The coffee Abbas Pasha had sipped must have contained some powerful narcotic; for, little as he had taken, his slumbers did not resemble ordinary sleep, even in its restlessness. He seemed more in the somnambulistic than in the natural state; for occasionally his eyes would unclose, and after staring wildly round — with no speculation in their dull orbs — would close heavily again. In those intervals it would seem as though two powers were contending for the mastery of the sleeping man; one, his will, which seemed wrestling to shake off the fetters of the drowsy languor which held him; the other, an external power, too potent for that will to resist.

In fact the Viceroy resembled one on whom the peculiar properties of that strange drug, haschisch, were at work; though in its stupefying and sedative, not its exciting influences; but as the Viceroy never partook of that drug, these phenomena were all the more strange in his case.

At length the two watchers by his divan observed that his breathing grew more regular, the fitful starts less frequent, and his slumber more natural, while the strange expression of his face relaxed, and the second stage of the hashisch drug manifested itself. This stage is that of mental excitement, coupled with bodily repose, when the enfranchised mind seems to soar away from its fleshy clogs, and disport itself at will in the regions of imagination; when the closed eyes see stranger things than human vision ever saw, even with the aid of the magic glass of fancy.

And as he lay sleeping there, watched by those two faithful Mamelukes, sent by his kinswoman to guard his slumbers and minister to his wishes, this was the dream of Abbas Pasha:

He dreamed that he had passed the portals of his earthly kingdom, and ushered by a shape that bore a strange resemblance to the Princess Nezlé, but supplied with long black wings, and with a strange lurid glow like a halo round her brow, had passed upon the bridge of Al Sirat, which spans the fiery gulf into which all unbelievers fall. Over the bridge he passed into a brighter world, lit up however by no soft glow, but illuminated by a lurid glare, like in intensity, but a thousand times more dazzling than that which encircled the brow of his guide. As he passed over the bridge, no wider than the edge of a scimetar, and looked down into the fiery flood beneath, he saw there the faces of all his enemies he had done to death by rapid or slow extinction; all of whom stretched up their arms, wildly striving to clutch him and drag him down among them, some almost reaching his robes, then ever falling back again — just as he shrunk from the touch, shivering with fear — hunted down again by Monkir and Nakir, the guardians of that pit of woe!

Prominent among them he recognized the face of old Askaros, his hoary beard tinged with the lurid red of the Lake of Fire; and on the extreme bank, in the Blessed Region of the Faithful, at the other end of the bridge, stood the fair face and tempting form of an houri, clad in her green robes, and beckoning him on the enjoyments of that paradise, which the Koran promises to all true believers. As he gazed eagerly upon her, the face changed suddenly to that of the American girl, who had so captivated his worn-out senses. Then Abbas strove to rush past his guide to clasp her in his arms; but that guide turned suddenly upon him, presenting no longer the features of Nezlé Khanum, but those of the Syrian he had caused to be so cruelly scourged; then seized him, clasped his arms tightly around his neck in a stifling embrace, and strove to hurl him from the bridge into the fiery pit below. Close-locked in that dread embrace, the stifling heat from below seemed rising up to scorch and suffocate him.

With that sensation of falling down — down — down from an immeasurable height into a fathomless abyss, Abbas Pasha awoke.

But he awoke from the vision of imaginary peril into the consciousness of a more dreadful reality — to find himself really suffocating under the cushion of his divan, pressed firmly down over his face, while strong hands bound his legs together, as though in fetters of iron!

He awoke at once to the full possession of his faculties, sharpened by the presence of the death so immi-

nent: for with the lightning-like rapidity of mental action in such emergencies, there flashed through his mind
full conviction of the treachery of Nezlé, and of her fell
design in sending the Mamelukes — now his only guardians in that chamber.

With that conviction came the strength of despair,
supplying courage to the craven heart, ever cowardly as
it was cruel; awakening in this dire extremity the slumbering wild-beast instinct of self-preservation, or signal
vengeance upon his murderers.   He felt the pressure
of the hands that held the cushion down upon his face
to the verge of suffocation; he felt the iron grasp of the
other upon his legs, as they were stretched out upon the
divan; and he felt, too, that a single minute more of that
pressure, and his laboring lungs would cease to breathe.

Summoning the last energies of his powerful frame
into one mighty effort, Abbas suddenly wrenched his
head free from the cushion held by those deadly hands,
and, drawing up his lower limbs convulsively, struck his
assailant there full in the chest, relaxing his grip and rolling him backward upon the floor, so violent and unexpected was the sudden blow.   Then, springing furiously
from the divan, purple in face, gasping for breath, his
jewelled tarbouche fallen from his shaven head, and his
rich dress torn and tumbled, with wild-rolling, blood-
shot eyes, and haggard face reflecting mingled rage
and fear, Abbas stood up glaring upon his destined murderers.

Ere his opened lips could utter the cry to summon his
guards, crouching as the wild cat crouches, the slighter
and darker of his two Mamelukes had bounded at his
throat, and he felt the lean, strong fingers, like the claws
of that savage beast, tearing and lacerating it.   That

fierce, fell pressure prevented outcry, as with the violence of the assault, assailant and assailed rolled over on the floor, the only spectator, petrified into stone, standing a mute and motionless witness of that struggle for life and death between those two, clutching and tearing each other like savage beasts in a death-grapple.

The contest was short as fierce. Though he could not shake off that desperate grasp which almost throttled him and partly paralyzed his powers, the greater weight and strength of Abbas soon told against his slight assailant. The Viceroy was over his enemy, his knee on his chest striving to crush it in, and cause him to relinquish his grasp upon the throat, to which he still clung with the tenacity of a wild cat, as the staring eyes of his adversary attested.

The strength and endurance of the Circassian were evidently failing fast under the superior strength of his enemy, and casting his despairing eyes around, wildly, in search of help in this extremity, they fell upon the Georgian, who stood with stupid, staring gaze fixed upon the conflict, as though it concerned him not. A last hope dawned upon the whirling, dizzy brain of the Circassian, and tightening his failing clutch upon his enemy's throat, he gasped out:

"Ali! for your life and mine, use the cord!"

As he spoke he could feel the vengeful grip of the Viceroy tighten upon him, the heavy knee crush down more heavily upon his laboring chest, as the fierce, dull eyes gleamed recognition and vengeance on him, within two feet of his own. But the same instant he heard the whizzing sound of the cord as it swept through the air, felt the thrill of sudden relief as the heavy pressure on his chest was removed — rather heard than saw the body of Abbas dragged backward to the floor — as the Georgian tugged at the tightening slip-knot round his master's neck, with all the energy of terror and despair.

The second after, sick, dizzy, half-fainting as he was — hate supplying the place of strength — the Circassian had risen to his feet — had seized again the fatal cushion, and — while the Georgian still strained at the ever tightening noose, till the tongue of the victim protruded — had thrown himself, with the cushion under him, upon the face of the writhing and struggling thing upon the floor.

It was over!   The desperate and convulsive struggles of the form grew fainter, then spasmodic — sunk into a mere twitching of the limbs!   Then, with a convulsive shudder, it ceased, and all was still!   The mission of the Mamelukes of the Princess Nezlé Khanum was performed!   They carefully laid him again upon the divan, replacing the jewelled tarbouche, smoothing the tumbled garments, and arranging the limbs in the attitude of one who slumbered.

Naught remained there upon the divan but the clay of him who was erewhile King of Egypt; the immortal part had gone to its judgment, and the meanest of Abbas Pasha's slaves could with impunity now spit on what was left of their dreaded master.

Strange and awful change, whether it happen to the leper or the king! when God's breath is withdrawn from the creation of His hands.

Mystery ever recurring in death as in birth!   When shall the awful secret ever be fathomed by the finite intelligence of man, striving ever to grasp the infinite? and ever falling back into darker depths after each presumptuous effort!

The dream of Abbas Pasha had found its fulfilment. So had the horoscope ; and as the two Mamelukes consulted together in whispers, the wild haggard face of a woman peered in upon the completed work, and the lips muttered :

"Said I not that the stars lied not! neither did the Khanum ! "

CHAPTER XXXIX.

THE DEAD MAN'S RIDE.

ELFY BEY, Governor of Cairo, sat in the citadel at midnight, and there was trouble on his brow. Before him stood the Kislar Aga, who had come in hot haste from the Abassieh at that unusual hour, and long and earnest had been the consultation between the two.

So eccentric and unaccountable are the movements of Eastern functionaries, that the household of Elfy Bey were not astonished when orders were given at that hour for an escort to accompany the Kislar Aga and himself back to the Abassieh; and the two, followed by a fitting retinue, were soon on their way to the Desert palace.

Arriving there, the Kislar Aga was told, in reply to his question, that his Highness was still sleeping, and they dared not disturb him, so strict had been his orders. Would the Kislar Aga, who was so great a favorite, take the responsibility of doing so? assuming as a reason the visit of the Governor of Cairo, who doubtless came on business.

"Have the Mamelukes yet come out?" asked the Kislar Aga.

"No; no one has seen them since Effendina sent away all the rest of his attendants."

434

"Then all is as it should be," responded the officer. "Has not his Highness the privilege of sleeping as long as he pleases, without being annoyed by your curiosity? Go to bed, all of you; I, myself, will call him in the morning. Let no one, as he values his tongue or his ears, intrude until I give the permission! Excellency," he added, turning to the Governor, "it grieves me that I cannot obtain for you an interview with his Highness; but you see the state of the case, and will pardon my waiting till sunrise, when he will doubtless accompany you back to Cairo. For the present, permit me to show you your apartments. All is safe," he continued, in a whisper. "These fools suspect nothing. In the morning you will take him to Cairo; we will send for El Hami, and the rest is easy."

"*Peki?*" answered Elfy Bey; "what you say has in it the wisdom of the serpent. I will do this. The faith I pledged to the living I will keep to the dead! Rely on me."

The eunuch nodded approving assent, and the two separated.

Scarcely had they gone, however, when the face of a woman, full of triumph and contempt, glared up from behind the same curtain, where she had heard the revelation of Abbas to the Kislar Aga.

"Is that your game?" she muttered. "Then shall it be frustrated. I shall be before you, and the friends of Saïd shall know what plot you are planning! What a good-looking man Elfy Bey is! Pity he should be such an ass!"

So saying, and chuckling to herself, the woman disappeared also.

The next morning there started at sunrise from the Abassieh the strangest cavalcade that probably ever went forth from palace-gates since the Cid Campeador took his ghastly ride — a dead man strapped to his saddle, with spear fastened to his stiff right hand — in advance of the Christian force, which went forth to do battle with the Paynim foe.

For the splendid state carriages of the Viceroy, with all the pride and pomp of place, were drawn up outside the palace-gates; and a retinue of two hundred cavalry, glittering in gorgeous array, were there as a guard; the drums beat, the banners flew and the trumpets brayed, as Elfy Bey, Governor of Cairo, and the Kislar Aga — one on each side — assisted his Highness, Abbas Pasha, Viceroy of Egypt, into his carriage at the private postern door, which was but one stride from the carriage-step.

The coachman and Syces were disposed to think the Viceroy ill, for, instead of pushing away impatiently those who sought to assist him, he allowed himself to be almost lifted into the carriage, into which Elfy Bey got also, taking the front seat. Then the whole *cortége* wound at full speed over the Desert plain, taking the road to Cairo.

What were the thoughts and emotions of Elfy Bey during that ghastly ride, seated in front of the dead man — that mockery of a monarch — can never be known; for he himself never confided to living man the reflections that must have crowded thick upon him at the strange farce, or melodrama, in which he was taking such active part.

On the *cortége* swept, the living Governor supporting with his knee in front, in the close carriage, the dead body of his late master, stark, stiff, and rigid — now leaning back against the luxurious cushions, now swaying forward as any impediment jolted them, until it almost fell into the arms of the faithful adherent.

Elfy Bey could not look out upon the surrounding prospect — for even the bare desert would have been a more pleasing object to survey than the hideous thing before him — for the blinds of the carriage were closed, to avoid detection. He could not look up, for there, with lids opened wide upon him, in a glazed stare of mortal agony and terror, were the protruding eyeballs starting from the livid and flaccid face of what was Abbas Pasha.

And outside, as though in mockery of the cold corpse within, and as if to insult the dull ear of Death, jingled the sabres of the guards in their rich uniforms; blazed the gilt panellings of the coaches; and — as they wound through the streets of Cairo to the citadel — rung the vivas and plaudits of the politic mob, to propitiate the Thing they still thought their living Tyrant!

At seeing the closed carriage and the evident precautions taken to avoid public scrutiny, many of the old gossips shook their heads, and said the Viceroy must be ill, or in a very bad humor.

"We shall hear something soon," they said; and this belief became more general when, shortly after reaching the citadel, its guns were pointed to cover and command the city, and unusual activity prevailed in the garrison.

Then by mid-day a rumor, creeping like the wind, as noiselessly and as suddenly, no man knowing whence it came nor how it went, swept over the city of Cairo, that a dead and not a living Viceroy had been brought by the Governor, Elfy Bey, that morning into the citadel; that El Hami was to be proclaimed Viceroy instead of Saïd,

37 *

the legitimate successor; with a general massacre of the Christians to inaugurate these measures.

Great was the alarm at these strange outgivings, and men looked fearfully in each other's faces for contradiction or confirmation of them, and crept quietly homeward to be out of harm's way. Therefore, the coffeeshops and places of public resort were almost empty; and the Ezbekieh, instead of its usual noise and animation, presented a look of blank desolation, such as it wore in seasons of the plague, when people feared the contact of each other.

The rumors however grew in consistency and became more positive as evening wore on; so that by nightfall some pretended to give the particulars of the death of Abbas; which of course were very wide of the truth. The general impression was he had died by poison, in vengeance for great cruelties inflicted on some of his slaves; others as confidently asserting that he had died of apoplexy.

The consul-general, who had befriended Askaros, and who had not left on his *congé*—as was generally supposed, and even believed by Abbas himself — had that day come up to Cairo. He was resting after the fatigues of his journey from Alexandria, and listening with a half-amused expression of countenance to the wild stories his excited subordinates were pouring into his ears, touching the death of Abbas, the dead man's ride, and the alarming intentions of Elfy Bey, who meditated the massacre of all Christians—native and foreign-— at Cairo, when two persons were announced as demanding immediate audience.

"Let them come in," was the order; and two men entered — one a black, clad as a servant; the other white, but covered face and person by a large coarse *abba*, or cloak, such as is worn by the common people. Both looked dirty, and the face of the black had that ashy hue indicating recent illness. He stepped up to the consul-general and prayed a private interview, as he and his friend had matters of grave importance to communicate to his ear alone.

The curious subordinates and attendants having un-willingly retired, the Nubian stepped back and his companion came forward — dropping the cloak that had hitherto concealed his person and face, and revealing to the gaze of the astonished consul-general the features of Askaros Kassis, though wan and worn from illness, and with suffering stamped upon them. From him he learned that Ferraj, who had long been an inmate of the citadel, had made himself so popular with the soldiers, that he had been allowed every liberty save that of egress. He had seen the entry of his master again into captivity, and had been allowed to attend upon him, without the knowledge of the Governor. That evening Ferraj had come in a great state of excitement, announced the fact of a dead, instead of a living Viceroy having been brought down from the Abassieh by Elfy Bey, and that the Governor and Kislar Aga — after consultation with some of the most trusted friends of Abbas — had determined to proclaim El Hami, Viceroy, instead of Saïd, the regular successor, and had already sent a confidential messenger to summon the youth, who was unfortunately at Constantinople — not in Egypt. Ferraj had further declared that so great was the confusion in the citadel, when the news leaked out, that they could escape by disguising themselves.

This they did; and had now come to give this news

to their best friend, and to ask tidings of the lost Edith.

The consul-general was much struck by these details, and advised Askaros to lose no time, but to proceed at once to Alexandria, and notify Saïd· Pasha — who was then residing in a palace near that city — of all he knew, and to urge him to come up at once and claim the sovereignty now his. He might also assure him that the consul-general would confer with his colleagues, as to the best means of checking the follies meditated by Elfy Bey, and the other adherents of Abbas.

But he grieved to inform him he could as yet give him no tidings of his wife.

The dejected countenance of Askaros grew more sombre still at this confession of ignorance from the lips of his friend; but seeing that her safety depended upon the solution of the existing difficulty, he prepared at once to carry out his protector's advice.

He sent Ferraj first to communicate his safety to El Warda, and then rejoin him at Boulak, where he proposed taking a boat which, manned by six rowers, would soon take him down the rapid current to the palace of Saïd.

What was his joy, on meeting Ferraj at the trysting-place, to learn that his wife was safe and well! A mysterious message from the Frenchwoman had notified El Warda of that fact, but she knew no more.

Still with a lightened heart Askaros, accompanied by his faithful Nubian, proceeded on his mission to warn the new Viceroy of his accession to the throne and honors of his predecessor, then lying dead at the citadel.

By midnight he had reached the palace of Saïd, and instead of finding everything still, and all the occupants buried in sleep, to his surprise he observed lights gleaming from every window, forms moving before them, and evident preparations being made for a movement in some direction. Surely, he thought, his tidings had either been anticipated by some earlier messenger, or the rumors that had disturbed Cairo had floated with the evening fog down the river to the palace of Saïd — hitherto more a gilded prison than a palace, from which he could not stir without the permission of his jealous and suspicious kinsman, Abbas.

Entering and demanding an audience, he was immediately shown into the presence of Saïd Pasha, a large handsome man, with reddish-brown beard and sanguine complexion, and a face indicating a frank and generous character. He was sitting on a divan, apparently in high good humor, surrounded by several friends, among whom Askaros recognized Zoulfikar Pasha.

Cordially greeting the Copt, Saïd burst into a loud laugh and cried:

"Why, Effendi, the news is stale which you come so mysteriously to bring me at midnight. Several hours since it was brought to me by a woman — by two women, in fact — one of whom I think you might like to see."

Clapping his hands, he ordered an attendant to take the Effendi to see the old Frenchwoman who had arrived a few hours before; and the next moment Askaros was locked in the embrace of his long lost wife, and attempting to answer a hundred questions of hers, and get answers to as many of his own at the same time.

The joy of both at this sudden and unexpected meeting may be imagined — it cannot be described. Both felt it almost a compensation for the trials and the sufferings through which they had passed to this blessed reunion, which they knew could never now be disturbed again·by mortal malice, or by aught save death.

Over a scene and a sentiment so holy, like the ancient painter let us drop a veil: for, as the pencil of Zeuxis failed to depict the agony of the bereaved father, so any pen would fail to paint the rapture of such a meeting, and at such a time.

How Elfy Bey, warned by the consul-general of the futility and folly of his project to set aside the regular succession of Saïd Pasha in favor of El Hami, renounced his design; how he welcomed Saïd to Cairo, and rode in at his right hand; how Saïd even praised his fidelity to his old master as the best guarantee for his faithfully serving the new; how Elfy Bey sat in the seat of honor next the Viceroy at dinner, and retired to rest full of hope and joy, only to be found dead in his bed next morning —all these are matters of history.

Whether the death of the Governor resulted from over-excitement of brain, or from a cup of coffee administered by some super-serviceable servant or ally of the new Viceroy, was never known, and probably it never will be until the great disclosure of secrets on the Final Day. But even the friends of Abbas and of Elfy Bey acquitted Saïd Pasha of any privity in the deed: if the Governor really died not by the visitation of God, instead of by the hand of man.

Such an act was felt by all to be utterly alien to the temper of the new monarch, who had enjoyed European training and culture, and was more a European in his tastes and habits than a Turk.

Abbas Pasha was interred with all befitting pomp and ceremony in the family vault of the descendants of Mehemet Ali, near the tombs of the old Mameluke Sultans: and a magnificent monument, placed over him at the public expense, now marks the resting place of his remains.

Elfy Bey was buried also with befitting honors: and the post vacated by his death was tendered by Saïd Pasha to Askaros Kassis. For the new Viceroy appreciated highly the good qualities and ability of the young Copt, and he desired by this appointment of a Christian to a position of such high trust, to mark the commencement of that new era of liberality which signalized his reign.

But Askaros gratefully, yet firmly, declined the great honor tendered him.

"Highness, never will I forget thy generous kindness, nor cease to hold it in my heart," he said. "But after all my wife has suffered, she needs rest, repose, and retirement—at least for a while—from this country. We will seek in the society of her old friends forgetfulness of past trials. Therefore the favor I shall seek from your Highness is the permission to sail next week for Europe."

This permission was graciously accorded by the Viceroy, who, nevertheless, renewed his persuasions, and his regrets at their want of effect; and the next week Askaros and Edith, with lighter hearts than they had known for many days, set sail for Europe, having vainly endeavored to persuade El Warda to accompany them.

CHAPTER XL.

EL WARDA'S VIGIL.

HOURS passed into days, and days into weeks.
The old reign was over, and the new one successfully inaugurated.

Her brother and sister had sailed, after vainly endeavoring to induce her to accompany them to Europe — and still El Warda neither saw nor heard from Daoud-ben-Youssouf, nor could gain any clue to his fate.

He had disappeared as suddenly, as mysteriously, and as thoroughly as a dissolving view in a panoramic picture, leaving behind him no clue by which to track his footsteps; had vanished from the sight of man, as utterly, as though the Khamseen wind of the desert had buried him beneath its sandy waves.

The mind and heart of El Warda had been the prey of many conflicting emotions since the hour of her last interview with the Syrian, when his strange revelation had been made to her, and she had sounded the depths of that strong and sullen soul. That fierce, passionate love for her which absorbed his every faculty: that unflinching will which would wade to her through peril and crime rather than lose her; and that atmosphere of strife and

444

sin, through which he moved and had his being — all
these things had impressed the imagination of the maiden
with a shuddering horror. But it was not unmixed with
reluctant admiration of the misdirected strength which
sustained him, making him the master of that fearful
situation in which he rose to the dignity of an arbiter.

As some one of the faithful angels, in the first great
revolt in heaven, might have looked upon the horrid splendor of Lucifer, when even over the burning marl, after
his fall, he trod defiant still — with pride unconquerable
after all was lost — so from the white heights of her purity looked down the spirit of El Warda upon the struggling, sinning — yet not utterly lost soul of Daoud-ben-
Youssouf!

With that horror and that admiration there blended
also pity for the perversion of powers so great; and a
lingering hope of the possibility of converting them into
the channels of good. For the young girl had in her
much of the spirit of the martyr, as well as of the devotee.
She had learnt self-sacrifice — the immolation of her own
hopes and wishes for the good of others — at an early
day; and in the way which appealed most directly to her
own heart — in accepting the last proposal of Daoud she
felt she had consummated that sacrifice as thoroughly as
though, like an Indian widow, she had mounted her own
funeral pyre!

Hence, on her return home to the convent on the night
after she had made that pledge, which she had intended
faithfully to keep, she felt the same spirit in her gentle
bosom of which she had read in stories of the blessed
martyrs of her church, whose sublime self-renunciation
she had often marvelled at, but never dreamed of imi-
tating.

38

Yet she never blenched nor faltered in her resolve, nor thought of evading the dread ordeal she had invoked. But she spent the whole of that night on her knees in prayer to the Virgin to sustain and strengthen her, and assoilize her soul from the sin — if such it was — by which she had sought to save her brother and sister by the sacrifice of herself. Morning had dawned upon her while thus engaged; and as she rose from her holy vigil, the patient endurance she had prayed for seemed to have descended on her agitated spirit from above, and she felt ready to accept the martyrdom she had challenged.

From that moment no shadow of doubt or of distrust disturbed her serene spirit, as to her own ability to bear her own burden; but the gentle spirit had undergone endless alternations of doubt and fear as to the safety of her friends, and as to the success of that mysterious mission of Daoud, of which she comprehended neither the necessity nor the purport. Had she for one moment imagined the criminal nature of that mission, or the dreadful tragedy it involved, not for a single instant could she have countenanced or encouraged it. But, while concealing no one thing in the past, the Syrian instinctively recoiled from even hinting the means by which the liberation of her friends was to be effected; and she had imagined that craft and stratagem — not violence and crime — were to accomplish it.

Ignorant as she was of all such matters, the very disguise assumed by Daoud confirmed her in this belief: and she supposed that only his safety was concerned in the venture, which he had undertaken solely for love of her. And she would not have been a woman — and a very young woman — had not the consciousness of this fact sent a pleasing thrill through her heart, and lent a favorable light to her judgment of both the acts and impulses of the Syrian — base as some of them had seemed — when palliated by a motive so strong as that which he had avowed.

The sentiment of compassion, of pity, grew stronger in that gentle breast when she thought over the isolation, and suppressed sympathies of that lonely life; of that strong soul struggling in the cold waters of poverty and contempt, while feeling the consciousness of capacity to rise — like the angel with shorn wings unwilling to sink, yet unable to soar, the divine element struggling ever against the diabolic.

Poor Daoud! he was not so very bad after all. Circumstances had much to do with his evil acts, and her interposition had never failed to turn him from the paths of evil to those of good. And now he had gone, even at the risk of his own life, to rescue from danger and worse than death those who were dear to her, for her sake only! She must have been more or less than woman to have resisted the appeal that the memory of that fact pressed upon her.

She felt a warm blush rise to her cheek as she recalled the impassioned fervor of his prayer to her; the total self-abnegation, the devoted heroism with which he had consecrated his life to secure her hand; and she thought that she could not fail to make his future life better than his past had been, while such was her influence over him.

Thus she dreamed, and meditated, and prayed, while the first hour passed after their decisive interview; and she knew not whether hopes or her fears predominated.

But another sensation took possession of her, when, the ensuing evening, she received the mysterious message from the old Frenchwoman that her sister was free —

when a few hours later Ferraj brought the welcome tidings that her brother was also safe, and that the tyrant, who had caused all their sufferings, had been sent to his dread account — how, she neither knew nor fancied.

When she found later that neither Askaros nor Edith could explain aught of the means of their deliverance, or of the hand which had stricken the blow that liberated them and Egypt at one stroke — though both thought the Princess Nezlé had some mysterious connection with it — a vague suspicion began to creep into her mind — a horrible dread lest she, in some innocent way, had taken part in that fearful tragedy that had sent a soul so ill-prepared to its dread account. Struggle as she would against it, this strange new horror rose up before her, and appalled her like some shapeless spectre !

These formless and spectral terrors assumed more substantial shape after her brother and sister had gone. Then the Frenchwoman had made a visit, in which she told all El Warda had not known before, and showed the black gulf of crime and sin, over which she had helped to build the bridge that bore her brother and sister into safety.

The Frenchwoman's love for El Warda was as that of a mother for a daughter; but her energy and courage seemed strangely to have collapsed, since the recent scenes in which she had displayed so much of both. She related this black and painful history to the young girl, to warn her against any future intercourse with the Syrian, whom she now showed her to be the executor of the wicked plot of her mistress — Nezlé Khanum. For the Frenchwoman well knew the love of Daoud for El Warda, though she suspected nothing of secret compact between the two.

These awful revelations threw a new and ghastly light upon the compact she had formed with Daoud, unwitting of its dreadful import; and the soul of the pure maiden was harrowed up by the thought of the fearful crime, in which she had innocently been made an accomplice.

In an agony of prayer and supplication she again invoked the Virgin all night at the convent; and the morning dawned upon her, pale, haggard, and tortured with internal doubts—not as before, calm and self-possessed in the serenity of a soul at peace with itself and with the world. She saw now, as if by flashes of lightning, the dreadful gulf which yawned behind and before her, both in her complicity in the accomplished crime, and in her pledge to the chief criminal, after its accomplishment.

Which way could she turn? How escape the dreadful doom she had rashly invoked on her own head, in linking her fate with that of one whom she knew to be a premeditated assassin — yet an assassin by her deliberate act and will — unconsciously it might be, yet none the less surely so?

Ought she now — after having tempted, as it were, the unhappy Daoud to the commission of his crime — ought she now abandon him — conscious as she was, that without her restraining and purifying influence, "his latter end would be worse than his first"?

Was it not rather her duty — all innocent though she might judge herself of actual complicity in his crime — to seek to remedy its after influences, and to turn him from his wickedness that he might live hereafter?

Should she shrink from this duty because it was repugnant and painful to her? Should she allow a soul to be lost, through her own weak, selfish scruples as to her own personal comfort or happiness?

No! a thousand times no!

She would sacrifice herself—all her own future happiness—to save this soul, staggering in the dark depths of sin, and almost, though not entirely lost; for gleams of native nobleness and self-sacrifice irradiated its blackness still!

Poor Daoud! sorely had he been tried and tempted; terribly had he suffered — foully had he been wronged by the man whom he had finally slain! And the motive for which he had perilled life to perpetrate that dreadful deed had not been low, or base, but one of the highest and 'most unselfish which can animate our frail humanity —at least in a maiden's eyes.

So, sadly torn and tossed by conflicting doubts and emotions, the maiden watched and waited for the Syrian's return; not quite decided how she would receive him, or what course she would finally adopt, but reserving her decision for the time of his return. Upon the impression that this interview — his explanations and his manner — should have upon her, she must depend.

And so she contented herself.

But that explanation and that decision were never to take place — at least on this side of eternity! For never again was the face of Daoud-ben-Youssouf seen of men in the city of Cairo; and his name and his memory passed away like a vapor that comes and vanishes into the void: leaving no trace behind it, even as substantial as the ripples left by a bubble broken on the water, ere it disappears forever.

CHAPTER XLI.

THE SYRIAN'S REWARD.

BUT where was the Syrian, that he came not to claim the reward for which he had risked life and soul? Where was he?

Let us return to the Abassieh, on the night of the murder of Abbas Pasha, and follow the footsteps of the Mamelukes, who wrought the will of that fell woman who sent them, knowing the choice was between his life and her own.

No sooner had the two Mamelukes arranged the body of their victim on the divan, so as to give it the appearance of natural death, than they glided out of the room. Through the silent and deserted passages of the hareem apartments — on to the postern gate that led to the outer court, they passed swiftly and noiselessly.

There stood expectant the shadowy form of a veiled woman, with whom the Circassian exchanged a few words, showing her a signet-ring. The door immediately opened, and the same eunuch who had brought them there appeared, and preceded them, without a word, to the palace-gate. At a whisper from him, that too opened, and the three passed out into the desert, beyond the bar-

racks surrounding the palace.   Here they found two fleet
dromedaries in charge of a Bedouin.

The eunuch mounting one of these, signed to the Mamelukes to mount the other, first giving each of them a
coarse Bedouin bournous, which concealed their glittering uniforms, and gave them the appearance of ordinary
Bedouins.   He also enveloped himself in one of these,
and the three rapidly traversed the road toward Cairo,
without a single word having been uttered.

The night was clear and beautiful.   Not a cloud obscured the deep blue vault of heaven, in which the stars
shone, white and lustrous, like the silver lamps hung in
an azure dome.   The moon was waning, but its silvery
sheen still illuminated earth and sky with a flood of mel-
low radiance, as though it designed its last lingering
glances to be its brightest, before withdrawing them from
the eyes of man.

Not a sight or sound disturbed the unbroken void and
stillness of the plain; and the desert-ships — as the dromedaries have been aptly termed — traversed it at a pace
more swift than that of a race-horse.   At length, striking
the city and entering the lower gate to pass direct toward
Boulak, the three traversed the silent and deserted streets
of Cairo — through the Syrian quarter, and avoiding the
Ezbekieh — and reached Boulak just about midnight.

Then stepping to the side of Daoud-ben-Youssouf, the
eunuch broke silence, for the first time, during the long
mysterious ride.

"I am charged by the Great Lady we all serve to
speak to thee these things," he said in Arabic.   "Firstly,
that thou and thy companion will find her at Rhoda
Island, on the other side of the Nile — not here.   At
that place she will listen to the tale thou mayst have to

tell. Next, that thou wilt find the boat to bear thee to her palace — where thy ring will admit thee — at the point thou knowest of amid the rushes, where tradition tells that the infant Moussa was found by the daughter of Thotmes in olden time.

"And finally, our mistress bids me charge thee, the Circassian, to well remember her charge — that when thou didst return to her, thou shouldst do so — *alone!*

"The princess bids me recall to thee the verse of the Persian poet —' That is a secret which two have in keeping. Admit a third, and it is none!' Such are the words of thy mistress and mine. *Bakaloum!*"

A shudder passed through the frame of the Syrian at the incentive to new crime, which lurked under the ambiguous message he had just received. Its meaning he could not doubt. He was ordered to remove the only witness who might testify hereafter against the princess and himself.

Was the labyrinth of crime into which he had entered, to have no clue by which he could retrace his steps into pure air, and into paths open to all men? Dare he disobey the princess, and risk all he had perilled so much to secure?

How did he know but her power with the new Viceroy might be greater than with the old? that she was not the agent of Saïd Pasha, making him her tool in the act which had opened the throne to him; and that Daoud, the instrument, was not now at the mercy of that pitiless woman? She bade him slay his accomplice — might she not afterward remove him, too, so that no witness should be left?

Yet, were he to listen to these craven doubts and fly to his own home, or to Syria — what then? He would have

stained his hands and his soul with blood to no purpose!
He would have committed an useless crime, and his reward — El Warda! — would be further from him than
ever! — more remote than yonder planet, Saturn, whose
dull red disk he saw dipping down to disappear behind
the horizon — its last, lingering rays gleaming like blood
on the Nile.

No; he would not turn back at this late hour! He
would go on — on! — and fulfil his Kismet, wherever it
might lead him!

Long as it has taken to record these doubts, they
passed with lightning-like rapidity through the brain of
the Syrian; and but a few seconds after the eunuch had
spoken, the two Mamelukes had dismounted, bidden him
farewell, and taken the path alongside the river, leading to the crossing to Rhoda Island, with its marble
palace gleaming ghost-like in the distance under the
white rays of the moon.

The Georgian went in advance along the narrow path,
the shrubberies of which grew denser as they proceeded;
the Circassian following a few steps behind him. In the
busy brain of the latter were fermenting a chaos of
thoughts and passions, little suspected by his companion;
and chief among them loomed the necessity of execut-
ing the order given him — which he shuddered to obey,
yet dared not disobey — if he were to face the implacable princess.

Twice — with the stealthy, gliding step of the panther
— he pressed close upon the footsteps of his unsuspecting companion, loosened his long, keen dagger in its
sheath, and prepared to strike him a mortal blow!

Twice his heart failed him; a numb, cold sickness
crept over brow, heart, and brain. He could not strike!

And the steel, innocent of blood, stole back to its scabbard.

So they wended their painful way, the path growing narrower still, and the jungle thicker ; until the Georgian at length turned his head, and with a laugh announced that a few steps more would bring them out of the thicket, on to the river-bank, where they would find the boat among the rushes.

As the other spoke, the necessity for prompt action forced itself on the Syrian. Now he must decide! — must either finish the work assigned him, claim and receive his reward from the princess ; or turn back with the Georgian, seek safety in flight from the country, and relinquish the prize for which he had perilled so much! For he never dreamt he could remain in Egypt — far less claim that reward — after disobeying the last orders of the she-devil, who seemed to have bought him, body and soul!

Then arose before his distracted vision the image of El Warda, pure, bright, and lovely even as he had last beheld her, stretching out her hand and beckoning him into an earthly paradise — even as the Houris beckon to the Faithful after death.

That vision, sent by the evil spirit Ahriman, turned the wavering balance. A mist seemed to pass before the eyes of Daoud, a fierce thrill of wrath and hatred shot through his heart.

"Shall I lose *her* for *him ?*" he hissed through his clinched teeth — "after all! and so near fulfilment? No! not though I swim through blood!"

Crouching as the tiger crouches, he bounded forward upon his late friend — now his foe. The keen, bright steel glistened in the moonlight over his unconscious

head, descended over his left shoulder, and, driven by
the force of madness, penetrated his heart!

The Georgian fell upon his face — the crimson tide
gushing from his lips ere they could syllable a sound —
dead ere he felt the felon blow, that dismissed his soul
from Time to Eternity!   .

Daoud paused not longer to survey the victim of his
treachery, than to pluck his dagger from the wound.
Then raising the body with difficulty in his arms, he
dragged it to the river's bank, and hurled it into the turbid waters — racing with a hoarse murmur down toward
the sea ; for the current set in near the bank on which he
stood.

Then by a sudden impulse, throwing himself wildly on
his knees, with the tears streaming from his eyes, the unhappy man burst into an incoherent rhapsody of remorse,
prayer and supplication to the Virgin Mary, that she
might cleanse and purify his soul from this, as from previous sins ; vowing that he would devote the rest of his
life to her service — to works of kindness and of charity ;
beseeching her not so much for his own sinful sake, as
for that of her vestal virgin, El Warda, whom he would
henceforth make the guide and guardian of his life ;
pleading for pardon on the bank of that lone river, with
all the fervor and earnestness of a criminal to an earthly
judge, sitting in judgment on him.

When he had finished his prayer — heard, perhaps at
that higher bar, but to which no answer was vouchsafed
by sign or portent, to his excited senses — the Syrian
rose, wiped carefully all signs of blood from his dagger,
which he again stuck into his sash, and descending the
bank, again peered anxiously into the rushes for the bark

which was to bear him across to Rhoda Island to see the
Princess Nezlé Khanum.

At length he found it; a small boat like a caique, very
frail and slight, with two slender oars. The river was
at low water, yet the current was very strong still, and
dangerous to be upset in, from the undertow which was
apt to drown any one who sunk in its tide, however good
a swimmer.

The Syrian, however, was intent on other things, and
eager to finish the interview with the princess, on which
so much depended. He took but little heed of the skiff,
but launched it into the stream, seized the oars and pulled
rapidly away from shore. Scarcely had he reached the
strong current, however, when he was surprised to find
the water rising round his ankles in the bottom of the
boat, which had been dry when he got into it. His subtle mind immediately suspected treachery; and a minute's
investigation showed the trap set for him by the princess,
whose cunning had devised the means of removing the
sole surviving witness of the tragedy planned by her,
although she took no part in it.

With that conviction rose in the Syrian's mind all the
hatred and all the courage of which his late thoughts had
robbed him. He would baffle this wicked woman yet;
save himself and secure from El Warda herself — without
the intervention of another — the performance of her
promise! He turned the rapidly sinking boat back
toward the shore he had left; allowing it to float downward with the current and inclining it gradually toward
the bank, that he might swim ashore at a point lower
down than he had launched it, and escape the possible
watch of the people of the princess.

When at last the boat settled down, the Syrian, plung-

ing into the stream and keeping his head well above it,
struck out for the shore at a point where he saw it shelv-
ing down to the water's edge, fringed with long rushes.
Strong as the current was, he breasted it successfully, and
was reaching shoal water — with a heart full of good resolves and thankfulness for his preservation, and rebound-
ing from his late despair — when suddenly he saw, to his
surprise, a dark object resembling an old log floating
from the muddy bank toward him.

As there was no current *from* the shore, this struck him
as strange; but his surprise was changed into horror
when the object approached nearer, disclosing to his
gaze, under the bright moonlight, the scaly back and un-
shapely bulk of the crocodile! most dreaded of all the
tenants of that slimy flood, though but rarely seen so low
down the river.

As the monster moved through the water, with a movement indicating the vast propulsive power in its short
forearms and muscular tail — lashing the river into foam
as it forged onward — Daoud could distinguish its sharp
snout elevated above the flood, and the small, glittering,
serpent-like eyes it fixed on its destined prey.

Each second brought the fell monster nearer the man;
while the huge jaws would occasionally open — displaying the sharp double row of glistening teeth which armed
them — then close again with a snap like the music of
castanets, resounding through the stillness.

Imminent and deadly was the peril, as Daoud well
knew; but he lost not heart nor hope. His nerves,
steeled to danger in its most fearful shape during his recent trials, did not fail him now. But he felt a deadly
sickness of heart, for an instant at the new and hideous
form of peril, thus suddenly confronting him at the very

moment of his fancied escape from all his danger; just when he was making his good resolves for a tranquil future.

Never before had he encountered this dread monster: but he knew its nature and its habits well; for he had often heard the Arabs of the Upper Nile tell of their encounters with, and victories over it: and he therefore understood which way the path of safety lay.

He allowed the greedy monster to approach within two lengths of him — simply floating himself on the surface of the water, with a wary eye fixed on every movement of his adversary. Flight he knew would be speedy and certain death. He waited till he could see the very twinkle of its hungry eye — then dived down into the flood, his dagger bare in his right hand!

The moment after, the huge bulk of the crocodile seemed convulsed with a sudden pang, as it abruptly twisted itself round — lashing the water into foam with its terrible tail, and snapping its jaws fiercely together, while its snaky eye emitted sparks of fire!

Then it sullenly sunk under the water too; and the calm moonlight shone on the rippling river, showing no form of man nor reptile on its agitated surface. But the water where the crocodile had sunk was discolored with a dark red stain, which showed the Syrian's dagger had found a vulnerable spot.

He had dived beneath the scaly armor which protected it from above, and struck an upward blow.

Next moment the man rose again to the surface, twenty yards further down stream, and struck out vigorously for the shore: but the current seized and bore him down still further. And on it, floated in pursuit his wounded, but not disabled enemy — fiercer and more savage from its injury, and displaying now those vast energies hidden under its cumbrous and mail-clad carcass.

Thrice when on the very eve of being seized and crushed between those mighty jaws — which vainly snapped together like the huge portcullis of some feudal castle — did the Syrian narrowly escape destruction by suddenly diving down!   And thrice did he stab with his keen poniard into the unprotected flesh of his foe, under its forearm; while deeper grew the tinge of the waters, as the red stream gushed out, though the great vital energies of the amphibium still sustained it under the deep wounds of its desperate antagonist — whose human intelligence, craft, and courage waged war against its superior strength.

At length it seemed human intellect, when backed by courage, was destined to conquer brute force — even in a conflict so apparently unequal as this, for, after the third plunge, the huge scaly bulk seemed to float almost helplessly upon the water; while the river ran red with the life-tide ebbing from its ghastly wounds, and the dim eye shone no more with hungry hate, but had an almost human expression of agony and despair lurking in its filmy and glazing orbs.

The crocodile was evidently well-nigh struggling in its death-throes, and the mighty frame seemed contracted and convulsed with the near approach of the final spasm.

The man was nowhere to be seen.

Just then, panting, worn, exhausted, but still unwounded, Daoud, the dagger in his right hand, rose again to the surface; but unhappily within a yard of the drifting body of the almost vanquished monster.

The scaly thing saw him! and with a mighty effort of expiring energy, struck out wildly with his strong tail.

It fell, like a flail, on the head of the Syrian, stretching him senseless and powerless beside his enemy ! The next moment the dying crocodile twisted its body round, opened its mighty jaws with a final and convulsive effort —and when they closed again, within them was the writhing body of the Syrian ; caught as in some huge trap, which crushed bone, muscle, sinew, and flesh into one undistinguishable mass !

And locked tight in the death-spasm those jaws never unclosed again !

But the scaly bulk of the crocodile, bearing in its dead jaws the corpse of its destroyer, floated down the rapid current of the Nile, under the still moonlight, to the open sea ; which was to retain the relics of both, until the hour shall come, when that sea shall give up its dead.

And so — although endowed with the craft and the courage which could cope successfully with the Great Ones of the earth — could punish princes, and defy both heaven and hell to thwart his designs — perished Daoud-ben-Youssouf; his only tomb the jaws of a hideous reptile — his only reward at last a fearful retribution.

His fate was never known. The silent river, the twinkling stars, and the solemn sea, which alone knew, kept their secret; and the bright eyes of El Warda grew dim watching and waiting — whether in fear or in hope, she herself finally could not tell — in vain for his return.

As the weeks glided into months, and the months rolled into years, that hope or fear, whichever it might be, faded away from the maiden's heart; and she felt herself absolved from the rash vow she had made to the lost man ; more utterly lost to human sight and to the

39 *

memory of all — save one — than ever was mortal man before !

Yet that One did not forget the Syrian — her brother that had been, her spouse that might have been — whose mysterious disappearance had softened down the harsh judgment she had formed of him, when she thought he would return and claim her promise.

Morning and night, for many, many long and weary years, did heartfelt prayers go up to the Throne of Grace from the holy lips of a Coptish nun, for the repose of the soul of Daoud-ben-Youssouf, who had found — sinner as he was, and stained with crime — a shrine in one pure and devoted heart, whose orisons for him may finally have been heard at the Great Mercy Seat.

FINIS

www.ingramcontent.com/pod-product-compliance
Lightning Source LLC
Chambersburg PA
CBHW031822270326
41932CB00008B/505